$7.61

D0561014

RELIGION IN
PUBLIC
EDUCATION

problems and prospects

edited by
David E. Engel

PAULIST PRESS
New York / Paramus / Toronto

Library of Congress
Catalog Card Number: 73-93471

ISBN 0-8091-1821-1

Published by Paulist Press
Editorial Office: 1865 Broadway, N.Y., N.Y. 10023
Business Office: 400 Sette Drive, Paramus, N.J. 07652

Printed and bound in the
United States of America

ACKNOWLEDGMENTS

Religion, Constitutional Federalism, Rights, and the Court by Sidney E.
Mead: Reprinted with permission of the publisher from *Journal of Church
and State,* Vol. 14, No. 2, Spring 1972, pp. 191-209.

Religion in Public Education: Principles and Issues by Philip H. Phenix:
Reprinted from the July/August 1972 issue of *Religious Education,* by permission of the publisher, The Religious Education Association, 545 West
111th St., New York, N.Y. 10025.

*Teaching about Religion in the Public Schools: New Ventures in Public
Education* by Edwin Scott Gaustad: Reprinted with permission of the publisher from *Journal of Church and State,* Vol. XI, No. 2, Spring 1969, pp.
265-276.

Introducing Religious Literature in Pennsylvania Secondary Schools by John
R. Whitney: Reprinted from the March/April 1968 issue of *Religious Education,* by permission of the publisher, The Religious Education Association,
545 West 111th St., New York, N.Y. 10025.

The First Year with Religious Literature in Pennsylvania High Schools
by John R. Whitney: Reprinted from the March/April 1969 issue of *Religious Education,* by permission of the publisher, The Religious Education
Association, 545 West 111th St., New York, N.Y. 10025.

Further Issues on Religious Literature in Pennsylvania by David E. Engel:
Reprinted from the March/April 1969 issue of *Religious Education,* by

permission of the publisher, The Religious Education Association, 545 West 111th St., New York, N.Y. 10025.

A New Shape for Religion and Public Education in Changing Times by Robert A. Spivey: Reprinted with permission of the publisher from *Journal of Church and State,* Vol. 14, No. 3, Autumn 1972, pp. 441-456.

Teacher Certification: Michigan's Approach to Teaching about Religion by Paul J. Will: This essay was originally written for presentation at a consultation at the Public Education Religion Study Center, Dayton, Ohio, June, 1973 and is printed here with permission of the author.

The Academic Study of Religions in the State of Michigan by the State of Michigan Department of Education: Reprinted with permission of the Division of Teacher Preparation and Professional Development, State of Michigan, Lansing, Michigan 48902.

Teacher Certification for Religion Studies in Wisconsin by Frank L. Steeves: Reprinted with permission of the author. This report was originally given at a consultation sponsored by the Public Education Religion Studies Center, Wright State University, Dayton, Ohio, June 15-16, 1973.

Some Unfinished Business by Robert W. Lynn: Reprinted with permission of the publisher from *Protestant Strategies in Education.* New York: Association Press, 1964, pp. 74-82.

A New Perspective in Religion and Education by David E. Engel: Reprinted from the November/December 1972 issue of *Religious Education,* by permission of the publisher, The Religious Education Association, 545 111th St., New York., N.Y. 10025.

Some Issues in Teaching Values by David E. Engel: Reprinted from the January/February 1970 issue of *Religious Education,* by permission of the publisher, The Religious Education Association, 545 West 111th St., New York, N.Y. 10025.

Developing Values by Louis E. Raths, Merrill Harmin, and Sidney B. Simon: Reprinted with permission of the publisher from *Values and Teaching.* Columbus, Ohio: Charles E. Merrill Books, 1966, pp. 15-26 and 38-48.

Moral and Religious Education and the Public Schools: A Developmental View by Lawrence Kohlberg: Reprinted with permission of the publisher from *Religion and Public Education,* edited by Theodore R. Sizer. Boston: Houghton Mifflin Co., 1967, pp. 164-183.

A Theory of Justice by John Rawls: Reprinted with permission of the publishers, from *A Theory of Justice.* Cambridge, Mass.: The Belknap Press of Harvard University Press, and Oxford: The Clarendon Press, Copyright, 1971, by the President and Fellows of Harvard College.

Contents

III

PROGRAMS OF INSTRUCTION

IV

ISSUES AND PROBLEMS FOR THE FUTURE

Preface

Throughout the history of the United States the relation between religion and education has been intense and problem-laden. The American experiment has been indeed that, an experiment, with respect to the trial and error manner in which the schools have treated religion. But especially in recent years the question of religion in public education has become a field of considerable activity and greater clarity.

Some of the problems of the past, of course, continue to exist. But the development of American society has posed new issues and presented new prospects. Especially since 1945 significant activity in the maturing relation between religion and education has occurred. Three phenomena stand out: America's changing social and religious climate, legal definition, and program development including more refined theoretical rationales for studying religion in public schools. Each of these matters is analyzed and explicated in the readings presented in this book.

Religious pluralism has certainly become a reality to most, if not all, Americans. Once the nation rejected a Catholic candidate for the Presidency. Then later a Catholic became the 35th President—but hardly because he was a Catholic. Apparently one's traditional religious affiliation made less difference in 1960 than had been the case in 1928. While religious prejudices still exist, the expectations of most citizens have changed. No longer is it broadly assumed that Protestantism is the religious norm or the only acceptable cultural identity. The United States is recognized as religiously pluralistic. And the secularist and non-believer suffer no social stigma for their views.

With respect to legal definition, the reader should note the extent of what has occurred since World War II. Although the First Amendment to the United States Constitution remains the basic document in this regard, it has only been in recent times that the U.S. Supreme Court has concerned itself with religion in public

1

education. And the majority of those Court decisions have been
issued since 1947.

While the religious situation has become more pluralistic and
legal guidelines about religious practice have become clearer, interest in serious study about religion has increased. For years religion has been studied in higher education. But especially since
1963, interest in studying about religion in public schools has
heightened. That interest has developed from varied interests and
mixed motivations. Some program developments occurred before
it could be clearly discerned what might warrant such studies in
public institutions. But the activity of the last decade or so by
scholars in the field of religion, university personnel reflecting on
and theorizing about educational development, as well as countless dedicated teachers in basic education, has greatly clarified
what can be done, how religion can appropriately be taught and
what value such an enterprise may have.

This book is, in the first instance, concerned to document
and explain these developments. Part I provides readings to clarify legal developments and the social evolution which has led to
religious pluralism and an increased need to respect the individual's religious liberty before the law. Part II contains two examples
of how studies about religion may be justified as an important part
of one's formal education. Part III documents some of the varied
programs for religion in public education which have been generated during the period following the *Schempp* decision in 1963.

Much has occurred. But much more can occur in the near
future. Part IV suggests some of the issues which educators and
those concerned with studies about religion face in coming days.
Two questions summarize the readings in this section: (1) What
is the role and responsibility of the religious institution and/or the
religiously concerned individual for the maintenance and development of education generally? (2) What is the nature and function of education in regard to value formation and development?
While these two questions do not exhaust the issues about religion in public education for the future, they certainly typify the
kind of future problems and prospects one may anticipate.

One of the most difficult tasks anyone can attempt is to be
objective or openly subjective about religious ideas and religious

experience. Yet that is the task for religion in public education. Perhaps in this regard the principle of "justice as fairness" as articulated by Professor Rawls in the last reading in this book is a practical necessity for teacher and student alike if religion in public schools is to serve the people's interest.

Acknowledgment of the assistance and cooperation of a number of parties is in order. Special thanks is given to the *Journal of Church and State* and the journal of *Religious Education* for permission to reprint key articles. Also, appreciation is hereby given to the Department of Education of the State of Michigan for furnishing their standards for the certification of teachers in religion and their informal guidelines for program development in religion studies.

Several individuals played roles that relieved editorial tedium. I am grateful to Reni Robinson who spent numerous hours typing major portions of the original manuscript and to Alexandra Scott Engel who assisted in coordinating pages.

I am particularly grateful to Philip H. Phenix from whom I never cease to learn and who originally suggested this undertaking. My departmental colleagues at the University of Pittsburgh have always provided a climate of freedom and critical acumen which is a continuing support for whatever good work I might do. My family's contribution is somewhat intangible, but nevertheless important. I thank them for being there and just being themselves.

The following postscript is also in order as an acknowledgment to a heritage Americans share and a consequent responsibility all of us carry together. The framers of the Constitution had a rare genius in political history. Their achievement has lasted almost two hundred years so far. And an important part of that contribution is a governmental blueprint which values the individual. Although threatened at times, this emphasis is not forgotten. Surely this is an important part of the meaning of the Constitution, especially the meaning found in the First Amendment. Through the years and the changes in society, the Framers' belief in the rights of individuals—their interdependent religious and secular liberties—is numbered among the best of human visions. Particularly today, in a complex society and after substantial assaults on individual rights, we can all be grateful that the wisdom of our Constitutional fathers is significantly preserved. We can also dedicate ourselves to insuring the continuance of their vision.

David E. Engel
Pittsburgh, Pa.
September, 1973

I

LAW
AND
SOCIETY

Introduction

Legal considerations are basic to an understanding of questions pertaining to religion in public education. Although there are variations by state in law applicable to school practice, the basic guidelines for religious education and practice stem from the Constitution and decisions rendered by the United States Supreme Court.

No attempt is made here to cover the full range of documents in Federal Law which deal with religion and public education. Such material is accessible in a number of anthologies dealing with church-state relations and religion and education. Some of the standard references are included in the bibliography at the end of this section.

Here two amendments to the United States Constitution are printed with brief commentary. The First Amendment articulates the basic right of religious freedom and the Fourteenth Amendment in Court interpretation over the years has extended that right to the states. That is, no state law can be interposed which denies the right of religious freedom.

The second chapter contains selected passages from the 1963 Supreme Court decision: *Abington School District v. Schempp* and *Curlett v. Murray*. The case as it was considered by the Court involved two cases from lower courts in Pennsylvania and Maryland. In each situation required prayers and Bible readings had been challenged. Although public school children could be excused from these religious exercises at the beginning of the day upon written request, the Supreme Court in this decision declared the practice itself in violation of the "establishment" clause of the First Amendment. It is also noteworthy that at the end of his opinion for the majority Justice Clark suggests that instruction about religion is not necessarily a similar violation. On the basis of Clark's statement ("Nothing we have said here indicates that such study of the Bible or of religion, when presented objectively as part

7

of a secular program of education, may not be effected consistent with the First Amendment") programs for religion in public education have been generated in several regions of the country.

Although the question of objectivity in such religious study has not been fully clarified (see Part II), curriculum designs for religion in public education have generally followed the mode of instruction in other areas, e.g., literature and social studies. Part III provides some background on representative developments in curriculum.

The third chapter in this section is an historical analysis of the function of the Supreme Court with respect to religion and civil rights. Sidney F. Mead notes that the Court is not an instrument for the majority, but a means for adjudicating among the several interest groups in the society. Because such interests, including religious interests, are plural, the Court's role is a secular one insuring that the rights guaranteed to individuals are not trespassed by the tyranny of some majority. In Mead's view this is of critical importance with respect to religion in public schools. Religious freedom, as all the rights outlined in the Bill of Rights, is not subject to vote within some jurisdiction. Guaranteed rights may only be changed through the process of Constitutional amendment which involves all the people.

The fourth chapter is an analysis of the social and legal factors relevant to religion in public education. The author describes general features of the social climate following the *Schempp* decision in 1963 and shows how sensitive an issue consideration of religion can be in such areas as public education. Despite continuing legal tension over the place of religion in public education, religion may be taught if such instruction is clearly directed at the education of the public and not to further some religious practice.

1 Amendments to the United States Constitution

DAVID E. ENGEL

The first eight Amendments to the Constitution are commonly known as "The Bill of Rights." Together with two others, these Amendments were proposed on September 25, 1789 and have been in effect following ratification since December 15, 1791.

Here the complete statement of the First Amendment is printed with brief commentary following. In addition, section 1 of the Fourteenth Amendment is printed with appropriate commentary relating the Fourteenth to the First Amendment. In effect, this Amendment extends The Bill of Rights to the individual states. states.

First Amendment

Congress shall make no law respecting an establishment of religion, or prohibiting the free exercise thereof; or abridging the freedom of speech or the press; or the right of the people peaceably to assemble, and to petition the government for a redress of grievances.

At the time this amendment was written and adopted, the nations from which American settlers had emigrated commonly had mandated one religious body as an official or "established" church. Varying degrees of toleration or persecution were accorded to non-conformist groups. The First Amendment eliminated the possibility of any such practices in the states drawn together following the Revolutionary War. The substance of several decisions of the U.S. Supreme Court has generally upheld such neutrality with respect to all religious groups over the years.

While the Amendment disallowed establishment and granted religious liberty to the citizenry, freedom of religion is not to be construed as an absolute right. Although the Congress cannot enact laws which prohibit the free exercise of religion, legal restraint can limit the freedom in some cases. One of the striking examples of such limitation was legislation against polygamy among Mormons. However, restraints in this area have been few. Although in recent years decisions by the Supreme Court have banned religious practices in public schools, notably the saying of stated prayers and the devotional use of the Bible, no such restraints on individual or church practice would be consonant with the First Amendment.

Fourteenth Amendment

Section 1. All persons born or naturalized in the United States, and subject to the jurisdication thereof, are citizens of the United States and of the State wherein they reside. No State shall make or enforce any law which shall abridge the privileges or immunities of citizens of the United States; nor shall any State deprive any person of life, liberty, or property, without due process of law; nor deny to any person within its jurisdiction the equal protection of the laws.

This amendment was originally proposed at the close of the Civil War and ratified in 1868. Its major purpose at that time was to enfranchise former slaves. In order to do so, it was necessary to clarify the meaning of citizenship. Some had held that citizenship was not existent unless one was a citizen of a state. With respect to the slavery question this "states rights" dictum would have meant that former slaves would have remained outside of the guaranteed privileges and rights of the Constitution if an individual state so ruled. As such emancipation would have remained legally meaningless.

In time, however, the Amendment has been instrumental to more groups than former slaves. Indeed the language in this first section extends to "all citizens." The principle articulated by the Amendment denies the priority of state citizenship in defining the meaning of United States citizenship. In effect, even though one may not be a legal resident or "citizen" of a state, if he was born or naturalized in the United States the guarantees of the Constitution may not be denied him.

Specifically, this section of the Amendment repeats one phrase which also appears in the Fifth Amendment to the Constitution (". . . nor shall any State deprive any person of life, liberty, or property, without due process of law"). Commonly referred to as the Due Process clause, the repetition of this clause in the Fourteenth Amendment compels states to afford all citizens in their domain the rights articulated in the Fifth Amendment and, by extension, the First Amendment. Hence among the rights protected both in Federal courts and in state and local courts are religious freedom, freedom of speech, freedom of the press, etc.

2 Abington v. Schempp; Murray v. Curlett

DAVID E. ENGEL

Two cases on religious practices in public schools were considered simultaneously by the United States Supreme Court, and because the Constitutional issues involved were closely similar, a common decision was rendered for both. The *Abington v. Schempp* case involved a Pennsylvania law which required the following:

> At least ten verses from the Holy Bible shall be read, without comment, at the opening of each public school on each school day. Any child shall be excused from such Bible reading, or attending such Bible reading, upon the written request of his parent or guardian.

The Schempp family (mother, father and two of three children) enjoined the Abington public school district and the Pennsylvania Superintendent of Public Instruction from continuing the practice. In addition to the mandated Bible reading, the Abington Senior High School, similar to other schools in Pennsylvania and other states, followed the reading with a recitation of the Lord's Prayer, salute to the flag and announcements to the students. The

12

District Court held that the Pennsylvania statute was in violation of the Establishment Clause of the First Amendment as applied to the States by the Due Process Clause of the Fourteenth Amendment. The school district appealed the decision to the U.S. Supreme Court.

Similarly the Board of School Commissioners in Baltimore, Maryland enforced a 1905 rule directing that schools conduct opening exercises which consisted of the "reading, without comment, of a chapter in the Holy Bible and/or the use of the Lord's Prayer." Mrs. Madalyn Murray and her son, both professed atheists, petitioned the Commissioners asserting that the rule was a violation of William Murray's rights under the First and Fourteenth Amendments. The Maryland Court of Appeals affirmed the Board's demurrer to the Murrays' petition. Although the case was not appealed directly to the U.S. Supreme Court, the Justices considered the Baltimore situation on a writ of certiorari at the same time it heard arguments on the Abington case.

The result of the so-called *Schempp-Murray* decision was that the practices of reading scripture and saying prayers (although the latter practice had been adjudicated in the 1962 *Engel v. Vitale* decision) in public schools was held to be in violation of Constitutional rights. In other words, the U.S. Supreme Court upheld the ruling of the Pennsylvania court and reversed the decision of the Maryland court.

Excerpts from the decision follow.

*   *   *   *   *

[June 17, 1963]

MR. JUSTICE CLARK delivered the opinion of the Court.

Once again we are called upon to consider the scope of the provision of the First Amendment to the United States Constitution which declares that "Congress shall make no law respecting an establishment of religion or prohibiting the free exercise thereof. . . ." These companion cases present the issues in the context of state action requiring that schools begin each day with readings from the Bible. While raising the basic questions under slightly different factual situations, the cases permit of joint treatment. In light of the history of the First Amendment and of our cases interpreting and applying its requirements, we hold that the practices at issue and the laws requiring them are unconstitutional under the Establishment Clause, as applied to the states through the Fourteenth Amendment. . . .

It is true that religion has been closely identified with our history and government. As we said in ENGEL v. VITALE . . . "The history of man is inseparable from the history of religion. And . . . since the beginning of that history many people have devoutly believed that 'more things are wrought by prayer than this world dreams of.' " In ZORACH v. CLAUSON . . . we gave specific recognition to the proposition that "we are a religious people whose institutions presuppose a Supreme Being." The fact that the Founding Fathers believed devotedly that there was a God and that the unalienable rights of man were rooted in Him is clearly evidenced in their writings, from the Mayflower Compact to the Constitution itself. . . .

This is not to say, however, that religion has been so identified with our history and government that religious freedom is not likewise as strongly imbedded in our public and private life. . . . This freedom to worship was indispensable in a country whose people came from the four quarters of the earth and brought with them a diversity of religious opinion. . . .

Extent of the First Amendment

Before examining . . . (the) "neutral" position in which the Establishment and Free Exercise Clauses of the First Amendment place our government it is well that we discuss the reach of the Amendment under the cases of this Court. . . .

First, this Court has decisively settled that the First Amendment's mandate that "Congress shall make no law respecting an establishment of religion, or prohibiting the free exercise thereof" has been made wholly applicable to the states by the Fourteenth Amendment. . . .

Second, this Court has rejected unequivocally the contention that the establishment clause forbids only governmental preference of one religion over another. . . .

Establishment and Free Exercise

The interrelationship of the Establishment and the Free Exercise Clauses was first touched upon by MR. JUSTICE ROBERTS for the Court in CANTWELL v. CONNECTICUT . . . where it was said that their "inhibition of legislation" had

> a double aspect. On the one hand, it forestalls compulsion by law of the acceptance of any creed or the practice of any form of worship. Freedom of conscience and freedom to adhere to such religious organization or form of worship as the individual may choose cannot be restricted by law. On the other hand, it safeguards the free exercise of the chosen form of religion. Thus the Amendment embraces two concepts—freedom to believe and freedom to act. The first is absolute but, in the nature of things, the second cannot be.

*　*　*　*　*

[In ENGEL v. VITALE] only last year, these principles were so universally recognized that the Court without the citation of a single case and over the sole dissent of MR. JUSTICE STEWART reaffirmed them. The Court found the 22-word prayer used in "New York's program of daily classroom invocation of God's blessings as prescribed in the Regents' prayer . . . [to be] a religious activity. . . ." It held that "it is no part of the business of government to compose official prayers for any group of the American people to recite as a part of a religious program carried on by the government. . . ." In discussing the reach of the Establishment and Free Exercise Clauses of the First Amendment the Court said:

> Although these two clauses may in certain instances overlap, they forbid two quite different kinds of governmental encroachment upon religious freedom. The Establishment Clause, unlike the Free Exercise Clause, does not depend upon any showing of direct governmental compulsion and is violated by the enactment of laws which establish an official religion whether those laws operate directly to coerce non-observing individuals or not. This is not to say, of course, that laws officially prescribing a particular form of religious worship do not involve coercion of such individuals. When the power, prestige and financial support of government is placed behind a particular religious belief, the indirect coercive pressure upon religious minorities to conform to the prevailing officially approved religion is plain.

And in further elaboration the Court found that the "first and most immediate purpose [of the Establishment Clause] rested on a belief that a union of government and religion tends to destroy government and to degrade religion. . . ." When government, the Court said, allies itself with one particular form of religion, the inevitable result is that it incurs "the hatred, disrespect and even contempt of those who held contrary beliefs. . . ."

Neutrality

The whole "neutrality" of which this Court's cases speak thus stems from a recognition of the teachings of history that powerful sects or groups might bring about a fusion of governmental and religious functions or a concert or dependency of one upon the other to the end that official support of the State or Federal Government would be placed behind the tenets of one or of all orthodoxies. This the Establishment Clause prohibits. And a further reason for neutrality is found in the Free Exercise Clause, which recognizes the value of religious training, teaching and observance and, more particularly, the right of every person to freely choose his own course with reference thereto, free of any compulsion from the State. This the Free Exercise Clause guarantees. Thus, as we have seen, the two clauses may overlap. . . .

Applying the Establishment Clause principles to the cases at bar we find that the States are requiring the selection and reading at the opening of the school day of verses from the Holy Bible and the recitation of the Lord's Prayer by the students in unison. These exercises are prescribed as part of the curricular activities of students who are required by law to attend school. They are held in the school buildings under the supervision and with the participation of teachers employed in those schools. . . . The trial court in . . . (ABINGTON v. SCHEMPP) has found that such an opening exercise is a religious ceremony and was intended by the State to be so. We agree with the trial court's finding as to the religious character of the exercises. Given that finding the exercises and the law requiring them are in violation of the Establishment Clause.

There is no such specific finding as to the religious character of the exercises in . . . (MURRAY v. CURLETT) and the State contends . . . that the program is an effort to extend its benefits to all public school children without regard to their religious belief. Included within its secular purposes, it says, are the promotion of moral values, the contradiction to the materialistic trends of our times, the perpetuation of our institutions and the teaching of literature. The case came up on demurrer, of course, to a petition which alleged that the uniform practice under the rule had been to read from the King James version of the Bible and that the exercise was sectarian. The short answer, therefore, is that the religious character of the exercise was admitted by the State. But even if its purpose is not strictly religious, it is sought to be accomplished through readings, without comment, from the Bible. Surely the place of the Bible as an instrument of religion cannot be gainsaid, and the State's recognition of the pervading religious character of the ceremony is evident from the rule's specific permission of the alternative use of the Catholic Douay version as well as the recent amendment permitting nonattendance at the exercises. None of these factors is consistent with the contention that the Bible is here used either as an instrument for nonreligious moral inspiration or as a reference for the teaching of secular subjects.

The conclusion follows that in both cases the laws require religious exercises and such exercises are being conducted in direct violation of the rights of the appellees and petitioners. Nor are these required exercises mitigated by the fact that individual students may absent themselves upon parental request, for that fact furnishes no defense to a claim of unconstitutionality under the Establishment Clause. . . . Further, it is no defense to urge that the religious practices here may be relatively minor encroachments on the First Amendment. The breach of neutrality that is today a trickling stream may all too soon become a raging torrent. . . .

It is insisted that unless these religious exercises are permitted a "religion of secularism" is established in the schools. We agree, of course, that the State may not establish a "religion of secularism" in the sense of affirmatively opposing or showing hostility to religion, thus "preferring those who believe in no religion over those who do believe. . . ." We do not agree, however, that this decision in any sense has that effect. In addition, it might well be said that one's education is not complete without a study of comparative religion or the history of religion and its relationship to the advancement of civilization. It certainly may be said that the Bible is worthy of study for its literary and historic qualities. Nothing we have said here indicates that such study of the Bible or religion, when presented objectively as part of a secular program of education, may not be effected consistent with the First Amendment. But the exercises here do not fall into those categories. They are religious exercises, required by the States in violation of the command of the First Amendment that the Government maintain strict neutrality, neither aiding nor opposing religion.

Finally, we cannot accept that the concept of neutrality, which does not permit a State to require a religious exercise even with the consent of the majority of those affected, collides with the majority's right to free exercise of religion. While the Free Exercise Clause clearly prohibits the use of State action to deny the rights of free exercise to *anyone,* it has never meant that a majority could use the machinery of the State to practice its beliefs. . . .

The place of religion in our society is an exalted one, achieved through a long tradition of reliance on the home, the church and the inviolable citadel of the individual heart and mind. We have come to recognize through bitter experience that it is not within the power of government to invade that citadel, whether its purpose or effect be to aid or oppose, to advance or retard. In the relationship between man and religion, the State is firmly committed to a position of neutrality. Though the application of that rule requires interpretation of a delicate sort, the rule itself is clearly and concisely stated in the words of the First Amendment. Applying that rule to the facts of these cases, we affirm the judgment in No. 142 (ABINGTON v. SCHEMPP). In No. 119 (MURRAY v. CURLETT) the judgment is reversed and the cause remanded to the Maryland Court of Appeals for further proceedings consistent with this opinion.

It is so ordered.

3 Religion, Constitutional Federalism, Rights, and the Court

SIDNEY E. MEAD *

"The legal profession in all countries knows that there are only two real choices of government open to a people. It may be governed by law or it may be governed by the will of one or a group of men. Law, as the expression of the ultimate will and wisdom of a people, has so far proven the safest guardian of liberty yet devised." [1]

Our nation is pluralistic by inheritance and nature. The United States, wrote Philip Schaff in 1855, presents "a motley sampler of all church history, and the results it has thus far attained." [2] During the century since Schaff wrote, to all the Christian denominations and sects that he noted have been added organized representatives of all the world's religions plus a few religions invented here. Each is an interest group competing with all the others.

Granted this multiplicity of competing religious groups there are bound to be disputes and conflicts that threaten the civil order. How one thinks such conflicts ought to be settled depends upon his

* Reprinted with permission of the publisher from *Journal of Church and State,* Vol. 14, No. 2, Spring 1972, pp. 191-209.

understanding of the nature of the democratic republic and especially of the rule of the law and the courts in it. It has seemed
to me that many attempts to discuss a "church-state" [3] issue in
the United States reveal a lack of such understanding. This essay
attempts only an elemental "map" of the system.

There are many definitions of "democracy." We may begin
with that of Judge Learned Hand: "Democracy is a political con-
trivance by which the group conflicts inevitable in all society should
find a relatively harmless outlet in the give and take of legislative
compromise." This means that democratic government is a method
—a means to an end, and not an end in itself. The end, in general
terms, is the securing of "life, liberty, and the pursuit of happiness."

In this context, as Professor Harry Jones noted, ". . . it is law's
unique role in a democratic society to accomplish a resolution, at
least a tolerable accommodation, of the conflicting interests and
opposed demands that are inevitable in any dynamic community." [4] The point is that in a pluralistic society such as ours compromise and accommodation of absolutistic claims in practice are
of the essence. If it is working no individual, no group, no faction,
or no interest can have his or its way completely. Every group must
learn to live with less than the whole pie precisely in order that the
others may live also in their way with their due part. This is difficult
for the religious groups, not only because religious commitment is
an all-or-nothing stance, but also because most of the old-line denominations grew up in national households like spoiled only
children, each accustomed to having its way while being fed,
clothed, and protected from interference by a civil power. The
attitudes developed during such upbringing are hard to eradicate,
and the persistence of "sectarianism" [5] is evidence that they still
exist in the religious groups.

But the law plays not only the negative role of preserving the
general welfare and outward peace. It also plays a positive role in
forming, shaping, and consolidating what Adolf Berle called the
"public consensus," [6] that binds society together. Laws may "encourage the virtuous" as well as "restrain the vicious." [7]

The law, for example, may induce some reluctant Christians
to live up to their Master's command. For, if Matthew 5:44 [8] be
interpreted as a command to every sect as well as to individual

Christians, then the civil law that forbids a sect to retaliate overtly against those who curse or despitefully use it plays a positive role in restraining Christians to act as if they were exhibiting the charity they profess. There is little evidence that they exercised such charity until the authority of a commonwealth constrained them to do so.[9] To civil authority the religious groups had become devisive and destructive. It could no longer maintain religious uniformity. Therefore it had to try to maintain peace and order between the sects, and in order to do so it had to become neutral so far as the sects' particularistic claims were concerned.

It may be admitted that charity and forbearance cannot be legislated. But overt action reflecting its absence may be controlled by positive law. As Martin Luther King put it, "A law can't force a man to love me, but it can keep him from lynching me. A law can't change the heart but it can restrain the heartless." [10] We too readily forget that at least from the time of the Toleration Act in Maryland in 1649 the outward appearance of the exercise of such charity and forbearance was again and again forced upon religious sectarians in the English colonies by law or authoritative decree.

I

FEDERALISM

Now let us look at the Constitutional federalism under which all the denominations live in the United States—and at its legal structure which was set up, negatively, to resolve conflicts, adjudicate differences, and accomplish tolerable accommodations in the commonwealth, and, positively, "to form a more perfect Union, establish Justice, insure domestic Tranquility, provide for the common defense, promote the general Welfare, and secure the blessings of Liberty to ourselves and our Posterity."

"Government" refers to the institution(s) accepted as the sole wielder(s) of coercive power—the locus (or loci) of legitimated authority—in the society. It is a truism that "the Government can suffer no rivals in the field of coercion." [11] The government of the United States is a federalism, in which governmental powers are

not concentrated in a unitary state, but are distributed between national and local authorities, each of which, in its defined realm, is
an institutionalized locus of the supreme sovereignty.[12]

In addition "the exercise of governmental power [by either or
both] is subject to limitations protective of the rights of the individual." [13] It is obvious that the distribution of power between the
national and local authorities is bound to lead to conflicts requiring adjudication. It is equally obvious that restrictions on the authority of both over the individual citizen are similarly bound to
lead to conflicts. For in the nature of things as Justice William J.
Brennan put it, ". . . no genius of constitution making could have
delineated the precise boundaries of the powers assigned the several repositories of governmental power . . . [or] fashioned precise
guide lines for the resolution of the myriad collisions between
power exercised by any of these repositories and the guarantees of
individual liberty erected to restrain governmental oppression whatever its source." In this situation "some institution had to referee
these conflicts, and the Framers chose the Supreme Court ultimately
to perform that duty"—an extremely difficult duty because necessarily "the guide lines are indistinct." [14]

But the guidelines are there, "in the Constitution"—which
phrase I put in quotation marks to remind us again that what is "in"
the Constitution is in practice something that the Court decides. In
other words, for the time being at least, the Constitution means in
any particular justiciable issue what the majority of the Court says
it means. To understand this, one must see it in the context of the
inclusive meaning and implications of government under a written
Constitution.

II
CONSTITUTIONALISM

Constitutionalism means government by defined law rather
than by "one [man] or a group of men." A written Constitution is,
first of all, a statement of the fundamental principles of a body
politic that defines the locus of the sovereign power (e.g., in "the
people"); its distribution (e.g., federalism); the structure of the

government and the relation between the parts (e.g., legislative, executive, and judicial). Second, it is a statement of the rules governing the forming and perpetuation of the government (e.g., for adopting the Constitution, eligibility for office, elections); for adjudicating differences that arise within the body; and amending the Constitution itself. Necessarily the principles have to be stated on a level of high generality, the rules somewhat less so. Together they constitute the guidelines and their indistinctness is commensurate with their generality. That is why umpires or referees are necessary, namely, to decide what a particular generality in the Constitution means when applied to a specific controverted point. To ask if something is "Constitutional" is to ask if it is consistent with the fundamental principles of the nation. In this sense the Court functions as the guardian of the character of the Republic.

By the time the English colonies were firmly planted on the eastern seaboard of America, the ideas were well established that "the power of the ruler should be exercised in accordance with established fundamental law, and that the government should owe its existence to a compact of the governed." [15] Thomas Hooker, preaching at Hartford, Connecticut in 1638, insisted that "the foundation of authority is laid, firstly, in the free consent of the people." [16] And ten years later in his *A Survey of the Summe of Church Discipline* he argued that before a person has any power over another "there must of necessity be a mutuall ingagement, each of the other, by their free consent, before by any rule of God they have any right or power or can exercise either, each towards the other." [17]

The concept of the consent of the governed was rooted in the image of men in the "state of nature" wherein no person had any right of power over another. Because it is questionable that any thinker really supposed either that such a state had actually existed or that such a contract was a historical reality,[18] we may call this a myth. But it was a myth of tremendous motivational power during the seventeenth and eighteenth centuries in overthrowing old governments and establishing new forms.

The concept reflected the great conceptual revolution that inverted the traditional view of the flow of God's power for the creation of ordered communities. Traditionally the image had been of the flow of such power from the top down through a man or a group of men thought of as divine or peculiarly accessible to Deity. Now the image became that of the flow of such power from the bottom up—from and through "the people" to rulers chosen by them. "God," said John Locke, "who hath given the world to men in common, hath also given them reason to make use of it to the best advantage of life and convenience." [19] In this view, the law no longer originates on some mountain top above the clouds to be brought down to the people by some God-ordained Moses. Rather, the power of God for the formation of law is *in* "the people," and "Moses" becomes their elected deputy.

Government, it follows, is an instrument which men create by reason and choice because they see its advantages as well as its necessity. Conceptually all power is from God, and God ordains government. But now the power on earth is resident first in "the people," and rulers have power only as a "trust reposed in them" by "the people." It follows that such rulers must "govern by *declared* and *received Laws,* and not by extemporary Dictates and undetermined Resolutions." [20] And *"The People shall be Judge"* of whether or not their chosen legislators "act contrary to their Trust." [21] Hence, so far as the creation of ordered communities is concerned, the people might be said to be enjoined in the words of Philippians 2: 12-13, ". . . work out your own salvation with fear and trembling. For it is God which worketh in you both to will and to do of his good pleasure." [22]

The myth, then, is that the people institute government by entering into a covenant (compact, contract) with one another, primarily to secure their rights. The Constitution lays down the terms of the contract—the rule of conduct to be observed and followed—the "guidelines" adherence to which is deemed most efficacious in protecting the individual's rights while promoting and defending the general welfare. One *consents* to these terms of the contract, which implies that he accepts certain responsibilities and duties which, within defined limits, he can be coerced to assume.

But because the ultimate sovereign power *on earth* is in "the people" and the government is their instrument, the Constitution itself provides that the people may alter the fundamental law and, as part of the contract, lays down the rules to be followed in amending it. But the people also reserve the radical right when "any form of Government becomes destructive of these ends . . . to abolish it, and to institute new Government" deemed more likely to achieve their ends. Abraham Lincoln in his first Inaugural Address summarized these principles in classic style: "This country, with its institutions, belongs to the people who inhabit it. Whenever they shall grow weary of the existing Government, they can exercise their constitutional right of amending it or their revolutionary right to dismember or overthrow it." [23]

Constitutionalism plus religious pluralism forced the "secularization" of government—for "secularization" means the "desectarianization" of government, that is, the civil authority must become neutral where the particularistic claims of the sects are concerned.[24] For government is for *all* men in society, and *all* men enter into the compact that forms it. As Judge H. M. Brackenridge put it in 1819 in protesting the Maryland law excluding Jews from public office, "our political compacts are not entered into as brethren of the Christian faith—but as men, as members of a civilized society." [25]

Implicit here is the conception of appeal to a universal principle that transcends not only the particularities that distinguish the Christian denominations or sects from one another, but also the particularities that distinguish one world religion from another. "*All* men are created equal," of whatever religion, denomination, or sect whatsoever, and all are equally endowed "with certain unalienable rights." [26]

It is helpful to think of American constitutional government as a game which "we the people" have engaged to play for the high stakes of freedom. The game has defined and known rules that are consented to as a condition of entering the game. The rules define the nature of the game, and set limits to permissible conduct in playing it. Referees or umpires are recognized as having power to interpret the rule-book of the game, and their decisions have the sanction of coercive power if necessary. The rules themselves include a provision for modifying them without changing the basic character of the game (the constitutional right to amend). And, of course, it is recognized that the players also have the right if they grow weary of the game, to change to another game with a different set of rules (the revolutionary right). Therefore it is very important if and when we question the decisions of the recognized referees to be very clear whether we are merely advocating amending the existing rules, or whether we are advocating shifting to a different kind of game. When uncomfortable or outraged with Supreme Court decisions striking down the Regent's prayer or Bible reading and recitation of the Lord's Prayer in the schools, people advocated the Becker, Dirkson, or similar amendments, they were playing the game according to the rules. But if, as reported in the papers, a speaker in southern California declared that the Chief Justice ought to be hanged because of a decision the Court made, he was advocating that we change to another kind of game.

III
RIGHTS

The concept of inalienable rights of the individual citizen was the corollary of constitutionalism. Anciently the power of God for the creation of ordered human communities, conceived primarily as coercive, was channeled through specially designated *powers* on earth—a priest-king or an elite—who wielded it to create ordered communities. Rather early in Christendom even the power of God for salvation (grace) came under the monopolistic control of a self-perpetuating line of priests (the "Church") through whom alone grace was made available to ordinary mortals. With the emergence of the nations a particular church became coextensive with a state.[27] The Reformation's "right-wing" churches were the tribal cults of the new nations.

The individual as a citizen-church member had no inherent rights that he could assert against the supposedly ordained repositories of power. He had, it was argued, "no other Remedy but Patience" for "that an Inferior should punish a Superior, is against Nature."[28] That the people must not defend themselves even against a "King imperiously domineering over them"[29] was sometimes deduced from Romans 13: 1-2: ". . . there is no power but of God; and the *powers* that be are ordained of God. Therefore he that resisteth the powers, withstandeth the ordinance of God; and they that withstand shall receive to themselves judgment." Resistance was a sin as well as a civil offense. To be sure the hard lot of the individual under the laws civil-ecclesiastical might be alleviated by monarch or priest. But such alleviation was an act of grace—a sheer gift. Some gifts of grace might become habitual in a society as "privileges" customarily granted by "the *powers*" but subject to withdrawal at their whim. We should not confuse such "privileges" with "rights."

The conceptual revolution noted above inverted this order, placing the power of God for the forming of communities in the people, making all rulers their deputies. And "the *Fundamental law* of [their] Nature," said Locke, "Being *the preservation of Mankind,* no Humane Sanction can be good or valid against it." [30] Therefore the basic collective right of the people is self-defense against outside enemies *or* their own chosen rulers who may become derelict in their duties. This, said Locke, is "the common Refuge which God hath provided for all Men against Force and Violence." [31]

The concept of government by consent of the governed implies that some rights are reserved by the individual—"every Man has a Property in his own *Person*. This no Body has any Right to but himself." [32] The obverse side of a right is a duty. An "unalienable" right is one that a person cannot relinquish the responsibility for exercising even if he thinks he wants to. "The care of every man's soul belongs to himself," Jefferson said. "The magistrate has no power but what the people gave," and they "have not given him the care of souls because they could not; they could not, because no man has *right* to abandon the care of his salvation to another." [33]

In defining "federalism," as noted above, the conception of rights operates as a limitation on the exercise of both national and local governmental authority over the individual. It is important that we understand why this is so.

In the practice of constitutionalism all the major decisions are reached through majority vote. But it is a majority operating under defined law. Part of that fundamental law is the Bill of Rights that limits "the power of the majority [even when] duly expressed through governmental action." [34] As Mr. Justice Robert H. Jackson summarized in the *Barnette* case (1943): "The very purpose of a

Bill of Rights was to withdraw certain subjects from the vicissitudes of political controversy, to place them beyond the reach of majorities and officials and to establish them as legal principles to be applied by the courts. One's right to life, liberty, and property, to free speech, a free press, freedom of worship and assembly, and other fundamental rights may not be submitted to vote; they depend on the outcome of no elections." [35]

Where religion is concerned, the Bill of Rights exists to protect minorities against "the tyranny of a majority" after long experience had shown "that society cannot trust the conscience of a majority to keep its religious zeal within the limits that a free society can tolerate." [36] This has important bearing on the permission of religious exercises in the public schools. The forms of worship would presumably be determined by majority vote—local, state, or national. Therefore, the proper question to ask is not, "Would you approve of prayers and/or Bible reading in the public schools?" but rather, "Would you as a member of a minority religious group (and in the United States every religious group is a minority) want the majority given the power to impose its form of worship on all the children in the schools?"

While a Bill of Rights may be part of the fundamental law of a nation, "it is the first axiom of a constitutional government that declarations of rights are meaningless, or can be made so, if there are no remedies to enforce them." And in the Constitutionalism of the United States "that remedy is provided . . . by the power of the courts, the ordinary courts, to review the constitutionality of legislative and executive action, and, if it violates constitutional principles, declare it void and ineffective." [37]

In other words, the constitution enumerates only *some* of the rights of a citizen. The Ninth Amendment reminds us that there are other rights not listed. The principle of judicial review means that the citizen can appeal to the courts if and when he thinks a right is being infringed by any legislative or executive action. In this sense the courts are the protectors of the citizen against legislative or executive infringement of his rights. The Court, in interpreting what the Constitution means, speaks for "the people"— the Constitution being the symbol of the sovereignty of the people.

Or, as summarized by Justice Jackson in his *Barnette* case opinion, "the Fourteenth Amendment, as now applied to the states, protects the citizen against the State itself and all its creatures—Boards of Education not excepted." [38]

It is important to understand the nature and purpose of the Bill of Rights and how its provisions are enforced. Well meaning people, who apparently did not understand its implications, have argued that striking down a state or local law requiring religious exercises in its public schools—which law was enacted "with the consent of the majority of those affected, collides with the majority's right of free exercise of religion." Rightly Justice Tom Clark replied that "while the Free Exercise Clause clearly prohibits the use of state action to deny the rights of free exercise to *anyone,* it has never meant that a majority could use the machinery of the State to practice its beliefs," [39] and compel observance of its *religious* exercises by all. This would be to deny free exercise to all the minorities.

IV
The Court

"The Supreme Court," said Justice William J. Brennan, Jr., "has been assigned the unique responsibility for umpiring our federal system," and, we might add, it has shared the fate and fare of most umpires. [41]

The Constitution is the rule book of the game we are playing. But the game is so vast and so complex that the rules of necessity must be broad and inclusive. As Lincoln put it: ". . . no organic law can ever be framed with a provision specifically applicable to every question which may occur in practical administration. No foresight can anticipate nor any document of reasonable length contain express provisions for all possible questions." Echoing this view, Justice William O. Douglas stated that "the federal constitution, . . . is not a code but . . . a summation of [the] general principles, . . . of a regime which the Fathers designed for us." [42]

The provisions in the Bill of Rights have the form of inclusive propositions, general principles, and abstractions. The work of the Court is the translation of these general principles "into concrete constitutional commands," [43]—"the application of [these] universal principles to the endless and infinitely varied concrete instances that occur in the real world." [44] This requires careful definition of the meaning of the general principles, plus clear reasoning from them to detailed and practical fact. And this involves "arguable controversies, problems of judgment and choice on which reasonable men can [and do] disagree and reasonable Justices of the Supreme Court of the United States divide five to four, or six to three, or in some other ratio." [45] Or, as Lincoln said of emancipation in 1862, "the subject is difficult and good men do not agree." [46] Thus the work of the Court is "constitutional exegesis," [47] the work of "arbitrating the allocation of powers between different branches of the Federal Government, between state and nation, between state and state, and between majority government and minority rights." [48]

As such, the Court is a peculiar and fragile institution in the American system. On the one hand it has status as an independent unit of government. But it is "in vital respects a dependent body," [49] its make up, powers, and limitations ambiguously defined in the Constitution (Article III), and its most visible aspect, appellate jurisdiction, the creation of Congress in the Judiciary Act of 1789.[50] Its most impressive power is that of judicial review of the constitutionality of legislative or executive acts. But this power "is not expressly granted or hinted at in the Article defining judicial power, but rests on logical implication." [51] It is for this reason that "[John] Marshall's great constitutional decisions" establishing this power "cite no precedents . . . they are argued out of political philosophy. . . ." [52]

Because it is a court it is "a substantially passive instrument" of government that can be "moved only by the initiative of litigants." [53] This means that the Court cannot go out looking for controverted issues to be resolved. It follows that the issues brought to it closely reflect the primary areas of political conflict in the society at the time.[54] Further, to make the appellate work of the Court manageable, "Congress has found it necessary to make review in the Supreme Court not the right of the litigant but a discretionary matter with the Court itself." [55] In a typical year only 119 of 1,452 cases presented were allowed. Naturally there is a tendency to select those cases that present very pressing issues. It is for these reasons that "the Constitution has gone through several cycles of interpretation" during the years, each cycle of emphasis reflecting the "political and economic condition of the period." [56] Therefore it should be kept in mind that "when judges do not agree, it is a sign that they are dealing with problems on which society itself is divided." [57]

Perhaps the greatest limitation on the Court, and the one least understood, is that its judicial power "extends only to cases and controversies." [58] It has "but one function—that of deciding litigations. . . ." [59] This means that it cannot act unless an occasion to act is brought to it. Yet, in spite of all these ambiguities and limitations, the Court has thus far rather successfully operated in our system to "accomplish a resolution, [or] at least a tolerable accommodation" of the innumerable "conflicting interests and opposed demands" of the pluralistic nation. In other words, it has been the chief instrument for the maintenance of a government of law. [60]

The Court is a court is a court—on this we must be clear. It is not a philosophical club, not a debating society, not an academic discussion group that meets to discuss and define the ideal, abstract, and theological meanings of such terms as "religious freedom," "separation," "establishment," "free exercise," and so on. In fact it is precluded from "rendering . . . every form of pronouncement on abstract, contingent, or hypothetical issues." [61] It has been argued that because even scholars are not agreed on the "criteria for religious activity" that the Court can have no "competence to distinguish religious acts fom non-religious acts" and therefore, ought to "leave this area alone" or at least wait "until such time as . . . [it] has done its homework on the nature of religion in American society." [62] Aside from reflecting a "stop the world I want to get off" academic mentality, this exhibits a gross misunderstanding of the whole system deserving the charge Blaise Pascal directed at students of theology in his day—"A looseness of thought and language that would pass nowhere else in making what are professedly fine distinctions." [63]

For it is elemental, as Justice Jackson said, that the duty of the Court "to apply the Bill of Rights to assertions of official authority" does not "depend upon our possession of marked competence in the field where the invasion of rights occurs." [64]

Because the Court *is* a court the Justices "have to adjudicate" within a time limit. Once they have taken a case they have to publish a decision with all its multifarious implications and in the midst of all the ambiguities of the contending claims that usually involve the legitimate invocations of "more than one so-called principle." [65] Partisans and advocates tend to reduce a question to a simple either or choice, a misconception of the situation exposed by Mr. Justice Oliver W. Holmes:

All rights tend to declare themselves absolute to their logical extreme. Yet all in fact are limited by the neighborhood of principles of policy which are other than those on which the particular right is founded, and which become strong enough to hold their own when a certain point is reached. . . . The boundary at which the conflicting interests balance cannot be determined by any general formula in advance, but points in the line, or helping to establish it, are fixed by decisions that this or that concrete case falls on the nearer or farther side.

To this Mr. Justice Felix Frankfurter added, "If the conflict cannot be resolved, the task of the Court is to arrive at an accommodation of the contending claims. This is the core of the difficulties and misunderstandings about the judicial process. This, for any conscientious judge, is the agony of his duty." [66] This is the agony induced by the necessity to come to a definite decision in the midst of ambiguity, while knowing that the decision will have far-reaching consequences in the lives of human beings. In the context of the idea that the Court is the guardian of the character of the Republic . . . its decisions are moral decisions. And the consequences of a moral decision of this kind cannot be known in advance.

Finally, the Court has no coercive power at its command, and is completely "dependent upon the political branches for the execution of its mandates." Every schoolboy learns that President Jackson once withheld enforcement, saying, " 'John Marshall has made his decision: now let him enforce it!' " [67]

Here one can see the plausibility of Robert G. McCloskey's conclusion (a disputed interpretation to be sure) that Congress can "decide whether the Supreme Court will be a significant or a peripheral factor in American government." [68] For as the then emeritus Justice Owen J. Roberts put it, probably there is nothing but tradition to prevent Congress from taking away "all the appellate jurisdiction of the Supreme Court . . . ," because Congress defines "in what cases the Supreme Court can entertain an appeal." [69] Because judicial review alone places limits on the legislative power, to strip the Court of this power would have the effect of making the legislative power supreme with the judicial power subservient to it.[70] This, so long as the outward forms of the Republic prevailed, would in effect make a majority supreme, and against it minorities would have no appeal. This is why eternal vigilance in support of freedom in the pluralistic society entails a perpetual "fuss over the rights of minorities" which well-meaning citizens have railed against.[71]

And "the people shall be judge" of what they want, and deserve what they get. For the whole system rests on the public consensus. Thus far, as Mr. Justice Jackson noted, public opinion has seemed "always to sustain the power of the Court, even against attack by popular executives and even though the public more than once has repudiated particular decisions." [72] This is to say that the people thus far have indicated that this is the game that they want to play for the high stakes of freedom, and they have been willing to stick to the rules of the game. "The people have seemed to feel that the Supreme Court, whatever its defects, is still the most detached, dispassionate, and trustworthy custodian that our system affords for the translation of abstract into concrete constitutional commands." [73]

It is clear that the whole system of constitutional federalism rests on the belief that the Constitution as interpreted by the Court is the highest authority of the nation for the resolution of conflicts in the society. I see no way to "prove" this. All one can do is point to the "fact" that this is the case. "Civil liberties had their origin and must find their ultimate guaranty in the faith of the people." [74] In practice this means their faith that the application of the principles laid down in the Constitution is the surest defense of their rights and freedoms.

Perhaps there is a lesson to be learned by thinking analogically of what happened to the visible church in Christendom when enough people ceased to believe that the Bible *as interpreted by the ecclesiastical institution* was the highest authority for the guidance of their lives. For when they rejected the institution's authority to interpret the concrete meaning of the Bible's principles for all, and insisted upon "no rule but the Scriptures" *and* the "right of private judgment" in its interpretation, the visible universal church was fragmented into mutually murderous warring sects, and, as some predicted, belief in the Bible as highest authority followed apace.[75] When in the society there was no longer an agreed upon institutionalized locus for the adjudication of differences between members of the Christian household of faith, the centripetal force of a common authority was overcome by the centrifugal force of individual freedom and the *catholic* church flew apart. I think that an analogous situation would follow in the nation if every minority began to insist on the "right of private judgment" in interpreting the Constitution. Then as the consequent threat of anarchy and chaos was widely observed, we would expect some form of tyrannical control in the name of law and order for the preservation of outward unity in the face of enemies from without. As Lincoln said, a people have just three possibilities in government—anarchy (which is no-government), despotism, and consent (now called participatory authority).

At present fragmentation seems a less obvious threat than centralization—the tendency "to move the center of gravity from the state capital to that of the nation." [76] This tendency is understandable and justifiable enough in the context of technological development that, as Adlai Stevenson said, has made counties out of continents and lakes out of oceans. Nevertheless, the threat to individual freedom inherent in the workings of vast national bureaucracies is clear enough to make them a legitimate object of attack. But we must note that such necessary attack can take forms that tend to undermine the prevailing consensus that the Constitution *as interpreted by the Supreme Court* is the highest authority for the resolution of conflicts within the commonwealth.

The saving factor in the situation is that the Constitution is a flexible instrument, "designed for a developing nation." It delineates, as Mr. Justice Frankfurter put it, "the skeleton or framework of our society—the anatomical as against the physiological aspects." [77] Continued growth is possible because "those features of our Constitution which raise the most frequent perplexities for a decision by the Court . . . were drawn in many particulars with purposeful vagueness so as to leave room for the unfolding but undisclosed future." [78] What Chief Justice Hughes said of dissenting opinions can be applied to all the law as interpreted by the Court—it is "an appeal to the brooding spirit of the law, to the intelligence of a future day" when future decisions will perchance correct the error of the present time in the light of much discussion of the issues, more experience in living with the results of past decisions, and, hopefully, of greater wisdom in the people.

In summary, as Mr. Justice Jackson said, ". . . the destiny of this Court is inseparably linked to the fate of our democratic system of government, . . ." [79] and the fate of our democratic system hinges upon the vision and faith of the people. As the ancient wisdom had it, where there is no vision the people perish, so it might now be said that not only the just, but also the free, must live by faith.

NOTES

1. Robert H. Jackson, *The Supreme Court in the American System of Government* (New York: Harper & Row, 1963), p. 27.

2. Philip Schaff, *America: A Sketch of Its Political, Social and Religious Character,* ed. Perry Miller (Cambridge: Belknap Press of Harvard University Press, 1961), p. 20.

3. The use of traditional "church-state" terminology is a chief source of confusion when applied to the situation in the United States. For a summary view see my "Neither Church nor State: Reflections on James Madison's 'Line of Separation,' " *Journal of Church and State* 10 (Autumn 1968), 349-363.

4. "Church-State Relations: Our Constitutional Heritage," in Harold Stahmer, ed., *Religion and Contemporary Society* (New York: Macmillan Co., 1963), p. 158.

5. For what I mean by "sectarianism" see my article, "The Fact of Pluralism and the Persistence of Sectarianism," in Elwyn A. Smith, ed., *The Religion of the Republic* (Philadelphia: Fortress Press, 1971), pp. 247-266.

6. Adolph A. Berle, Jr., *Power Without Property: A New Development in American Political Economy* (New York: Harcourt, Brace & World, Harvest Book, 1959), pp. 90, 91, 110-116.

7. Virginia Presbyterian Petition of 1776 as quoted in H. Shelton Smith, Robert T. Handy, and Lefferts A. Loetscher, *American Christianity: An Historical Interpretation With Representative Documents*, 2 vols. (New York: Charles Scribner's Sons, 1960), 1, p. 445.

8. "But I say unto you, Love your enemies, bless them that curse you, do good to them that hate you, and pray for them which despitefully use you, and persecute you."

9. Compare William Pauck, *The Heritage of the Reformation* (Glencoe, Ill.: Free Press, 1950), p. 230; ". . . the separation of the church from the state was primarily due to the initiative of the modern state and not of the church." See also my *The Lively Experiment: The Shaping of Christianity in America* (New York: Harper & Row, 1963), pp. 20-22, 26, 27.

10. Speech at Grinnell College, reported in the *Iowa City Press Citizen,* October 30, 1967.

11. Robert H. Jackson, "The Supreme Court as a Political Institution," in Alan F. Westin, ed., *The Supreme Court: Views from Inside* (New York: W. W. Norton and Co., 1961), p. 163.

12. James Madison's Fifty-First Federalist Paper contains the classic statement of the difference between "a single republic" and the "compound republic" (federalism) of the United States. In Clinton Rossiter, ed., *The Federalist Papers* (New York: New American Library, Mentor Book, 1961), p. 323.

13. Felix Frankfurter, "The Process of Judging in the Supreme Court," in Westin, *The Supreme Court*, p. 35.

14. *Ibid.*, p. 109.

15. Perry Miller and Thomas H. Johnson, eds., *The Puritans* (New York: American Book Company, 1938), p. 187.

16. As quoted in Karl Herbert Hertz, "Bible Commonwealth and Holy Experiment: A Study of the Relations Between Theology and Politics in the Puritan and Quaker Colonies" (Ph.D. diss., University of Chicago, n.d.), p. 107.

17. As quoted in *ibid.*, p. 188.

18. Compare William Temple: "It is now generally recognized that theories of a Social Contract cannot in any case be more than mythological; probably this was the intention of their several authors. There never was a moment when a contract was made. But a contract between Sovereign and people is implicit in their relations to one another." *Citizen and Churchman* (London: Eyre & Spottiswoode, 1941), p. 24. For some, America apparently made the image of a state of nature real. John Locke in discussing property

in money declared, "Thus in the beginning all the World was *America*. . . . for no such thing as *Money* was anywhere known." "An Essay Concerning the True Original Extent, and End of Civil Government" (The Second Treatise of Government), chap. 5, sec. 49, in Peter Laslett, ed., *John Locke, Two Treatises of Government: A Critical Edition With An Introduction and Apparatus Criticus* (New York: New American Library, 1965), p. 343.

19. *Ibid.*, p. 328.
20. *Ibid.*, pp. 413, 405.
21. *Ibid.*, p. 476.
22. This might receive literal application as with the Reverend John Davenport who argued that in an election "there are not two several and distinct actions, one of God, another of the People; but in one and the same action God, by the Peoples suffrages, make such an one Governour, or Magistrate, and not another." As quoted in Miller and Johnson, *The Puritans,* p. 109. It was not supposed that such magistrates had divinely given wisdom for ruling. John Winthrop reminded the people ". . . to consider, that when you choose magistrates, you take them from among yourselves, men subject to like passions as you are. . . . When you call one to be a magistrate he doth not profess nor undertake to have sufficient skill for that office, nor can you furnish him with gifts, etc., therefore you must run the hazard of his skill and ability," from Winthrop's speech to the General Court, 3 July 1645, in Miller and Johnson, *The Puritans,* p. 206.
23. The emphasis on the revolutionary right tended to fall into disrepute, and citizens have been penalized for mentioning it. "Roger Baldwin, director of the American Civil Liberties Union, was arrested when he started to read the Declaration of Independence in front of the city hall in Patterson [New Jersey] and was convicted of conducting an unlawful assembly"—Leo Pfeffer, *The Liberties of An American: The Supreme Court Speaks,* 2nd ed. (Boston: Beacon Press, 1963), p. 106.
24. In the *Zorach* case (1952) Justice Douglas argued that "government may not . . . blend secular and sectarian education." Here "secular" means simply "nonsectarian." This meaning seems apt in the context of pluralism. Here is rooted the concept of "neutrality" which the Justices invoked in the *Schempp-Murray* decision of 17 June 1963: "The government is neutral, and, while protecting all, it prefers none, and it disparages none," and "in the relationship between man and religion, the State is firmly committed to a position of neutrality." In Arthur Frommer, ed., *The Bible and the Public Schools* (New York: Liberal Press, 1963), pp. 67, 69.
25. As quoted in Joseph L. Blau, ed., *Cornerstones of Religious Freedom in America* (New York: Harper & Row, 1949), p. 107.
26. Compare Elwyn A. Smith, "Religious Liberty as a Secular Concept, *Journal of Ecumenical Studies* 2 (Spring 1965), p. 275.
27. Ernest Barker, *Church, State and Education* (Ann Arbor: University of Michigan Press, 1957), p. 139.
28. Noted by Locke in Laslett, *John Locke,* p. 469.
29. *Ibid.*, p. 472.
30. *Ibid.*, p. 403. For a scholarly discussion of what I have called

the inversion of the view of the flow of God's power that ushers in modern democracy, see Walter Ullman, *Principles of Government and Politics in the Middle Ages* (New York: Barnes & Noble, 1966), pp. 19-26.

31. Noted by Locke in Laslett, *John Locke,* p. 461.

32. *Ibid.,* p. 328.

33. Thomas Jefferson, "Notes on Religion," in Saul K. Padover, ed., *The Complete Jefferson: Containing His Major Writings, Published and Unpublished Except His Letters* (New York: Duell, Sloan & Pearce, 1943), pp. 943, 944.

34. Jackson, "The Supreme Court," pp. 4, 77.

35. *West Virginia State Board of Education* v. *Barnette,* 319 US 624 (1943), as found in Joseph Tussman, ed., *The Supreme Court on Church and State* (New York: Oxford University Press, 1962), p. 148. This passage was quoted by Justice Clark in his *Murray-Schempp* opinion. Frommer, *The Bible and the Public Schools,* p. 79.

36. Jackson in opinion in *Douglas* v. *City of Jeannette,* 319 US 157 (1943), as found in Tussman, *The Supreme Court on Church and State,* p. 140.

37. Harry Jones, "Church-State Relations: Our Constitutional Heritage," in Stahmer, *Religion and Contemporary Society,* p. 166.

38. Tussman, *The Supreme Court on Church and State,* pp. 147, 148.

39. Majority opinion, *Murray-Schempp* case, in Frommer, *The Bible and the Public Schools,* p. 78.

40. Westin, *The Supreme Court,* p. 103.

41. *Ibid.,* p. 104.

42. William O. Douglas, "In Defense of Dissent," in Westin, *The Supreme Court,* p. 52.

43. Jackson, "The Supreme Court," p. 23.

44. Jones, "Church-State Relations," p. 168.

45. *Ibid.,* pp. 168, 169.

46. Disagreement is expressed in majority and dissenting opinions. The majority opinion becomes the law, although it "actually binds, in most instances, only the parties to the case. As to others, it is merely a weather vane showing which way the judicial wind is blowing—a precedent that the Court in a similar case is likely to follow." Jackson, "The Supreme Court," pp. 13, 17, 19.

47. Jones, "Church-State Relations," p. 158.

48. Jackson, "The Supreme Court," p. 9.

49. *Ibid.,* p. 10.

50. *Ibid.,* pp. 10-13. McCloskey, *The American Supreme Court,* pp. 3, 4.

51. Jackson, "The Supreme Court," p. 22.

52. *Ibid.,* p. 57.

53. *Ibid.,* p. 12.

54. Westin, *The Supreme Court,* pp. 34, 54.

55. Jackson, "The Supreme Court," pp. 13, 14. Westin, *The Supreme Court,* pp. 104, 108.

56. Jackson, "The Supreme Court," p. 23.

57. Westin, *The Supreme Court,* p. 54.

58. Jackson, "The Supreme Court," p. 11. Robert H. Jackson, *The Struggle for Judicial Supremacy: A Study of a Crisis in American Power Politics* (New York: Vintage Books, 1941), ix.

59. Jackson, "The Supreme Court," p. 12.

60. "Struggles over power that in Europe call out regiments of troops, in America call out battalions of lawyers. . . ." Jackson, *The Struggle for Judicial Supremacy*, p. xi.

61. Jackson, "The Supreme Court," p. 12.

62. Clyde A. Holbrook, "Religious Scholarship and the Court," *The Christian Century* 80 (4 September 1963): 1076-1078. See my reply in *The Christian Century* 80 (October 30, 1963), pp. 1342, 1343.

63. Felix Frankfurter, "Reflections on Reading Statutes," in Westin, *The Supreme Court*, p. 92.

64. Tussman, *The Supreme Court on Church and State*, p. 149.

65. For a striking example see *Everson* v. *Board of Education*, 330 US 1 (1947), in Tussman, *The Supreme Court on Church and State*, p. 211.

66. Felix Frankfurter, "The Process of Judging in the Supreme Court," in Westin, *The Supreme Court*, pp. 43, 44.

67. Jackson, "The Supreme Court," p. 11.

68. McCloskey, *The American Supreme Court*, p. 7.

69. Owen J. Roberts, "Protecting the Court's Independence," in Westin, *The Supreme Court*, p. 100. For a thorough review of the issue see Leonard G. Ratner, "Congressional Power Over the Appellate Jurisdiction of the Supreme Court," *University of Pennsylvania Law Review* 109 (December 1960), pp. 157-202.

70. Douglas, "In Defense of Dissent," p. 52.

71. See my reply to Emmons E. White in *The Christian Century* 82 (March 10, 1965), p. 309.

72. Jackson, "The Supreme Court," p. 23.

73. *Ibid.*

74. Tussman, *The Supreme Court on Church and State*, p. 142.

75. In a conference with a Jesuit in 1622, Bishop William Laud anchored "his whole system to the arbitrary word of God," while the Catholic argued "that if the authority of the Universal Church were disowned, the Bible would prove an inadequate substitute, because the Bible would become subject to individual interpretation, no two men would agree on what it meant, Protestantism would split into a hundred differing sects, each one twisting Biblical meanings to suit its own convenience, and thus scripture would lose all the necessary attributes of an authority"—Miller and Johnson, *The Puritans*, pp. 41, 42.

76. Jackson, "The Supreme Court," p. 66.

77. Westin, *The Supreme Court*, p. 37.

78. *Ibid.*

79. Jackson, "The Supreme Court," p. 82.

4 Religion, Education and the Law

DAVID E. ENGEL *

I will begin by stating a proposition which summarizes the major legal constraint about religion in public schools: *You can lead a person to religion, but you can't make him religious.* Accordingly, you can expose meanings in religion, the history of religious developments, the content of religious literature, the relation between religious and secular phenomena, the significance of traditional days, etc. But, according to the Constitution, you cannot make a student (or anyone for that matter) be religious. That is, you cannot coerce someone to engage in some religious act or cultic practice.

If he should pray on his own without coercing others in school and without disrupting the school schedule, probably he can. In law the point is moot. And in actuality that is not a major problem. But if one should contrive to get someone else to pray, then the point is no longer moot. For you can lead a student to religion, but you can't make him religious.

Our Constitution has been sensitive to the tricky balance between religious institutions and the secular state since the adoption

* This essay was originally developed for presentation at a symposium at The Defiance College, Defiance, Ohio in February 1969. It appears here in revised form.

of the Bill of Rights. But only recently has our society generally been aware that issues about religion and religious institutions are difficult to resolve and at times assume a political character. There was no major problem about reading from a Protestant Bible in our common schools until some objected to the practice. The objectors, it became apparent, did not share some of the assumptions about our nation that had gone without challenge in the past. Unlike many, these objectors did not assume that the United States was a Christian nation. And the Supreme Court in evaluating both the position of the litigants and the phraseology of the Bill of Rights had to agree with these objectors (variously named McCollum, Engel, Schempp and Murray).

We should note that our courts, functioning in concert with the First Amendment to the Constitution, are not explicitly concerned with church affairs or theological questions. Instead they are mandated in our republic to preserve the civil integrity of the state and to maintain a climate where the voluntary exercise of religion is possible. That is to say, the concern of government about religion is appropriately secular. I might add that we as citizens generally or as educators specifically share that concern.

Hence it behooves us to be acquainted with the legal guidelines for the relation between religion and education. Without being lawyers, it is possible for us to know salient facts and pertinent theories in this regard.

I

Since 1925 the Supreme Court has entertained a growing number of cases which have to do with religion and education. Without going into the specifics of each case, it can be noted that those decisions have dealt with such diverse issues as: the rights of parents to send their children to non-public schools, the constitutionality of state subsidy for secular textbooks in church-controlled schools, the place of "released time" religious education, the constitutionality of prayers and devotional Bible readings at the opening of the school day. While some critics of the Court may feel that these several decisions were capricious, contradictory, even politically motivated, or, at worst, subversive, I would argue that in the main they are complementary and form the basis for a consistent legal position.

In each case the majority in the Court has been concerned to preserve individual religious liberty, such as in allowing parents to send their children to parochial schools (the *Oregon* case) or in upholding the constitutionality of voluntary released time religious instruction off school premises (the *Zorach* case). At the same time the Court has attempted to prohibit the establishment of a particular religious faith or practice within the public institutions of education of this nation (the *Schempp-Murray* case). While some may be dissatisfied with the outcome of the 1947 *Everson* decision allowing financial rebate for bus fees to parents of children attending parochial schools, the Court in that instance was careful to say that such a practice was valid only as a benefit to the child and not as a direct benefit to the schools themselves. Whether or not you agree with that reasoning, the decision represents an attempt to maintain separation without jeopardizing one's general freedom or his religious liberty.

II

It must be recognized that the public has not received these decisions with universal accord. Following the latest in this series of Court decisions in 1963, a movement to amend the Constitution and legalize prayers and devotional Bible readings in schools has arisen. In some school districts, officials and/or teachers have chosen to ignore what the Supreme Court has said. Continuing devotional practices in public schools is scarcely a good example of teaching students the meaning of due process. In any case, these maneuvers are certainly a symptom of considerable dissatisfaction and unrest over the Supreme Court's decisions in this regard. Instead of dodging such unrest, we should understand its assumptions and dynamics.

In large measure, the issue over religion and education in the popular mind has resulted in a curious polarity which is based neither on constitutional mandate nor on informed sociology. On the one hand, some have criticized the Court for dereligionizing the schools. In brief, it has been felt that reading the Bible and saying a prayer, however uninspired and perfunctory, somehow preserved the religious dimension of life in our schools. There is an obvious educational and religious shallowness of this assertion. Philip Phenix has noted that this is a practice which actually encourages "the view that religion is a specialized activity which can be taken care of in five or ten minutes . . . and then be put out of mind until the next day." [1] But, more importantly, in a pluralistic society the practice invariably violates someone's religious liberty. Which version of the Bible is to be read? What prayers are to be said? What is the object of devotion? Whatever way the issue is resolved, state enforcement of the practice contributes to the establishment of some cult. It is important on this side of the issue that we not read too much into the Court's decisions.

Frequently the rhetoric opposing the *Engel v. Vitale* and the *Schempp-Murray* case has included charges against action which the Supreme Court never took. Declaring Bible readings and prayers in our public schools as contrary to the Constitution is not a decision against religion or God. It is a decision against establishing specific cultic devotional practices.

At the other end of the polarity is the charge that the Court has not gone far enough. Not only are prayers and Bible readings inappropriate. So, some would contend, is any consideration of religion in the classroom. According to this view, it is felt that there is no way to teach religion without making someone adopt a particular faith. The study of religion in public schools is thus seen to be doubly problematic.

In the first place, it is assumed that religion unlike science is not aimed at discovery. It provides a set of answers. Once one learns the answers, then he has adopted a faith or is committed to a position. One does not question religion, so this view would contend, because it is authoritative. It makes its final appeal to some form of revelation from an inscrutable deity. Thus, it might be argued that religious belief is not compatible with knowledge. Faith and reason, belief and knowledge are caught up in a tension which cannot be resolved. The schools are concerned with reason and knowledge; hence belief or faith should be omitted from general education.

Secondly, it would seem that in the field of religion there are a plethora of authorities. Not only is this a matter of divergence among the major religions of the world—Judaism, Christianity, Islam, Buddhism, Hinduism, Taoism, Confucianism, etc.—but even within a single major tradition there is no common agreement. Groups of Christians hold different positions with respect to Scripture, the Church, the nature of man, the activity of God, the questions of justification and sanctification. Nor is sectarian proliferation limited to Christianity. Within Judaism there are at least three or four major groups or emphases. In terms of religious practices and general outlook toward the world it is well nigh impossible to reconcile such disparate bodies as the Hasidim and the Reform community.

Further, because religion tends to generate emotion, those attached to a particular religious outlook are inclined to view other persuasions as erroneous. Why should one be taught error, one camp might charge. As a result, the educator throws up his hands in horror at the impossible task of being fair to all groups. The principle of separation, not merely of church from state, but of religion from education, thus seems to be a reasonable way to avoid a battle which could threaten the integrity and possibly even the existence of the public school.

It is not my intention to minimize this latter argument. Without doubt it takes no little skill to traverse this ground without violating some group's conscience and piety.

But I indicated earlier that neither of these extremes was based on Constitutional grounds or adequate sociology. The first extreme usually assumes that this nation was fundamentally religious in its founding and that this heritage should not be lost. America is thus conceived as a Christian nation. And what is meant by "Christian" usually turns out to be "Protestant" or, in some quarters, WASP. While Protestantism may have been the major faith of our country through the nineteenth century, there is no sociological warrant for such an assertion today.

Will Herberg in his landmark study *Catholic, Protestant, Jew,*[2] showed how we had moved by the 1950's from a Protestant culture to become a three-religion society. We might today, more than fifteen years after Herberg's work, agree to John Courtney Murray's additional thought on this topic. Murray contended that in our nation there were not three but four faiths: Protestant, Catholic, Jew and Secularist.

In any case, it is clear that the United States cannot be viewed as a one-religion nation. Religious pluralism is a sociological fact. From a Constitutional point of view each of the three or four major faiths is to enjoy full freedom of expression except insofar as such freedom may infringe upon the free exercise of another faith and lead, consequently, to the establishment of any one religion in the land.

On the other hand, for those who view religious pluralism in horror at the tensions among faith groupings and conclude that religion has no place in the school, there is another danger. If one contends that a consideration of religion in the public domain is barred by the separation of church and state, then he opens up the possibility of establishing secularism as the faith of the school.

Even though jurists have utilized the concept of separation, we should recognize its extra-legal and extra-Constitutional character. The idea of a "wall of separation" or even the specific term "separation" is not to be found in the Constitution with respect to church-state relations. Jefferson is the author of idea in its secular form,[3] and it has functioned as one way to interpret the First Amendment. But it is not a normative legal definition for all time.

Further, even if one should agree with such a Constitutional interpretation, the "wall" metaphor would not separate religion from the public—clearly that could block free exercise—but would serve to mark out the parameters of two institutions, church and state. Thus, while one may wish to be cautious about including religious studies in public schools, there is no Constitutional prohibition of such a move. Indeed, a recent Supreme Court decision on religion and education makes this conclusion eminently clear. By now, all of us are familiar with Justice Clark's often-quoted postscript to the majority decision in the *Schempp-Murray* case. "Nothing we have said here," Justice Clark pointed out, "indicates that such study of the Bible or of religion, when presented objectively as part of a secular program of education, may not be effected consistent with the First Amendment."

So far, we have viewed the substance of some of the decisions of the Supreme Court with respect to religion and education. While there is a general coherence to the Court's position, the public has not always recognized this. In fact, some have reacted to these decisions, especially those in the 1960's (*Engel v. Vitale* and *Schempp-Murray*) as if they were not based on the Constitution and court precedent. So, as well as understand the guidelines set down by the Supreme Court for relations between religion and education, it has also been necessary for us to consider the attitude of two polar groups: those who feel that there is no justification for any consideration of religion in public schools and those who would legalize prayers and Bible readings.

III

None of this is to say that there is no continuing legal tension in this area. There is. Nor is it to suggest that if we choose some safe *via media* all will be smooth going in the future. Such a prediction seems improbable on the basis of the past difficulties over the question at hand.

Let us, therefore, recognize a fundamental tension which continues to exist in relation to an understanding and employment of the First Amendment. This is not an argument outside of the law nor is it based on inadequate sociology. At bottom, what is involved is the way one reads the First Amendment.

Leo Pfeffer, a constitutional lawyer, has tended to emphasize the priority of the so-called "establishment clause." In turn, this position has lead Pfeffer to emphasize the idea of separation between church and state. Citing precedent from British and United States legal theory, he concludes: "The fathers of the First Amendment were convinced that the free exercise of religion and the separation of church and state were two ways of saying the same thing: that separation guaranteed freedom and freedom required separation." [4]

It must be admitted that it is well-nigh impossible in this time to gain a clear perception of the intention of either the framers of the Amendment or those who advocated its adoption. To be sure, Jefferson seemed to have held a strong separatist view. Yet at his beloved institution, the University of Virginia, he settled for less than complete separation. It is also true that Madison in his *Memorial and Remonstrance* articulated a position consonant with Jefferson's. Still in the years after Madison's writing and the adoption of the First Amendment itself general practice suggests that the nation was less than unanimous about the priority of the separation guarantee. Prayers and Bible readings, certainly a vestige of church devotional practice, lasted in our public schools for over a hundred years.

In addition, it can be pointed out that even if schools were free of religious practices or even religious instruction, then another more subtle form of religion could arise. I refer, of course, to the possibility that secularism itself can form its own ideology which evokes an adherence that is religious in character. Thus the separation of some forms of religious practice from the schools can lead to the institution of others. As a result, religious liberty is not necessarily guaranteed by the separation principle. Actually, to assert the priority of separation can lead in practice to establishment of secularism as a religion or secular credo.

The point need not be labored. Pfeffer's is not the normative legal interpretation. However, it is one of considerable force and popularity. But one will find other positions quite in contrast to Pfeffer's articulation of the principle of separation. Wilbur Katz has noted: "Separation obviously promotes religious freedom." [5] But then he adds that the principle of separation "is defensible so long as it does, and only so long." [6]

What Katz intends to show is that the idea of church-state separation is an instrumental principle. In this connection, he makes two main points. First, and here he is at variance with Pfeffer, the concept of separation is subordinate to the maintenance of religious liberty. Second, separation prohibits governmental support of religious institutions. There are practical ambiguities associated with this second point, such as indirect support to religious institutions in the form of tax exemption and even subsidies for secular textbooks in religious schools deemed Constitutional by the Supreme Court in the 1930 *Cochran* decision. I do not propose to go into these ambiguities here, except to note that they exist. The central point that Professor Katz makes is that the separation principle does not take priority over a view of religious liberty. Instead, he feels that separation is subordinate to religious liberty and is a valid instrumental principle "only so long" as it promotes religious liberty.

With regard to religion and education, Katz further notes the sociological realities of the situation. Government's responsibility here, he says, is to avoid "the use of its power to promote religion— however impartially—and avoiding, at the same time, the promotion of secularism." [7] In this connection, the 1952 *Zorach* case dealing with released time is extremely important. In Katz's view, that opinion can be taken as a decision "to prevent the secular public school system from impliedly teaching the unimportance of religion or its irrelevance to week-day concerns." [8]

IV

Where does this leave us? In the light of the tension in law and the diversity of popular opinion about the proper place of religion in the schools, educators must recognize the delicate character of the issue. Like it or not, you cannot include any consideration of religion in our schools without great care and a feeling for the sensitivity of others. Ordinarily we do not have to be thoughtful of legal opinion and public sentiment or even the academic character of a subject when we plan a curriculum. In this sense—perhaps only in this sense—religion is different from other subjects and activities in our schools.

Despite this difference, however (a difference in emotive reaction to subject matter pertaining to religion), some notable programs of study about religion have been developed in recent times. If they are academically successful as well as legally responsible, it is because they are developed as instruments for the education of the public and not as vehicles for the practice of religion.

NOTES

1. Philip Phenix, *Religious Concerns in Contemporary Education* (New York: Bureau of Publications, Teachers College, Columbia University, 1959).

2. Will Herberg, *Protestant, Catholic, Jew* (New York: Doubleday & Co., 1955).

3. It should be noted that Roger Williams also used the phrase in a somewhat different fashion. See William A. Clebsch, *From Sacred to Profane America* (New York: Harper & Row, 1968), pp. 209f.

4. Leo Pfeffer, "The Case for Separation," in John Cogley, ed., *Religion in America* (New York: Meridian Books, 1958), p. 60.

5. Wilbur Katz, "The Case for Religious Liberty," in Cogley, *op. cit.*, p. 97.

6. *Ibid.*

7. *Ibid.*, p. 106.

8. *Ibid.*, p. 107.

Bibliography

There are a number of volumes which provide more detailed selections from major legal cases treating religion in public education as well as commentary about their meaning for educators. The following annotated list contains some key works to which the reader may profitably refer.

Religion in the Public Schools: A report by the Commission on Religion in the Public Schools of the American Association of School Administrators. New York: Harper & Row, 1964.

In addition to providing an overview of legal considerations, this book makes concrete suggestions for the school teacher and administrator in the light of religious pluralism in the United States.

Donald Boles, *The Bible, Religion, and the Public Schools*. Ames, Iowa: Iowa State University Press, 1965.

————, *The Two Swords*. Ames, Iowa: Iowa State University Press, 1967.

These two books are companion pieces detailing court cases and legal dynamics associated with religion and public education. Boles' attention to detail is valuable in that it reveals subtleties and complexities often overlooked in other volumes.

David Fellman, editor. *The Supreme Court and Education* (revised edition). New York: Teachers College Press, 1969.

This is one of the best collections of relevant decisions by the U.S. Supreme Court on religion and education. Fellman's introductory analysis is generally helpful. The book also includes excerpts from cases dealing with racial segregation and academic freedom.

Herbert M. Kliebard, editor. *Religion and Education in America: A Documentary History*. Scranton, Pa.: International Textbook Co., 1969.

In addition to reasonably full excerpts from Supreme Court decisions on religion and education since 1923, the volume also provides useful historical background over the broad range of American history on Constitutional and educational developments. Kliebard's introduction, different in emphasis and outlook from Fellman's, is useful.

Robert Michaelson, *Piety in the Public Schools*. New York: The Macmillan Co., 1970.

Michaelson's approach is historical. Yet his analysis of trends in the relationship between religion and the public schools over the years has contemporary relevance. By putting issues in historical perspective, this book provides a thorough explication of the questions and problems the public educator faces today.

James V. Panoch and David L. Barr, *Religion Goes to School*. New York: Harper & Row, 1968.

This has the quality of a primer. Opening chapters tend to be sketchy, but some may find its question and answer approach a good introduction. Although later sections are dated, they contain ample amounts of information on programs developed and materials available.

Philip H. Phenix, *Religious Concerns in Contemporary Education*. New York: Bureau of Publications, Teachers College, Columbia University, 1959.

Although this study of the reciprocity between religion and education is dated in the sense that it was written before the landmark Court decisions of the 1960's, it is still insightful. Phenix is able to apply his theoretical understandings to practical situations. As such, the classroom teacher will find this little book very helpful.

II
THEORETICAL
BASES

Introduction

Issues about religion in public education have been treated in the previous chapter from a legal and social point of view. To be sure, it is essential in understanding the place of the academic study of religion to be clear about legal guidelines. But such understanding is more relevant to a definition of *what* may be done without a developed explication of *why* and *how* religion may be a part of the education of the public.

The following two essays are theoretical in character. In different ways they develop a rationale on which the educator may base the study of religion in public institutions of education. Phenix' argument importantly contributes to this matter in several ways. First, he notes that the recognition of religious pluralism can be furthered by studying its dimensions and components. Secondly, he attempts to take Justice Clark's dictum about studying religion a step further by defining objectivity as "disciplined inter-subjectivity." Finally, Phenix cites twelve questions frequently asked about religion in public education and, on the basis of his theoretical analysis, provides preliminary answers relevant for application in specific circumstances.

The second essay is generally critical of the distinction between the teaching *of* religion and teaching *about* religion. Somewhat comparable to Phenix' notion of "disciplined inter-subjectivity," the author of the second essay suggests that an objective study is based on a frank admission of biases. He then suggests that the function of religion in public education is to extend the student's understanding or vision, not to channel it into one mode of faith and practice or another. Similar to the view articulated by Phenix, the author of the second essay notes that study about religion actually raises more questions for the learner than it answers. Instead, then, of arriving at some predetermined answer or doctrinal stance, the function of religion in public education is to highlight for the learner what is known in tension with what is believed so that he might arrive at his own religious understandings and commitments.

In a postscript to the second essay, the author states that religion study is but one option in relating religion to public education. The same theme is more fully developed in Part IV of this book. There, the reader should note especially the readings by Lynn and Engel (Chapters 15 and 16).

5 Religion in Public Education: Principles and Issues

PHILIP H. PHENIX *

The present time is particularly propitious for giving serious consideration to the principles and issues concerning religion in public education. If one looks back over the last 40 years, one can see a number of different centers of interest in public education which can be characterized somewhat as follows: In the 1930's the schools were taken up with the kind of emphasis that appears in George Counts' celebrated pamphlet, *Dare the Schools Build a New Social Order?* [1] In the 1940's the schools confronted the problems of war and reconstruction from war—the kind of issues that were raised in the Harvard Report.[2]

The 1950's were taken up with competing with the USSR, with getting our own Sputniks into orbit, and with retooling our curriculum in mathematics, natural science, and language. The 1960's were an era centered primarily in the movement for civil rights; student protests and critical questions about the nature of higher education and of all lower level institutions which lead up to it—these were certainly the great issues in that era.

* Reprinted from the July/August 1972, No. 2 issue of *Religious Education,* by permission of the publisher, The Religious Education Association, 545 West 111th St., New York, N.Y. 10025.

Now, it seems to me, the greatest questions that confront our people are those of personal and national purpose and of values —of trying to reorder national priorities in such a way that the educational system does justice to the needs of our time. The kind of question which many serious students are asking today is: "What is really worthwhile?"; "What does existence really add up to?"; "What is the meaning of the human situation?" The piecemeal, pragmatic, and analytic American temperament, which has characterized our tradition, and which has been evident in our educational research and planning—our concern for detailed technique—fails when we come to these deeper questions. Thus, the determinative factor in education today is the overall orientation, the "why" of the entire educative effort. I am increasingly convinced that the basic problem in education is not how to organize the curriculum or how to administer the schools. The basic problem is *moral*. This is the great background problem against which all the foreground problems have to be set. The question of morale is at root a religious question.

Whitehead said, "The essence of education is that it be religious." I think that is profoundly true. We need to discover the sense of that affirmation: What does it mean to say that education is basically religious? How can the fundamental educational problem of morale, of orientation of the "why" of life be dealt with effectively in the American context? I suggest that it is by the "academic," or "objective," or "factual" study of religion that the proper recognition of the religious factor in education can be achieved.

Influential Agencies

The problem of the proper treatment of religion in the schools is one with which many agencies and many groups in society must concern themselves, in order to create the requisite climate of understanding. Let me outline some of the agencies through which this climate may be created. There are, first, governmental agencies, chief among them the courts, culminating in the United States

Supreme Court. No agency has been more effective in our history than the Supreme Court in helping us as a people to untangle the meaning of the "American way" in respect to religion and education. There are also legislative bodies, representing various constituencies of citizens, that can do much to clarify the issues. One thinks, for example, of a man like Congressman Emanuel Celler and the fight he has carried on, in the matter of school prayers, for insuring the proper relationship between religion and public education. The Executive branch has a role to play, too. Here, unfortunately, we have not had enough leadership on these issues. The President of the United States, governors, and various lesser government officials, particularly those in the field of education, can and ought to help the people who are part of their constituency to understand the meaning of these issues. ·

Next, there are ecclesiastical agencies. None are more important than those created by various national and regional bodies, like the National Council of Churches, the United States Catholic Conference, state and local councils of churches, the Synagogue Council of America and other religious groups. Such religious organizations can be and have been of great importance in educating their constituencies regarding the relation of religion and education. One thinks of the effect, for example, of official statements of these bodies in changing national attitudes on such questions as the saying of prayers and the reading of the Bible in public schools. Important, too, is the work of individual pastors and directors of religious education in educating members of their congregations, through sermons and discussions, in this policy area.

Third, educational institutions themselves have a responsibility, through college and university departments of religion, the social sciences, history, and education, particularly in programs of teacher education. Nor do I believe any theological student is properly prepared without some exposure to these questions of religion in education. Then there are the various national associations, including the National Educational Association, the American Association of School Administrators (who some years ago published an important report on the study of religion in schools [3]), the American Association of Colleges for Teacher Education, the

American Federation of Teachers, the National Council of Teachers of English, the National Council for the Social Studies, and the like. All these national professional groups should be concerned with the religious element in teaching; all can alert their members and have discussions at their national and local meetings dealing with this question.

Finally, there are the civic and cultural voluntary associations, service organizations, clubs, fraternal societies, and the like, that are concerned with the welfare of their members and the advancement of the common good, and that can include this question on their agenda.

In sum, there are governmental, ecclesiastical, educational, civic and cultural agencies, all of which can and should be concerned with this question. All can deal with it through a number of different channels: through publications, including newspapers, journals of opinion, and religious journals; through broadcasts, over radio or television, or by films; or through face-to-face meetings in lectures, panel discussions, religious services, political meetings, and the like. Thus all of the agencies, through many channels, can concern themselves with the issues that we are here to discuss.

The point I want to make in outlining these agencies and channels is to remind you that the responsibility for dealing with these issues does not lie primarily or solely with professional religious educators, but with a whole range of persons and organizations in both the "religious" and "secular" spheres.

Fundamental Principles

Having said that, let me move to the question of what it is that should lie behind the activity of persons interested in the issues. I suggest that there are a number of principles which characterize what might be called the American Way in religion and education, and that whenever one is confronted in whatever context with issues of religion in education, the proper procedure is to refer to the fundamental principles by means of which the issues can be resolved. Much of the discussion of religion in education proceeds on relatively superficial levels because it never gets back to theoretical fundamentals.

Political Principles

I shall group the principles in three categories: political, theological, and pedagogical. The first political principle is the basic American principle of pluralism and equality. We are a society of many ways but comprehended within a fundamental unity. Our national motto is "E Pluribus Unum." The oneness is comprehended in the ideal of equality, in the sense that each of the many that constitute our society has its due, where this "many" refers to both persons and to groups. We are a society of many persons and many sub-groups within the society. In particular, we are a people of many faiths, all of which, in the political sense, are equal—equal before the law. It is important to note that this principle does not mean indifferentism. Politically, equality means rather the right to be oneself, to have oneself represented in the public arena.

In schools, the practice of the principle of pluralism and unity is crucial. In general, schools tend to be homogenizers, and to organize learning in terms of "classes," that is, in terms of similarities. The principle of pluralism and equality implies that there must be an attempt also to introduce non-homogenizing experiences and non-harmonized materials. We need to encourage the non-settlement of important issues. All religious studies undertaken in the schools must accordingly be conducted on a multi-faith basis. Each faith must be represented in its own terms and in such a way that the best representations of each faith are included, avoiding thereby the "straw man" technique in which the teacher presents a position in such a way as to be able easily to refute it. The teacher should serve as a referee of equality of representation, not as an advocate of any particular position. He is in effect a judge who insures that the case is optimally stated for each position; he is not an advocate for one position over another.

The second political principle is that the civic covenant is separate from the ecclesiastical covenant, to use Franklin Littell's helpful terminology. A covenant is an agreement on standards of conduct involving other persons—the rules by which persons live together in a commonwealth. There are various spheres of covenant-making—for example, in clubs, families, professions, and nations. Two of the most decisive ones are those of the nation and the religious group. Both have to do with matters of the highest moment. The nation is the highest authority concerning the common good, especially the security of life. The religious organization is the highest authority as regards a person's destiny and the supreme values of his existence.

Every covenant has specific functions in the commonwealth as a whole, and it is necessary to organize life into a compatible series of covenants. The goal of "E Pluribus Unum" is to organize a mutually compatible series of covenants. American civilization makes the independence of the covenants of the nation and of the religious organization absolutely central. This is the meaning of the doctrine of the "Separation of Church and State," which, I think, should not be stated quite in those terms, but that is how the American way has come to be formulated. It is a principle that says that the human rules for organizing the life of the person in the nation and in the religious organization must not overlap. This requires careful articulation of the domains and norms that are applicable to the two kinds of organization. For example, in the matter of conscientious objection to military service, a delicate question arises as to whether the covenant of the religious organization or the covenant of the nation should apply. What is required by the civic covenant and what is required by the ecclesiastical covenant, and can these two requirements be made compatible?

In education, the role of covenant creation and limitation is an important feature. A primary educational objective should be to understand the limitations of the promises one engages to keep. A person should learn to map out his loyalties and to understand the relationship between commitments made and the consequences which follow from them. I recommend teaching a "process" view of civic covenant rather than a "substantive" one, that is, to devise a concept of covenant based on principles of procedure that will encourage substantive divergence within a convergence on process.

The third political principle is freedom of worship—a principle which follows from the first two and which articulates the positive purpose in the first two principles. American civilization implicitly recognizes that worship is a high if not the highest form of human activity. It is remarkable that a political system should have this orientation. Contrast the commitments of a Communist regime, where there is official hostility to worship unless it be to the state or the Party. Or contrast a welfare state which aims supremely at maximizing security or economic benefits, and is indifferent to religious interests.

The American tradition is one that in its political structure sets a high value on worship. The problem is how to reflect this political principle in public school practice. Clearly, it cannot be done by denying the principle of the separation of civic and religious covenants, for that would be to limit the freedom of worship and to destroy the very pluralism on which the society is based. Certainly, it cannot be done by being indifferent to religion as if it were non-existent. The American aim is fulfilled by emphasizing the preciousness of worshipful attitudes in our tradition and by opening up the religious domain of human experience to deliberate consideration. The impulse to give a proper place to religion in public schools, such as articulated by some members of the Supreme Court in their decisions, is based on this implicit recognition of the centrality of worship in human life. Accordingly, schools have a responsibility to develop a climate in which worship can flourish. This is perhaps what is really behind the "prayer amendment," which contradicts the principle of separation of covenants and is therefore improper; nevertheless, it symbolizes the conviction that worship is important and should not be eliminated from human life, and this is a vital part of the American tradition, to which the objective study of religion can make an appropriate contribution.

Theological Principles

So much for the political principles. What are the theological principles? The first concerns the nature of religion. I suggest that we need both a functional and a cultural description of what reli-

gion is. If one is to talk intelligibly about religion in public education, the concept of religion has to be sufficiently broad to include
the kinds of human situations out of which religious experience
arises together with the various specific cultural manifestations of
those human concerns.

A functional definition of religion may be framed in terms of
the kinds of fundamental life situations in which every human
being finds himself: anxiety, guilt, meaninglessness, indecisiveness,
doubt and fragmentation, for example. These are ultimate concerns that every person has regardless of his particular historical or
personal situation. They are problems to which one seeks answers
that appear as: courage, forgiveness, direction, purpose, faith,
power, and wholeness.

These are universal and inescapable questions and answers.
They are the source of religion, and from them arise the cultural
manifestations in the form of beliefs or creeds—the intellectual
formulations of these questions and answers; of rites or symbolic
actions, which are objectifications of the feeling element; of codes or
systems of ethical response to the questions of fundamental life
concerns; and of institutional agencies—churches, synagogues and
religious societies—the social structures that express the fundamental questions and answers. These are the visible, concrete,
historical expressions of the religious concerns.

Both the functional and the cultural aspects are needed for a
full understanding of religion. One needs both the universal human
elements in experience which lead to the religious concerns and the
kinds of concrete historical and practical formulations that have
been given to these questions in beliefs, rites, codes, and social
organizations. Moreover, the meaning of "E Pluribus Unum," the
one in the many, is found precisely in this interplay of the unity of
fundamental religious concerns and the multiplicity of the concrete
expression of those concerns. The answers given to the question of
the place of religion in public education depends upon a theoretical
understanding of the nature of religion which enables one to take
hold of both the multiplicity and the unity within the same context.

The second theological principle is that of transcendence,
which is a basic concept of religion. By transcendence I mean a
sense of the infinite, of the less-than-final status of any given object,

institution, or belief. This is the source of the prophetic judgement which the great religions of mankind have always made on human absolutes. It is the source of human hope and human freedom. It is associated with the attitudes of humility and of tentativeness before the vastness of the cosmos and before the profundity of the problems that confront human beings.

In public life, including that of the schools, transcendence means that government and its agencies are not the final authorities. The American tradition has had an implicit theological element of concern for transcendence. The denial of the ultimacy of government in matters of personal human concern is evidence of this recognition of transcendence. This recognition is not to be confused with indifference: to deny that any given entity is absolute does not mean that one may not argue about the relative worth of different finite elements in culture. Transcendence simply excludes closedness; it requires openness, and willingness to entertain alternative possibilities. It demands the practice of tolerating ambiguity. To reiterate what I said earlier: the schools should encourage the nonsettlement of fundamental issues. Educational practice with transcendence is practice concerned with inquiry, dialogue, and plurality of perspective.

The third theological principle is that of the primacy of faith. All human actions have a faith basis, using "faith" in the sense of commitment to or trust in a principle which at the time is not itself in question. There is a vital, dynamic, personal element in all conduct. Man is a whole. He is not an abstraction. This is what one means by an existential orientation to human activity. A human being is not merely a thinking apparatus. All reason is shot through with faith pre-suppositions. This truth is recognized not only in theological circles, but also in secular thought. Recall, for example, the position of Michael Polonyi in his concern for the element of faith, or personal engagement, which underlies all human cognition.[4]

In education, it is a commonplace that one should be concerned for the whole person. To this end are directed the contemporary efforts on behalf of feeling and sensitivity, and of relevance and creativity. This concern for wholeness is precisely that of religion as total life-orientation. To say that faith has primacy in

education is to point to the inescapability of the religious foundations in the educative process.

The school is inevitably involved in the substance of religion.
The issues of faith are at stake, either implicitly or explicitly. The
desirable goal is to make them explicit, that is to say, to bring into
self-consciousness the faith commitments that underlie the activities
of human culture. This argues for conscious attention to the faith
bases of all human conduct as a primary reason for the study of
religion in the schools. This objective suggests teaching about religion through subjects that are not labeled "religion," for example,
in studies that examine the religious perspective in the so-called
"secular" disciplines. One can usefully ask: What are the faith bases
of science, of language, of the social studies, of art, and of history?

Pedagogical Principles

Turning now to the three pedagogical principles, the first is
the distinctiveness of the educative commitment as compared to
that of worship. It is fundamental to the American tradition to
recognize that a school is not a church. This is part of the doctrine
of the separation of the civic and the ecclesiastical covenants.
Teaching and learning have their own special presuppositions, at
least within the tradition of the liberal West. I do not propose to
state here precisely what that commitment is, but intend only to
indicate that it is a commitment to inquiry in which understanding
is sought. It is a commitment which does not permit indoctrination
and does not exclude any domain from inquiry, which does not
allow for any foregone conclusions, but develops canons of inquiry that themselves constitute the covenant of the educative
community.

Worship, on the other hand, presupposes some historic faith
community in the cultic sense. It is not primarily an inquiry activity. It is not an attempt to teach, but to proclaim and to cele-
brate. It is pedagogically essential to understand that proclamation
and celebration are different functionally from education and inquiry, that the pre-suppositions of worship are quite different from
those of study. It follows that educative activity in public schools

does not include the practice of worship. This was the point of the Supreme Court's declaration about the inadmissability of prayers in the public schools. If the nation should vote in a "prayer amendment" to the Constitution, a fundamental pedagogical principle would be violated, as well as a basic theological principle of the American tradition.

The second pedagogical principle is that of the possibility of objectivity in religious studies. This is a principle about which there has been a great deal of misunderstanding. Every study in every school, public or private, should be objective. No teaching, no educative activity, in any school ought to be indoctrinative, but should be based upon evidence and fair-minded inquiry rather than upon subjective opinion or special pleading. Knowledge in education properly conceived is everybody's knowledge, in the public domain. But "objective" does not mean value-free, abstracted from the domain of human interest. It is better interpreted as *disciplined intersubjectivity*. To be objective is to enter into the subjectivity of persons other than oneself in a disciplined way. It betokens a person's capacity to enter imaginatively into the position of another. This is the fundamental mark of human intelligence. We are humanly intelligent to the degree that we are capable of accepting points of view other than our own, in a way that is genuinely appreciative.

The methods of obtaining objectivity comprise what are called the disciplines. A discipline is simply a set of procedures for insuring that the kinds of intersubjectivity that will be developed are responsible to evidence and are available to public scrutiny by all those who will enter into the covenant of the discipline. Every discipline is a covenant, a particular kind of agreement about procedure. Once those procedures are adopted, one can enter imaginatively into the subjectivity of other persons.

Religious studies are susceptible to disciplined treatment like any other subject. There is no reason why any person, no matter what his own faith is, may not study theology—Christian, Jewish, or Buddhist—objectively. To do so requires understanding the subjectivities which each particular faith system has. Other disciplines, too, may be applied to the phenomena of religion. The most productive way of dealing with religion in most school situations, I believe, is to take the secular disciplines of history, of literature, of art and architecture, of music and dance, of geography, of sociology and anthropology, of psychology and philosophy, using them to enter responsively and evidentially into the study of the rites, institutions, beliefs, and codes of religion. The most productive way of setting up a curriculum of religious studies is to apply these disciplines, which have their own covenants of objectivity, so as to make explicit and vivid the subjectivities that constitute the meaning of faith in the various religions of mankind.

A third pedagogical principle is that of developmental sequence. Educators are increasingly aware of the stages of human growth and of the effect that these stages have on learning. Religious and moral meanings also grow in developmental sequence, as men like Allport, Piaget, Kohlberg, and Erikson have shown. The principle of developmental sequence helps us form an optional sequence of studies and of concepts which are significant for each of the various stages. Adult theology may make no sense at all to the very young. The educator must know how to place the religious studies he recommends in appropriate order. In this respect I find Erik Erikson's analysis of stages particularly suggestive. In his work, *Childhood and Society*,[5] he suggests the following stages: Trust (the first year of life), autonomy (1-4), initiative (4-6), industry (6-12), identity (12-16), intimacy (16-25), creativity (25-), and finally, integrity. Each of these stages presupposes the successful working through of the earlier stages. Such analyses provide valuable insight into the kinds of religious teachings that are feasible for students in various periods in their development.

I suggest that the curriculum should move from the more concrete and particular in religious studies to the more abstract and universal. Unfortunately, most teachers of religion want to start at the end, with abstract theology, rather than at the beginning. My preference for the sequence of disciplines applied to religious study would begin with the application of music, dance, art, and architecture to the understanding of religion. These are the concrete sense expressions of the content of faith. Then would come the study of literature, reading the Scriptures of mankind and engaging in literary analysis of these writings. Then would follow the history of religion, which is still a fairly concrete approach. Next would come the social studies: geography, then anthropology, and then sociology—sociology being the most abstract of the social sciences, in comparison with the more concrete whole-culture approach of anthropology and the still more concrete approach of geography. Still later would appear the psychology of religion, and last would come philosophy of religion and theology. These last, concerned with questions of truth and meaning, are the most difficult and the most abstract kinds of disciplined intersubjectivity. Much of the teaching of religion has been mismanaged because too many think that teaching religion is teaching philosophy and theology. The question "Is the belief true?" is the last question one should ask. It should wait until one has entered in a much more concrete way into the phenomena being discussed.

Fundamental Issues of Religion and Public Education

Finally, I propose to suggest some of the issues that the foregoing principles help to resolve. Most discussions of the questions of religion and education start with the issues, but they never get back to principles. I am arguing that the only intelligent way to approach these matters in dispute—the kinds of issues that are discussed in Parent-Teachers Associations, school boards, and faculty meetings—is to know what the basic principles are upon which one can appeal for their solution.

1. Many people ask, "Will not religious studies create divisions and hostilities and destroy the unity that characterizes American civilization?" My answer is that if there are faith differences—and there are—it does not help to suppress awareness of them. They become even more troublesome that way. Differences can be constructive and enriching. That is the essence of pluralism. We must teach so as to build on differences, to help sharpen insight. We need more differences in our schools and not fewer differences. Only idolatrous differences are destructive, that is, differences based on absolutisms in which people do not understand the possibility of what I call disciplined intersubjectivity. The deeper unity of the human situation, beneath all of the differences of creed, code, cult, and institution, is what we must depend upon in order to be

able to unify in a more fundamental way the differences that appear on the surface. Creative tension is an important value in education. I have little sympathy for the notion that, above all, students must be made to feel comfortable. There should be creative, constructive tension.

2. "How can schools do justice to the many different faiths? Isn't it impossible to cover the extensive, exuberant variety of cults in human civilization?" The answer is yes, it is impossible to cover completely all the different cults, but it is not necessary either. The major types can be dealt with. This is a problem in any subject. It is never possible to cover everything. Imagine a course in geography that tried to cover the globe in all of its details. The important aim is to help students with ways of understanding religious phenomena. Once they have learned how to proceed, they can continue their explorations on their own. The basic principles of the nature of religion, of transcendence, of faith, and of the disciplined intersubjective understanding of religion are what the student needs to learn and not all the details of all the religions of mankind.

3. "Isn't religion a private, personal matter that doesn't belong in public education? Isn't it a matter between the soul and God, not for scrutiny in the public arena?" Yes, in the last analysis, as Whitehead said, religion is what man does with his solitariness. But also it is the case that man is not an island, that we are all members one of another and that we need to share our life at the deepest levels. Each needs help, insight, and inspiration from other persons and all are united in a divine ground of being, in a reality that is common to all. There is no such thing as religion without shared expressions in symbol, act and organization. These worldly embodiments need to be articulated, criticized, and understood by other persons. To relegate religion to the private sphere exclusively is to invite superstition and isolation. Revelation (as the disclosure of the hidden), proclamation, and witness are basic. Public forms of religious expression are essential to all religious understanding.

4. "Will not the impressionable young be indoctrinated by religious studies?" Many people object to the teaching of religion on the grounds that the influence of the teacher is decisive. He is an impressive adult and the child will simply follow what he says. In

reply, I submit that even a teacher of the young can teach about religion objectively, not just as a matter of rational argument but as a matter of sympathetic treatment of the faith of persons with different persuasions. Young children are quite capable of getting outside of their own perspective and inside others' minds. They are less prejudiced than older children. It is not necessary for teachers to indoctrinate. One requires, in some sense, an open classroom, with a non-authoritarian, seeking, hospitable, and appreciative spirit. This is where developmental sequence must be understood so as to meet every student where he is and to build on that.

5. "Will not the academic study of religion create doubt rather than faith? Will not the study of many religions and openness to many alternatives sow doubt in the minds of students? Don't the young need the security of a clear, definite belief?" There are two kinds of doubts: destructive and constructive. The former arises from skeptical negations, when a person believes there is nothing to seek for. The latter is a consequence of profound faith in transcendence. Doubt of this right kind is necessary for any significant faith. Without it one lapses into idolatry and fanaticism, into a closed mind, into intolerance. Engendering constructive doubt is a primary objective of all effective education, even in the very young, where it might better be termed "wonder."

6. "Can teachers really present other faiths fairly? Will they not misrepresent other faiths?" Many parents and clergy want all religious instruction in the hands of their own co-religionists. Fairness to a faith, seeing and feeling it as from the inside, is the very essence of objectivity. A competent teacher can present other views fairly in any subject. This is the distinctive quality of self-transcending personhood. In fact, a competent teacher can do better with other faiths than with his own. If I am a good teacher, it is possible for me as a Protestant to present Roman Catholicism with more passion, with more understanding, and with more insight than I can present my own faith. As a good teacher I will be careful not to present simply my own subjectivity, but will do my utmost to get inside the faith that other persons have. Even professed atheists can, in principle, teach religion and teach it well, and many do. No teacher is a good one unless he understands passionate commitments to political systems, to economic systems, to scientific

methodologies, and to religious faiths. That is the essence of being a good teacher. It does not mean being objective in the cold sense.

7. "If religion is treated objectively, it is not religion but abstract intellectuality." I do not need to dwell on this issue, since I have already explained that this statement betrays a misunderstanding of objectivity in the full sense. Objectivity means full inward appreciation, i.e., intersubjectivity. The competent teacher aims not at intellectual understanding only but seeks a subtle interplay between intelligence and emotion.

8. "Is it not impractical to expect teachers to be able to teach religion this way?" Teachers who are really competent are in short supply in any subject. The objective sympathetic treatment of religion does require persons of great capacity, but so does exciting teaching of mathematics, language, or history. The kind and level of teacher achievement are not essentially different in religion from any other field. It is true that teacher preparation programs have in the past given little attention to the teaching of religion. In recent years many colleges and universities have introduced the teaching of religion in a way which satisfies the highest canons of scholarship and of teaching. Religion should be part of any teacher's preparation, regardless of his specialty. Every teacher ought to know something about religion from a disciplined academic approach, just as every teacher needs to know something in a disciplined way about mathematics and economics.

9. "Are there suitable materials for the appropriate study and teaching of religion?" The answer is no, not in sufficient numbers and variety. Here also progress is being made, as in the Pennsylvania and the Florida state programs. With increasing demand and use, the supply will increase. This is a promising field for properly prepared curriculum writers. What we need is not so much a set of textbooks as a variety of books on special topics in religion done by the best writers and thinkers in the field.

Three final issues of a somewhat different kind are raised by people who think that teaching of religion objectively is not enough.

10. "We need strong positive religious teaching because we are a religious nation. 'In God We Trust' say our coins, and the public schools need to make good this commitment." It is true

that a majority of our citizens make some sort of formal religious profession. It is true that most Americans are committed to religion as persons. But as a nation, we are secular. We admit no establishment of religion. We are not a religious people politically speaking. The school must be the school and not the church. Thus secularity has an important place. In fact, secularity has a profoundly religious basis because to say that we are a secular nation is to say that the nation is not absolute. This means that we believe implicitly that there is a theological dimension that transcends the dimension of civic authority.

11. "Religion is needed to sustain the people's morality. The moral decline of our times is due to the absence of positive religious sanctions in the school." This argument is empirically false, for it can be shown that there is no evidence of a positive correlation, or even evidence of a negative correlation, between religious profession and moral strength. On the other hand, I believe that, in a more profound sense, real religious commitment does have moral effect. What counts are personal maturation and transformation that are due to deep understanding. In the long run, real understanding of the kinds of life commitments people make will make a difference also in what they do in relation to other persons.

12. "The minority objections to religion should not deprive the majority of their rights to religion in the schools. If more people want to pray than those who don't want to pray, we believe that majority will should prevail!" The answer to this is that this is not a country in which what the majority says goes for everybody. We believe that the principle of minority rights is fundamental, that truth is not determined by majority, that the protection of the civic covenant as separate from the sacred covenant is an important distinction. How different this is from the notion that the majority rules, and if there are objections to prayer, so much the worse for those who object. That is a quite mistaken view of American democracy.

I conclude by reiterating that there was never a better time to take the religious question seriously as educators. There are great values in exploring the riches of meaning in the faiths of mankind. The hunger of today's young people is for the deeper realities of

existence. We have before us in the schools an unparalleled opportunity. Let us make the most of it.

NOTES

1. John Day Co., New York, 1932.
2. *General Education in a Free Society* (Cambridge, Mass., Harvard
University Press, 1945).
3. *Religion in the Public Schools* (New York: Harper & Row, 1965).
4. See, for example, his book *Personal Knowledge* (Chicago: The
University of Chicago Press), p. 959.
5. W. W. Norton and Co., New York, 1950.

6 Toward a Theory of Religion in General Education

DAVID E. ENGEL *

The *Schempp* decision in 1963 has helped to clarify the way in which religion may be handled in public education. Bible readings and the recital of prayers, widely the practice in schools during this century, have been eliminated from public education except in some few cases where their unconstitutionality is disregarded. In place of such practices, interest has grown in studying about religion. Courses of study in religious literature, religion and social studies, comparative religion and the like have been generated at the state and district level.

But on what grounds may such studies be warranted? An initial justification for teaching about religion in general education is that such studies can provide learners with important sociocultural understandings. In an intellectually pluralistic society where not only the traditionally religious but also secularists advocate ultimate worldviews, it can scarcely be said that that society

* This essay was originally presented at the November 1973 meeting of the American Educational Studies Association in Denver, Colorado and is a revision of an earlier article by the same title which appeared in the July/August 1970 issue of *Religious Education*.

is non-religious. Study about religion can assist the learner in understanding his and others' commitments.

Accordingly if one asks why religion should be part of a general education curriculum, the warrant can be made in terms of needed understanding in a pluralistic society. Justice Clark's remarks at the end of the *Schempp* decision (". . . it might well be said that one's education is not complete without a study of comparative religion or the history of religion and its relationship to the advancement of civilization") might be so viewed. Because our society is multi-religious, the school—not the religious school but the public school—needs to include instruction about religion as one means to promote cultural awareness. Such religious instruction is not necessarily the job of a Sunday school or a parochial school or a weekday religious school (although they are certainly free to consider social and cultural issues). It is the job of the public school. In brief, then, it can be said that insofar as religion is an important cultural phenomenon, it becomes a major concern of general education.

But how can religion be taught in public schools? The Supreme Court has said that teaching about religion must be done objectively. What does that mean? In order to approach such questions, it is necessary to attempt to develop a theory of religion in general education.

I

A common way to view the theory of teaching religion, especially in the public sector, has been to make distinction between the teaching *of* religion and the teaching *about* religion. Teaching *about* putatively is not aimed at evoking commitment. First and foremost it attempts to transmit facts associated with religion. Instead, for example, of making the claim that Jesus is Lord, this approach would teach that a central notion of Christianity is the claim that Jesus is Lord. Presumably such a method insures greater objectivity than the teaching *of* religion. The implication is that the teaching *of* religion is more concerned with gaining converts and retaining believers than fully explicating the subject matter at hand.

But there are difficulties with this distinction. For example, it can be questioned whether commitment and the full development of any subject matter are mutually exclusive. To assert that one who is committed to a particular perspective or approach to a given body of subject matter cannot teach it either fully or fairly seems hardly warranted. An astronomer who believes in the "big bang" theory of the origin of the universe is no more or less able, on the basis of that commitment, to teach his subject than one who holds to the "steady state" theory or even one who is neutral in this regard. Ordinarily one would not judge an astronomer's adequacy on the basis of such commitments, but on the basis of the completeness of his knowledge of astronomy and his ability to justify and criticize any astronomical theory.

Similarly, one who teaches religion may or may not hold a belief in God. If he does hold a theistic belief, the chances are, of course, that it will be a specific kind or, at least, colored by one tradition. But that is really not an issue. Theoretically an atheist who has been well educated in theology could teach it as adequately as the most fervent theist. The basis on which a judgment is made about the adequacy of one's teaching is his ability to communicate what religious phenomena are and what they mean.

What is at stake is whether religion can be approached openly and extend one's understanding. One need not soft-pedal his commitments, no matter what they are, when he teaches religion. It is more open to admit commitments than to pretend they do not exist. In the classroom, however, one's commitments are only of incidental importance. What is educationally important is whether the interaction between the form of one's perception and the content of some subject enlarges the learner's vision and teaches him how that subject might or might not be employed in his experience.

Two illustrations may clarify the point. Consider contrasting ways in which one might approach the discovery of the American continent. A teacher, on the one hand, may tell a student that Columbus discovered America. Subsequently the teacher asks him the question: "Who discovered America?" Every time the student gives an answer other than "Columbus" the teacher offers some negative reinforcement, such as verbal denial or a poor grade. Every time the student gives the answer "Columbus" the teacher

offers some positive reinforcement. In time the student realizes that
the answer sought by the teacher's question is "Columbus."

On the other hand, the teacher may not give the student any
answer at all. Instead he gives the student the resources by which
an answer might be found. Suppose, however, that the student does
not then conclude that Columbus did discover America. Is his
answer wrong? Has there been no teaching or merely unsuccessful
teaching? Actually the student may have found that there is considerable evidence to suggest that several centuries before Columbus certain Scandinavian tribesmen journeyed to this continent.
Consequently, he is able to present a justifiable argument for a
discovery of America prior to Columbus.[1]

Notice what has occurred in each instance. In the first case,
the answer "Columbus" was predetermined before any teaching
took place. No other answer would have been deemed correct.
There is a marked lack of openness in the process. At the same
time, the extension of the student's knowledge is limited to the
adoption of a certain verbal behavior. He has learned how to re-
spond to a question about the discovery of America in a set way.
That is, he has learned how to conform to an authority pattern. In
the second case, the student has a significantly greater degree of
cognitive freedom. He may give any response he can justify. Thus
he not only extends his knowledge in respect to the discovery of
America, but he is also given a lesson in the way in which knowledge generally is discovered and acquired.

The opportunity of the student for further interplay with the
teacher and with the materials is preserved in the second instance
where it is blocked in the first. In the second case, the teacher may
be impressed with the student's ingenuity. Still he may not abandon his view that it really was Columbus who discovered America.
Then, by a deeper consideration of each position, it is possible for
the student to realize that while the probable Norse journeys to
the American continent do appear to pre-date Columbus' discovery
in the fifteenth century, these earlier sea probes had none of the
significant economic and social consequences that Columbus' later
voyage did. At the same time, the teacher is stimulated to examine
again the pertinence of his own pattern of understanding.

In the first case, the form of teaching and learning was set from the beginning. The teacher prescribed what the learning was to be and went about eliciting the response which corresponded verbally with the predetermined answer. In the process there was little or no exercise of the critical intelligence. The student learned an answer. He did not learn how to find an answer for himself and evaluate its adequacy.

That is exactly what the second case provides. The student finds his answer from the materials suggested by the teacher. But his answer is at variance with the teacher's. The two answers confront and openly interact. Each is extended. It is important that the teacher does not play an entirely detached or non-directive role. He does not feign ignorance or profess a lack of opinion in regard to the question at hand. He does not tell the student that it makes no difference where he seeks an answer. The student is directed to the resources the teacher deems relevant. When the student arrives at his conclusion, the teacher does not say that the answer is as good as any other. The teacher challenges the student with a contrasting conclusion. But throughout it is apparent that teaching is not simply a matter of dispensing facts. It is also a matter of critically evaluating the way in which facts are interpreted or patterned.

II

It might well be questioned how such an approach can be employed in studies about religion. Suppose the aim of a teacher is to develop with students an understanding of the significance of a major religious figure like Jesus. He may simply supply a normative response for students to repeat, such as some traditional phrase asserting that Jesus is Lord and Savior of men. Every time the question "What is the nature of Jesus Christ?" is asked, the student is directed to answer: "Jesus is Lord and Savior of mankind." As in the case with the instruction about Columbus, the teacher employs appropriate reinforcement and in time the student realizes the response sought by the question is the one specified by the teacher or some curriculum.

But again, similar to the Columbus illustration, there is no exercise of the student's critical intelligence in the process. What is learned is one response to a question. What has not been learned is the way in which that assertion may be evaluated or justified.

There are sources on which such a religious claim might be based. Instead of furnishing a set response, the teacher might rather direct the student to such sources. In the process of his investigation, the student might also discover that other traditions, religious and secular, make contrasting claims. Subsequently the student may conclude that Jesus Christ is not the Lord and Savior of men. He has considered that possibility; but to him it seems more reasonable to say that man is the Lord of his own destiny and that salvation is a question of psychological health, economic well-being and political freedom, all of which are not materially affected by a supernatural force or the man Jesus.

The teacher, in turn, confronts the student with a counterargument. Certainly, he admits, man is responsible for his destiny to a degree. Religious belief does not necessarily preclude freedom. Rather it helps to define its extent. The teachings of Jesus, especially as they relate to interpersonal relations, provide a vision of life which serves to promote the give and take and the necessary social responsibility where there is popular sovereignty and where economic well-being is defined as a common aim as well as an individual opportunity. While other religious figures may speak of social justice, it is Jesus who has dramatized it in such a way that men have been inspired to improve their lives and the lives of others even under adverse conditions.

The illustration need not be drawn out further except to note that the argument or conversation associated with it does not end at any predetermined point. It can continue beyond the point I have described. A subject has been opened up, one might say. In the process one's understanding has been enlarged or extended. No fixed conclusion is reached. But the student has been shown how to examine and evaluate whatever conclusion he might reach with this and similar subject matter.

Teaching religion in this sense is not different from teaching other subjects. The question at issue is not whether one will learn and retain a certain viewpoint, but how thoroughly he can utilize given materials and evaluate his conclusions about them. What is involved in such a procedure is not merely learning a body of data, but analyzing the distinctive fashion in which a variety of data may be patterned and how his conclusions about both the form and the content of the subject matter may be justified.

Such an approach to education suggests a distinctive direction and style for religious instruction. Contrary to some catechetical practice, for instance, this kind of an approach is open-minded and open-ended. There are no predetermined, fixed answers. Where answers or conclusions appear, they are critically examined and evaluated in relation to other patterns of perception.

III

It can be noted in passing that such a view of religious instruction might also be appropriate for instruction in explicitly religious schools. Such a style of instruction as the one I have just outlined might help to eliminate the development of a naive faith. In religious education, attempting to communicate a certain outlook by the repetition of a series of set responses means that one has been conditioned to say certain words, not necessarily to understand what they mean. Although such an educational instrument as the Westminster Shorter Catechism is not in common use in church education today, religious educational practice in some instances is not radically different. Despite the use of more sophisticated curriculum material and aids, the teacher frequently attempts to have the student arrive at some profession of belief consonant with the institution's confession or point of view.

In the Westminster Shorter Catechism the very first question asks: "What is the chief end of man?" The matching answer is: "Man's chief end is to glorify God and enjoy him forever." The answer, however, raises at least as many questions as it answers. Assuming that one has settled for himself who and what God is —and it is debatable whether such issues are ever settled—the meaning of such crucial words as "glorify" and "enjoy" are far from clear. Even if one has arrived at some reasoned conclusion about them, the question of how the whole statement relates to actual experience needs still further consideration.

Instead, therefore, of furnishing firm answers, the process of question and answer in religious education is actually open-ended. The employment of a catechetical method, whether the catechism itself is traditional or arises from the questions formulated by modern curriculum writers, involves a process of question upon question. As Johannes C. Hoekendijk has put it: "In this era . . . a catechism would have to look somewhat different from the classic kind, which gives an immediate answer to each question. It would have to lead us on a course of thinking things through with question after question, thus inviting us to search things out for ourselves." [2]

No doubt such a style would be unsatisfying to some. For years many persons have sought answers from religion. Instruments of religious education have frequently been understood as providing answers. To turn around and say that the function of religious education is to raise questions may seem to be something of an anticlimax or a sell-out. It is, on the face of it, a less exalted role than supplying answers. Yet it can be questioned whether such a practice of raising questions has not actually been in operation where theology and biblical studies have been more than a recital of past opinion.

Religion is not a closed discipline, any more than philosophy or the natural sciences. Religion does not supply intellectual answers in a final sense. Instead it helps us to formulate questions about experience in a particular way and points us in a direction where some provisional resolutions may be discerned. In other words, even though religion involves devotional practice, it can also be studied as a subject or as a dimension of other subjects. And it can, accordingly, be viewed as an academic discipline which contributes to man's self-understanding. For some persons traditional religious notions may be *the* answer. But broadly understood, the study of religion is an approach to the issues and problems of life.

IV

Thus we have moved to another dimension of a theory of religion in education. The issue is the way in which religion can be treated in so-called secular disciplines. Here it is important to note that a clean separation cannot be made between what is secular and what is religious. Insofar as a secular discipline or orientation attempts to explain ultimate meanings, such as the nature of man or the purpose of life, it becomes in itself religious in character. That is, secular approaches to experience contain latent or implicit religious dimensions.

One problem with the distinction between the teaching *of* religion and teaching *about* religion is that it commonly assumes religion is a separate subject matter area. In some instances, of course, it is separate. In order to keep the educational process within manageable proportions, religious subject matter can sometimes be presented most efficiently as a single course of study or as a series of courses. At the same time, however, religious issues are to be discerned in such general areas as the history of ideas, literature, and art. One who teaches history can hardly do justice to sixteenth-century Europe, for example, without dealing with the theological issues inherent in the Reformation. While the teacher would give less than full treatment of the history of the period if he were to communicate a Lutheran or Calvinist or Roman Catholic viewpoint alone, it cannot be denied that the theological positions in each outlook are essential to understanding the period.

Similarly, religious motifs and ideas play an important role in the work of such poets as W. H. Auden, T. S. Eliot, William Blake and John Dryden. There are important religious dimensions in the work of such artists as Roualt, Rembrandt, and Michelangelo and such novelists of this period as Thornton Wilder, John Updike, Saul Bellow and Graham Greene. Without attention to the beliefs and religious themes imbedded in such works significant aspects of them are overlooked.

The point need not be labored further. To separate any subject matter from the commitments, passions and ultimate questions which surround it is to consider it incompletely. Accordingly, it follows that religion is part and parcel of the educational process as long as men raise ultimate questions, hold strong commitments and are subject to emotion as well as to reason. In other words, studies about religion are not restricted to the consideration of explicitly religious subject matter.

What this means for religion in general education is that it need not be restricted to a religious tradition or even to the comparative study of religion. The learner's attention can be directed to secular issues and questions which involve concerns and commitments that are implicitly religious. Religious instruction can occur outside formal courses in religion and outside religious institutions. Actually where no barriers impede the consideration of the religious dimensions of experience, religious instruction can and probably does occur.

From a different perspective, the teacher of religion himself may fail to recognize the continuities between the secular and the religious. That is, he may resort to the kind of fideism which either cannot or will not tolerate public scrutiny. His consideration of religious subject matter in such a case constitutes a retreat from the world. He would take sanctuary in the mystique of his private world of isolated subject matter because the experience he confronts is either too threatening or too confusing or both.

The correction of distortions in either direction, the world viewed as devoid of a religious dimension or religious experience viewed as an entirely personalistic affair with no meaningful, objective relationships, is the constant interaction of what is believed and what is known. It is always possible to concentrate on what one knows empirically at the expense of what one believes or values personally, or vice versa. But to keep knowledge and belief separated and fail to consider how they influence one another is to do justice, in the long run, to neither.

It would be a mistake to consider any example given in this analysis as a specific model for a given educational situation. Instead I have attempted to draw out some general guidelines upon which a theory for religion and education might be based. A theory in contrast to a fully developed program is more flexible in order to accommodate not only the variety among different situations, but also the changes which can occur in the course of time. At its best, a theory must be broad enough and flexible enough to serve many programs.

To suggest, for instance, that instruction about religion is a process of question upon question or, in other words, an instrument for investigation and discovery, constitutes no fixed rule. At some points, answers may be attained. They may be as far as anyone can go at the moment. Still it cannot be forgotten that the answers of one time can easily become the grounds for questions in the next. Similarly, what is believed at one time can be revised by what comes to be known. Or what is known can be rearranged if a more adequate interpretation or pattern of belief is discerned.

Educational theory, especially as it relates to religion and education, needs to be sensitive to such dynamics. When either what is known or what is believed becomes fixed or closed, each runs the danger of becoming perverted. For if either what is known or what is believed is elevated to a position of permanent dominance over the other, then the corrective power of each is accordingly diminished.

V

I could end at this point. What I take to be major issues or ingredients for a theory of religion and education have been underscored. But a brief postscript can be made. It is necessary, from my point of view, that one not gain the impression that teaching religion either as a separate course or as a dimension of another discipline is the only way to bring about some rapprochement between religion and education. It is one way, not the only way.

Robert Lynn [3] has stated that Protestants generally have accepted the public school as the normative instrument of education in our society, but he feels they have done so uncritically. That is, their acceptance has not been based on an informed understanding of the issues confronting education in the nation.

It takes very little insight to recognize that the schools of our nation are unsettled at the present moment. They face difficult issues which involve funding, governance and curriculum. What is to be taught and how is it to be taught? How can our schools be financed to meet the needs of an inflationary economy and a shifting tax base? What is the appropriate function of the schools with respect to the matters of race and urban pressures? What constitutes so-called quality education? To what values ought the schools be committed? To what degree can we legitimately expect the school to be a problem-solving institution? Is public support of independent and/or parochial schools constitutional, and if so, is it acceptable as a policy? And so on and so forth.

Lynn suggests that Protestants, instead of directing their efforts at religious matters, turn their attention to the larger questions, such as the ones just enumerated.[4] The suggestion need not be restricted to Protestants. It might just be that persons with theological insight can make a contribution to the further development of education in the United States. Educational practice might benefit from some of the experience and insight of religion.[5]

NOTES

1. This illustration has a curious history. Thomas F. Green notes it was suggested to him by one of his former students, Gerald Reagan. Green further states Reagan used it differently than he did. And I use it here to make a somewhat different point from Green. See Thomas F. Green "A Topology of the Teaching Concept," *Studies in Philosophy and Education,* III; 4 (Winter, 1964-65), pp. 284-319.

2. Johannes C. Hoekendijk, *The Church Inside Out.* Philadelphia: The Westminster Press, 1963, p. 80.

3. Robert W. Lynn, *Protestant Strategies in Education.* New York: Association Press, 1964.

4. *Ibid.,* p. 75.

5. E.g., Langdon B. Gilkey, "Religion and the Secular University," *Religious Education,* Vol. LXIV, No. 6, November-December 1969.

Bibliography

Philip H. Phenix, *Religious Concerns in Contemporary Education.* New York: Bureau of Publications, Teachers College, Columbia University, 1959.

Although this little volume pre-dates important Supreme Court decisions in the 1960s, it is still a very helpful and very readable approach to the subject. In addition to providing a theoretical foundation for religion in public education, Phenix relates his theory to the roles of teachers and administrators as well as to curriculum development.

Randolph C. Miller, *The Language Gap and God.* Philadelphia: The Pilgrim Press, 1970.

Ian T. Ramsey, *Religious Language: An Empirical Placing of Theological Phrases.* New York: The Macmillan Co., 1957.

Analytic philosophy has been a major approach to clarifying means in philosophy in the English-speaking world in this century. Both Miller and Ramsey show how this method may be employed in religious communication. Ramsey focuses on the unique character of religious language and shows how it evokes discernment and commitment. Miller reviews the work of major analytic philosophers and discusses their relevance for religious instruction.

Donald Vandenberg, *Being and Education: An Essay in Existential Phenomenology.* Englewood Cliffs, New Jersey: Prentice-Hall, Inc., 1971.

J. Gordon Chamberlin, *Toward a Phenomenology of Education.* Philadelphia: The Westminster Press, 1969.

Only recently has the phenomenological method been utilized

as a means for analyzing educational matters. Vandenberg and Chamberlin are among the few educational theorists to look at their field in this way. An understanding of this method will assist the reader in understanding the implications of what Phenix means by "disciplined inter-subjectivity" in his chapter in the foregoing section.

III

PROGRAMS
OF
INSTRUCTION

Introduction

Especially since the *Schempp* decision in 1963, programs of instruction about religion have emerged in a number of states and school districts. The readings in this chapter by no means treat them all. Instead the emphasis has been placed on predominant types which have been generated in key areas, notably in connection with secondary education in literature and social studies.

Edwin S. Gaustad provides an overview of state programs in Nebraska, Pennsylvania and Florida. The first two relate studies about religion to the study of literature. The Florida project, with which Gaustad has been identified, attempts to integrate an awareness about religious phenomena and developments with social studies. In addition, it has adopted an inquiry approach (what Gaustad calls "learning about religion" as opposed to "teaching about religion") common to emerging social studies curriculum developments.

The three essays which treat the developments in Pennsylvania not only describe the elements of the syllabus generated, but also some of the associated social, political and educational issues.

John R. Whitney has been the project director for the Pennsylvania curriculum. As such, he is able to describe the events which led to the publication of *Religious Literature of the West* [1] from the inside. As such, Whitney also sees, at the end of his second essay, the need for serious consideration of teacher training for courses on religion in public schools. Engel's article highlights some educational and social issues surrounding events in the development of the Pennsylvania syllabus.

The question of teacher education for religion studies has been most graphically raised and approached in such states as Michigan and Wisconsin. Paul J. Will reports in his essay on the way in which Michigan has devised a process for teacher certification in religion. Following his essay the reader will find printed the Michigan certification standards and the state's informal program suggestions. As distinct from such states as Florida and Pennsylvania where teacher certification is in the field to which religion is related (literature or social studies), Michigan is among the few states where religion itself is the subject for certification. Similarly, Frank L. Steeves reports on developments in certification in religion in Wisconsin.

It would be a mistake for readers to assume that programs for instruction about religion must necessarily rely on some organized developments in a given state. Religion in some degree has been a part of secular instruction over the years without there being discrete courses on religion or emphases on religion in literature and social studies classes or materials.[2] Individual teachers have developed their own courses with explicit religious content.[3]

One conclusion that can be reached is that there is no one way for teaching about religion in public education. The examples and analyses furnished here demonstrate some of the various ways in which such instruction may proceed.

NOTES

1. John R. Whitney and Susan Howe, *Religious Literature of the West* (Minneapolis: Augsburg Press, 1971).

2. See especially Lawrence C. Little, editor, *Religion in the Social Studies* (New York: The National Conference of Christians and Jews, 1966); Lawrence C. Little, *Religion in Public School Social Studies Curricula* (Westminster, Maryland, 1968).

3. See James V. Panoch, "Why Not Inaugurate a Course?" *Religious Education,* Vol. LXIV, No. 2, March-April 1969; James V. Panoch and David L. Barr, *Religion Goes to School* (New York: Harper & Row, 1968), pp. 55-60.

7 Teaching about Religion in the Public Schools: New Ventures in Public Education

EDWIN SCOTT GAUSTAD *

I n any discussion of religion and public education these days, the "introductory remarks"
can easily go on at near-interminable length—thus preventing one
from ever getting to the principal fare. So much has happened in
the decade of the 1960s that needs to be digested before one can
order up provisions for the 1970s.

I

THE BACKGROUND

Even prior to the 1960s subtle shifts in American life were
taking place. Those shifts are sometimes dramatized by such
phrases as "from Protestantism to pluralism" or "the secular age"
or "the post-Christian era." In the confrontations between religion

* Reprinted with permission of the publisher from *Journal of Church
and State*, Vol. XI, No. 2, Spring 1969, pp. 265-276.

and education, the drama has been provided more often than not by the United States Supreme Court: *Minersville School District v. Gobitis, West Virginia State Board of Education v. Barnette, Everson v. Board of Education, McCollum v. Board of Education, Zorach v. Clauson, Engel v. Vitale,* and *Abington School District v. Schempp.* Just to ring these changes is to create Pavlovian responses in the minds (if not the mouths) of the public.

What once were common assumptions are not now so common. To speak of a consensus quietly shared, of goals collectively pursued, of patterns of behavior faithfully followed is to speak of an age that has passed. "Tradition" (to use the dairyman's good word in "Fiddler on the Roof") is more often subject to attack than it is a subject to venerate. In some of these things one may rejoice, for others one may weep. But whatever the reaction of one's glands and brains, neither education nor religion is irrelevant to changes in society and in men.[1]

The remarkable development in the academic attention to religion at the college, university and graduate school level should be noted. What has happened here in a brief span of ten or twenty years is at least a transformation; it may even be a revolution. Constitutional ghosts and administrative or faculty hallucinations have lost most of their power to terrify or paralyze. Now at the public school level, new and sometimes dramatic developments may be seen. Most of them take their cue from the 1963 Supreme Court decision in the case of *Abington v. Schempp.* Speaking for the Court, Justice Tom Clark said that the religious exercises then being adjudicated were clearly unconstitutional. It was equally clear, however, that the academic study of religion was not.

It might well be said that one's education is not complete without a study of comparative religion or the history of religion and its relationship to the advancement of civilization. It certainly may be said that the Bible is worthy of study for its literary and historic qualities. Nothing we have said here indicates that such study of the Bible or of religion, when presented objectively as part of a secular program of education, may not be effected consistent with the First Amendment.

However, once this vital distinction between the practice of religion and the study of religion was made, all did not become magnificently and gloriously clear. Nevertheless, the making of this distinction has opened up an area of broad endeavor and bold experimentation. Some of the efforts are purely local (a single school or even a single class), some are short-ranged or fleeting (a single unit, or even a single day). Others, however, emerge from careful, scholarly planning and involve the labors and insights of many schools and of entire communities. At least three adventures are being made at the level of state initiative and supervision.

II
The Pennsylvania and Nebraska Programs

In December 1965, the General Assembly of the Commonwealth of Pennylvania amended the public school code by adding the following section:

Section 1515. Religious Literature—(a) Courses in the literature of the Bible and other religious writings may be introduced and studied as regular courses in the literature branch of education by all pupils in the secondary public schools. Such courses shall be elective only and not required of any student.

(b) Such courses shall be prepared and adopted according to age levels by the Department of Public Instruction with the advice and counsel of the Council of Basic Education and the approval of the State Board of Education.

Under the authorization of this law, the Department of Public Instruction asked Pennsylvania State University and the University of Pennsylvania to assist in developing courses consistent with this mandate. At this stage two courses are being developed. The first in point of time is entitled *Religious Literature of the West*. The writing of student materials for this course, chiefly during 1966-

1967, was followed by arranging an institute for teachers in the summer of 1967. A Teacher's Guide was also written at that time and plans were made for field testing of the materials in 1967-1968. Revision and further field testing is continuing at the present time.

The student manual (195 pp.) is divided into five sections: (1) Introduction, (2) Hebrew Bible, (3) Rabbinic Writings, (4) New Testament, and (5) Koran. There is an accompanying seventy-four page Teacher's Guide. In 1967-1968, field testing was carried out in thirty-one high schools in Pennsylvania and in over seventy high schools during the current academic year (1968-1969). All of the material being tested is carefully labeled "Unrevised Experimental Working Papers," for one soon learns, in this type of venture, the wisdom of caution.

As this project in *Western* religious literature continues, a similar effort in the religious literature of the East is being developed at the University of Pennsylvania. There the Department of Religious Thought is preparing an anthology or sourcebook of literary materials from the Eastern religions. In addition, a student text and commentary to include considerable historical and social background will be provided. Along with these basic curricular items, such aids as a teacher's manual, audio-visual materials, and annotated bibliography will likewise be made available. The first teachers' institute for this phase of the Pennsylvania project will be held in the summer of 1970, followed by extensive field testing in 1970-1971.

Both of these ventures—first in the religious literature of the West and second in the religious literature of the East—are designed to be *elective courses*. They are not part of the existing curriculum, nor do they consist of lessons or units to be inserted into courses currently being taught. Also, by clear legislative prescription, these courses are "not [to be] required of any student."

In contrast, the Nebraska experiment is within the framework of the regular English curriculum and extends throughout the twelve years of public schooling. "Religion" as a specific designation appears nowhere in the description of the project. It is called simply "A Curriculum for English" and is under the direction of the Nebraska Curriculum Development Center. Publication of the materials, which began in 1965, is under the imprint of the University of Nebraska Press.

If this is merely a new curriculum in English, why is it brought up here? The answer is that the framers of the new program have paid to religious themes an attention—or respect—far above that normally found in the public school curriculum. "Hundreds of people collaborated in the creation of these materials," reads the preface to the units, with the writing and testing principally concentrated in the period from 1961 through 1967. According to the multiple and anonymous authors, this curriculum "is not a panacea for present problems in the teaching of English; it is more like a half formed slave struggling to free itself from the stone." Again, this particular kind of business promotes caution —as well as humility.

One example may be offered of the way in which the religious ideas and motifs in literature are treated. In the tenth through the twelfth grades, major attention is given to the theme of "Man and Moral Law: Sin and Loneliness." Students read such items as Tolstoy's *Resurrection* and Steinbeck's *Pearl* (tenth grade), Hawthorne's *Scarlet Letter* and Faulkner's *The Unvanquished* (eleventh grade), ending in the twelfth grade with the "Christian Epics," *The Faery Queene* and *Paradise Lost*. Certainly there is nothing especially radical or innovative in this (partial) list of texts. But the treatment *is* innovative as it focuses on religious themes, explains religious terms, and calls for the exercise of a religious imagination. Religion when encountered in literature is not seen as a regettable embarrassment to be evaded or muddled through as quickly as possible; instead, it is seen as a fundamental feature to be understood as comprehensively and as perceptively as possible. The preface to the teacher (in the tenth grade unit, for example) reads in part as follows:

Six works have been selected for study in this unit. Together they present three possible ways of looking at the theme of "Sin and Loneliness." The first is the psychological way having to do principally with man's relationship to man. . . . Another is a religious way having to do principally with man's relationship with God or his relationship with man seen in the light of his relationship with God. Still another is a strictly "Christian" concept in which the Christian concept of God operates.

Later remarks make it clear the whole purpose is educational, not evangelical, an exercise in illumination, not in indoctrination.

III
THE FLORIDA RELIGION-SOCIAL STUDIES
CURRICULUM PROJECT

In 1965 the Superintendent of Public Instruction for the State of Florida appointed a twelve-member State Committee on Study About Religion in the Public Schools under the chairmanship of Dr. Robert A. Spivey of Florida State University. This representative group of citizens, wholly agreeable to the recent decisions of the United States Supreme Court, began investigating constructive approaches to the study of religion. After considerable examination and discussion, the Committee decided that a project which worked within the existing curriculum offered the most promise. The members further decided on social studies as the area for initial concentration. This decision was based in part on the fact that Nebraska and Pennsylvania were already experimenting with two different approaches in the humanities, while no state had undertaken a project relating religion to the social studies curriculum. Upon application to the Danforth Foundation, a grant of approximately $150,000 was given to finance a two-year pilot program. In 1968 the project got underway and the writing of materials began. In March 1969, a conference was held in Orlando to inform the public of the nature and purpose of the statewide program. The banquet speaker for the occasion was Mr. Justice Tom Clark—the author of the critical *Abington v. Schempp* decision. His presence also served to dramatize the desire not to circumvent or nullify either the Court or the Constitution. In the summer of 1969, the project's first teacher training institute will be held; thirty fully certified social studies teachers have been selected from high schools across the state. Each of these thirty schools will become a pilot center for field testing during 1969-1970. Another group of thirty teachers will attend a similar institute in the summer of 1970. By the end of the 1970-1971 school year, the materials will have been tested in at least sixty Florida schools. During all this time, revision and evaluation are being carried on.

Now, what is the format or focus of this religion-social studies project? As indicated, it seeks to work within the secondary social studies curricular pattern. And what is that pattern? In Florida, it runs along these lines: eighth grade—American history (especially the earlier periods); ninth grade—world geography or civics; tenth grade—world history; eleventh grade—United States history (especially the later periods); and twelfth grade—problems of American democracy (including a required 30-hour minimum in "Americanism vs. Communism"). There are exceptions, of course, but this sequence is typical.

The project proposes a three-volume series on "Religious Issues in the Social Studies." Volume I deals with American culture, Volume II with Western Civilization, Volume III with World Cultures. The first volume will be ready for testing in 1969. Each volume consists of ten lessons or studies which may be used, as the teacher wishes, in the appropriate course and at the appropriate level. It is not necessary to use all ten lessons in any course, and of those used it is not essential (though it may sometimes be desirable) that they be studied in a specific sequence. The intent of the lessons is to provide greater depth, more competent guidance, and fuller treatment of religious questions or problems or topics than would normally appear in the regular course of study. Thus, the whole program may fairly be described as an *enrichment* of the social studies curriculum, not an *intrusion* of religion into education.

Some examples may illuminate. In World History, one certainly encounters the rise of Islam. A lesson of three or four days duration is provided. The lesson does not repeat the basic data to be found in any respectable world history text: a few facts about Mohammad, the Hegira, the Koran and the five pillars of Islam—sometimes in two whole paragraphs! Rather, emphasis is on a single facet, treating it in some depth, encouraging some analysis and evaluation, inviting some discussion and reaction. In this particular case, the lesson compares the doctrine of holy war (*jihad*) with the doctrine of compassion (*zakah*), asking how these are reflected in the history of Islam and, indeed, of the world. Because in this instance extensive use is made of maps (maps showing the expansion of Islam from the seventh century to the twentieth), it is obvious that the lesson could also be used in world geography—especially if the teacher follows a cultural approach.

Two other examples, this time in the American area where, of course, the exposure is greatest for the majority of high school students. A purely historical study deals with the religious factors that helped provoke the American revolution. Few if any textbooks pay adequate attention to the "episcopacy" crisis, and few if any teachers are prepared to discuss it—without help. Thus a lesson (again three or four days) drawing from the vigorous pamphlet and newspaper debate of the 1760s corrects an important deficiency. Its use is appropriate in either eighth grade or eleventh grade American history, and, conceivably, even in civics.

The second example is a lesson entitled "Protestantism or Pluralism," and this one requires two weeks of class time. The content of this lesson includes such issues as nativism, anti-Semitism, diversity, ecumenicity, and the patterns of pluralism in contemporary America. One could use this lesson in dealing with the nineteenth century Know-Nothings, with immigration, or with other historical phenomena. But with at least equal appropriateness, one could study this material as one of the continuing "problems of American democracy." Thus its use at the twelfth grade level might be the best of all. That many of these decisions are left to the option of the teacher may be seen as a liability. It may also be considered an asset, however, since the teacher's interest, attitude and capability are of absolutely critical importance in any classroom study.

A word about the nature of the materials provided. Each study utilizes primary sources. The basic reading is not predigested and tamed textbook-ese. Every effort is made to bring students into direct contact with men and women who felt strongly about the subject under investigation. So, for the most part, the student learns from the lips and pens of men and women who are themselves involved, committed, concerned, penitent, indignant, persuasive, earnest. In this way one may hope to avoid the danger of reductionism, of treating religion as though it consisted of nothing more than dates, names, places, quaint little costumes, and clever little notions. Even in the classroom, religion should have life. Learning about religion should be a process not of evisceration but of comprehension.

A second feature of the materials is that they seek student involvement through his own inquiry and discovery. For that reason the phrase, "learning about religion," is preferred to the more familiar one, "teaching about religion." The emphasis is not on the lecture which can more easily slide down from education into indoctrination, but on the analyses and discussions in which teacher and student jointly participate. This, too, seeks to avoid the danger of deadly dullness in the classroom. But in avoiding dullness, is there a risk of too much liveliness? Yes, there is such a risk. It is, however, a risk worth taking not only for the sake of a richer understanding of religion, but also for the sake of the educational enterprise itself. As Harvey Cox has written:

> When and if religion is taught in American public schools, it should be taught in such a way that pupils may experience and deal with conflicts of opinion over very basic matters. Students should learn as early as possible that, although some people believe the various religions are merely different roads to the same celestial destination, many others think the differences between religious systems are of crucial significance. How all this can be taught is a difficult matter, but teachers cannot even begin to work at it until initial agreement is reached that the classroom is a place to *handle* the most explosive issues, not [the place] to *avoid* them. Teaching religion in public school classrooms may have many educational values. Here I only wish to argue that, since religion is something about which people have had and still have strong, conflicting ideas and feelings, this is no reason to *exclude* it but a very good reason to *include* it in the public school classroom.[2]

Finally, the lessons are—so far as possible—self-contained: that is, they do not presume to ask the teacher to engage in elaborate research or to travel far afield to "round out" the lesson. The activities are all based on the materials given to each student. Audio-visual aids are provided where these are essential to the lesson. Extensive bibliography assistance is offered along with suggestions of additional films, records, filmstrips, and maps which may be used if desired. A "basic library" for American and world religion that each high school should acquire—gradually, if necessary—is suggested.

Among the many questions commonly raised, one is more insistent than all the others. How, in heaven's name, does one expect to cover all of Islam in one or two lessons, all of Judaism and Christianity in three or four, and probably all of Shinto in one? The question is earnest; the answer is simple. There is no such expectation. The project's curriculum becomes ridiculous only if one supposes that it pretends to cover "all" of anything. That pretension is not and cannot be made. Rather it is sought to introduce the student to some original material about religion, to some issues that are vital, to some human beings worth knowing, to some ideas worth entertaining, to some judgments worth weighing. And this is done within the limits of, or upon the opportunities offered by, the social studies curriculum.

IV
PROS AND CONS

This writer will now suggest—making a heroic lurch in the direction of objectivity—what he conceives to be some of the assets and some of the criticisms of the Florida venture. First, the positive side:

1. The use of the *regular* public school faculty avoids any necessity for separately labeled "religion" teachers. It thereby avoids the necessity of a special credential program in religion, or the adoption of any special hiring procedures and criteria. Specifically, it avoids the necessity of attempting to maintain some nice but artificial "balance" of Protestants, Catholics, Jews and secularists on the staff. What is hoped for is a well-qualified, effective teacher who takes his subject—social studies—seriously.

2. The use of the *regular* public school curriculum avoids the necessity for approval of new courses, separate departments, and special programs. (Naturally, it also avoids the hazards of disapproval!) No juggling of high school schedules is required, and principals do not have to shut their tortured ears to repetitive demands for just "one more course" to be added to the crowded curriculum.

3. The introduction of these lessons into the *general* student population avoids the possibility of invidious distinctions between pupils who "take religion" and pupils who do not. No artificial sifting takes place; no unfortunate categorizing or stereotyping becomes possible.

4. Finally, no compromise on the *educational* aspect of the program is likely to be tolerated in the context of the *regular* curriculum, taught by the *regular* faculty, and attended to by the *general* student population. And it must be made perfectly clear that the defense for religion in the schools is, and can only be, an educational one. The moment a program ceases to be educational both in intent and in effect, it ceases to be defensible either on constitutional or on moral grounds. Of course, "educational" covers a wide spectrum of scholastic efforts: good, bad, and indifferent. The fond hope, therefore, is that the program be not only "education" in some fashion or other, but that it be good education. Here, to be sure, there are no guarantees.

Now, are there problems, difficulties, uncertainties, criticisms? Yes to all; four will be noted in the form of questions—questions which are sometimes but not always asked rhetorically.

1. How objective can one possibly be? Rabbi Robert Gordis raises this very important question in the following manner:

> The danger of the "camel's head in the tent" is not imaginary. It cannot be denied that there are those who would regard teaching about religion merely as the opening wedge for the teaching *of* religion. . . . The study materials thus far produced in this area leave much to be desired from the standpoint of objectivity and content and raise the serious question whether adequate material can be prepared to meet the need.[3]

It is indeed a serious question and one which probably cannot be answered before the fact. "Adequate material" can be prepared if one does not raise his sights impossibly high. In the American judicial system it is not asked that a case be proved beyond all *possible* doubt, only that it be established beyond all *reasonable* doubt. So to the question, "How objective can one possibly be?" the answer is, "Reasonably." Will an objectivity beyond that within the grasp of the social sciences generally be obtained? No, of course not. But even as one can distinguish between good and bad history by the evidences of accuracy, impartiality, and comprehensiveness, so here one should—with some hope and much effort—seek a *reasonable* objectivity. In American pluralistic society, will there be immediate and unanimous agreement on the "reasonable"? The answer to that is, of course, again negative.

Here is one example of what appears unreasonable. Some persons measure objectivity by the number of scholars who represent various denominations, or by the number of books in a bibliography from specific ecclesiastical traditions, or by the number of lines devoted to a specific group. One might ask of the materials dealing with America: is 4.5% of the lesson Lutheran? 2.9% Jewish? 1.8% Episcopalian? 10% black? and 1.6% Eastern Orthodox? To these queries a negative response must be given. For this is not teaching social studies; it is playing a political game. Of course the picture of religion in America—or in any other society—must be presented as faithfully and as fairly as possible. But the role of religion in the affairs of nations and of cultures need not correspond precisely with the statistical profile of institutional religion at any given moment in time.

2. How much of an impact can one possibly hope to make? This question generally comes not in that form, but rather as a comment to the effect that only the surface is being scratched. What is being done about the elementary schools? Are any materials being written for the slow learner? So one may reach sixty high schools in two years: what is that out of a total of 100,000? Or what is sixty high school teachers out of a total of 800,000? Now, these are not especially helpful comments, but they are honest ones. What is being done is, in fact, only a drop in the

bucket, only a small beginning. One can only take refuge in the anecdote concerning Benjamin Franklin. Watching the first air-filled balloon carrying a man across the English channel, Franklin heard a Frenchman exclaim: "Humph! What good is it?" To which Franklin replied, "What good is a new-born babe?"

3. How can one possibly be sure that the lessons will "work?" That is, that they will reach the objectives in knowledge, in abilities, and in attitudes? What control groups are used? What behavioral changes are tested for? If the lesson works among whites, is there any reason to believe in its effectiveness among blacks? If in the ghetto, then what about suburbia? Is poison for the WASPs bound to be meat for the Mexican-Americans (and vice-versa)?

To all these questions, which are in effect only a single question, there are really not any good answers. The most meaningful evaluation will come only after extensive use, over a long period of time, and in a wide area of space. Even then, it will come clothed in ambiguity, wrapped in uncertainty. The validity of this experiment is not demonstrable to the fourth decimal place. Few things in life are, and one is not often permitted the luxury of waiting until all the evidence is in.

4. How genuinely relevant to *religion* can one hope to be? Here the critic is saying that a program of this kind deals with the part of religion that does not count. What men are truly committed to in their hearts is precisely what is left out. They do not teach about religion: they teach "around and about religion" (to use a phrase of Professor John Whitney's). Or, in the words of Frederick Olafson, Harvard Professor of Education and Philosophy, teaching about religion

> . . . might lead to a religious attitude in which any sense of reference beyond human history and culture is lost, and in which religion is finally and not just provisionally treated as a dimension of human existence. . . . In its more pernicious forms a religiosity motivated in this way amounts to little more than a worship of ourselves worshipping.[4]

These comments are manifestly worthy of the most probing analysis. They cannot be lightly disposed of—now or ever. In the Orlando Conference, Father Michael V. Gannon spoke of the difference between "true religion" and "academic religion." For good or ill, there is a difference and only the latter can be the stuff of formal, public education. That "academic religion" is not the whole of religion must be readily recognized, even confessed. In all of education, one must be ready to confess that man is not saved by transcripts alone. Learning about religion is but one segment of the total religious enterprise. It happens to be a segment in which public education can legitimately—and effectively—participate. That there are other segments, greater and transcendent ones, cannot and must not be denied. But these must be left to different agencies and institutions, to other programs and personnel, and—not least of all—to the grace of God.

NOTES

1. Ivan Illich of Cuernavaca believes that education has in fact become our religion. "Schooling is a craze, a mad religion, an initiation rite to power which is inaccessible to 95% of humanity, but which is being preached to them as their only way of salvation. . . . Schooling is the universal established church of our time—more evil than any before. Christians once shuddered at the thought of unbaptized babies going to hell. But today . . . it is a dogma that high school dropouts are condemned to the ghetto. This school system [is a] children's crusade that became a world religion. . . ." *Tempo* (March 15, 1969), p. 6.

2. In Theodore R. Sizer (ed.), *Religion and Public Education* (Boston: Houghton Mifflin Co., 1967), pp. 103f.

3. Quoted by Arthur Gilbert, *ibid.*, p. 47.

4. *Ibid.*, pp. 94f.

8 Introducing Religious Literature in Pennsylvania Secondary Schools

JOHN R. WHITNEY *

T his article reflects primarily the subjective experience of one who currently is involved in writing courses in the literature of religion. The courses must treat religion objectively. The account that follows conveys the implicaton that the objectivity of any meaningful event, including a course in religious literature, is at least as much a quality ascribed to it by one or more human subjects as it is a quality somehow inherent in the event itself. When therefore people through their law require that a school course be taught objectively, one can assume that something more is being pleaded here than some simplistic legalism. They are pleading, it would appear, by means of this positive statute, for the reconciliation of their various subjective attitudes as they mandate the course and converge their attention on its development and content.

* .Reprinted from the March/April 1968 issue of *Religious Education*, by permission of the publisher, The Religious Education Association, 545 West 111th St., New York, N.Y. 10025.

What follows constitutes neither a hearty recommendation nor a dire warning with regard to the *modus operandi* which has evolved in the course-building project in Pennsylvania described here. After all, each situation demonstrates its own peculiar aspects. One can assume that any success for this project will certainly be a function of the objectivity achieved in the course treatment of the literature. So goes the law. But one further can assume that any such objectivity in turn will be a function of the degree to which subjective attitudes turn out to be reconciled through the medium of such courses.

Perhaps one dares say that the achievement of objectivity in the Pennsylvania courses, or any courses, may be simply a way of referring to a subjective consensus among Pennsylvania folks that the courses serve to mediate the self-realizing and self-fulfilling experience of people involved with them, whether as students, as teachers, or as interested sponsors. Certainly the courses could be objective in another sense. They could be objective in the way that a table of random numbers is objective—carefully calculated to avoid the pitfalls of subjective communication altogether.

Thus objectivity can mean two quite different things with reference to a course in the literature of religion. It can mean either the enhancement of human community or else the meticulous avoidance of it.

However, this is not an article on subjectivity-objectivity, but the description of a project involving the acutely subjective task of making a course in religious literature a generally acceptable object—one way or the other. With no further introductory ado, and with frequent reference to experience rather than to footnotes, we now offer this subjective account of one particular project in the preparation of courses in religious literature for the public schools.

I

The Commonwealth of Pennsylvania, since late 1965, has been involved in an extensive state-sponsored project in the development of public school courses having to do with religion. During the current school year (1967-68), the Commonwealth's Department of Public Instruction is supporting the first field test of a course in "Religious Literature of the West." The field test, as part of a larger project in such course development, is progressing under the immediate aegis of the Department of Religious Studies at The Pennsylvania State University.

Thirty-one selected school districts throughout the Commonwealth are involved. They constitute a sample of districts drawn from urban, suburban, and rural localities of various ethnological community backgrounds. All of the teachers involved in the field test are selected faculty certified and experienced in the teaching of English. They have been prepared especially for teaching this course as part of the English curriculum. The project currently is producing two initial courses for the secondary schools: the one already mentioned plus one to be called "Religious Literature of the East."

Educators, politicians, and religionists around the nation have shown a remarkable interest in the purposes and methods of this course-building program. Press coverage of the project has been widespread and persistent. Editorials have dealt favorably if somewhat superficially with its implications. Television stations have carried interviews with its leadership, probing for news in the project's means and ends.

The object of all this interest involves a painstaking schedule of development and an extensive organization of personnel and scholarship. The current field test in high school classrooms concentrates on the use of unrevised working drafts of a Student's Guide and a Teacher's Guide for the selected readings in "Religious Literature of the West." The revised and finished material for this course will be available for the school year 1968-69. The Eastern course material should be complete for use in 1969-70.

II

The Western course consists of selections from the Hebrew Bible, the Apocalyptic Writings and the Talmud, the New Testament, and the Qur'an. These writings constitute the related classical expressions of the Jewish, Christian, and Islamic traditions. When revised into final units of instruction, this Western course probably will include fifteen units of selections. The units will occupy a one-semester schedule of five fifty-minute classes per week for eighteen weeks. Five of the units will deal with material from the Hebrew Bible, five with material from Apocalyptic, Rabbinic, and New Testament writings, and two with material from the Qur'an. Three introductory units will illuminate the historical and cultural background of the selections as well as some aspects of scriptural criticism.

The methodology of the course will emphasize verbal discussion rather than reading and writing in class. An individual approach to the selections by the students will be encouraged as much as possible, beginning with the students reading the selections apart from class.

The authors and consultants generally recognize the need for some provision of help through commentaries to be read with the selections. Just how much and what kind of commentary may be most conducive to an optimum student interest remains a moot question at least until the field test results are completed for evaluation. Some critics, the literati for the most part, see no need for any commentary at all except that provided for the classroom teachers. Others, largely from religion and education, see a need for some considerable commentary for students as well as for teachers.

The initial performance goals for the course anticipate that at the end of the course the student will be able to identify significant persons and events in the literature, to explain certain types of literature found in the readings, to discuss the influence of this literature on other literature, to distinguish between certain major motifs, and to relate the meaning of events in the literature to the events of his own experience as well as to those of contemporary public life.

Without finally committing the course to any of the elements herein-before described, the above review provides the reader with something of how the thinking and the Western course are developing during the winter of 1967-68.

What follows will provide a picture of the milieu in which the construction of the course is taking place as a joint project of the

Pennsylvania Department of Public Instruction and The Pennsylvania State University Department of Religious Studies.

III

The religious and political background to the project has taken shape about as one might expect. When the *Abington v. Schempp* decision came down from the United States Supreme Court in 1963, a large variety of proposals pressed themselves upon the Congress aiming to amend the Constitution and nullify the Court's decision. Related proposals reached Pennsylvania lawmakers bearing the intent to circumvent the Court's decision. But the legislature responded positively to other views and pressures, consequently promulgating the following law. It mandated action by the Department of Public Instruction.

Act of the General Assembly No. 442, dated December 22, 1965, provided "for a secondary course in the study of religious literature." It amended Section 1515 of Public Law 30 to read as follows:

Section 1515: Religious Literature.—(a) Courses in the literature of the Bible and other religious writings may be introduced and studied as regular courses in the literature branch of education by all pupils in the secondary public schools. Such courses shall be elective only and not required of any student. (b) Such courses shall be prepared and adopted according to age levels by the Department of Public Instruction with the advice and counsel of the Council of Basic Education and the approval of the State Board of Education.

Warrant for such a law had occurred to the legislature in the *obiter dictum* attending the *Abington v. Schempp* case.

We agree of course that the State may not establish a "religion of secularism" in the sense of affirmatively opposing or showing hostility to religion, thus "preferring those who believe in no religion over those who do believe." . . . We do not agree, however, that this decision in any sense has that effect. In addition, it might well be said that one's education is not complete without a study of comparative religion or the history of religion and its relationship to the advancement of civilization. It certainly may be said that the Bible is worthy of study for its literary and historic qualities. Nothing we have said here indicates that such study of the Bible or of religion, when presented objectively as part of a secular program of education, may not be effected consistent with the First Amendment.

Basing its view on the Supreme Court decision and accompanying interpretations, the State Department of Justice had said, prior to the enactment of the Pennsylvania law:

Group Bible reading and prayer, as the practices have heretofore existed as devotional exercises or ritual in the public schools of the Commonwealth, may no longer be conducted. . . .

In view of the foregoing, the following non-religious practices may be substituted lawfully in the public schools in place of corporate prayer and Bible reading without offending the First Amendment: daily recitation of the Pledge of Allegiance; a period of silent meditation; readings from great literature, passages and speeches of great Americans and from other documents of our heritage; presentation of inspirational music, poetry and art; the objective study about religion as a cultural force; objective study of comparative religion or the history of religion; and Bible study for literary and historic qualities as part of a secular program of education.

Apparently sensitive also to the contesting political pressures of both religious and non-religious interests in its constituencies, the legislature enacted the law mandating that the courses be offered as *elective* courses in the *literature* of the Bible and other religious writings. Whether by intent or not, this action avoided either making religion an autonomous course or submitting it directly to social science interpretation.

Consequently, and with equal political sensitivity, the Department of Public Instruction turned to The Pennsylvania State University. There, to the task of producing the desired courses, it could employ religious and literary scholarship that was not directly subordinate to either organized religion or the Commonwealth. At the University, the course development has proceeded with primary reference to the canons of good scholarship in literature, religious tradition, and cultural anthropology. Those responsible have made the operational assumption that balanced scholarship best reflects the best that can be meant by the term *objectively* as used in the Supreme Court's statement and as implied in the Pennsylvania law.

IV

During the initial period of conversations between the Department of Public Instruction and the University's Department of Religious Studies, the following structure for the program was projected. The basic principle of operation posited that the course should take the product of scholarly input from as wide a variety of interested parties as possible. The resolution of divergent opinions about the course content and method would rest, however, with the authorship team during the process of development. Final judgment as to the acceptability of the produced course would rest with the Department of Public Instruction as the directly sponsoring party of the contract.

The organizational structure of the project, in an order of immediacy and intensity of accountable involvement, began with the choice of an authorship team. This consisted of an author-administrator for the course program together with a research assistant and later a research associate. The original authorship and ensuing revision of the Western course guides, plus continuing responsibility for the negotiation and administration of the ancillary program, becoming the daily full-time task of the author and his co-author research assistant. Later research and planning for the Eastern course became the responsibility of the research associate expert in that field.

The daily work for the Western course during 1966-67 included: making final selections of readings; writing the Student's

Guide commentaries; planning, chairing and recording weekly Working Committee meetings; administering the project budget; negotiating contracts with the Department of Public Instruction; the intensive training of a local teacher who employed the drafted material experimentally in class as it was produced; responding to numerous inquiries from the public; addressing several interested educational and ecclesiastical groups; writing periodic reports for the Department of Public Instruction and the Advisory Panel; planning and teaching a four-week summer institute for secondary English teachers slated to teach the course in the field test; writing the Teacher's Guide draft; designing and administering the field test; the politic diffusion of credits for project inputs and achievements; and the systematic absorption of criticism with all possible alacrity and aplomb.

The second order of the project organization took the form of the Working Committee. This was a group largely of local and Department of Public Instruction persons whose task it was to stay in continuing consultation with the authorship team. This group counted in its membership the experimental teacher, Department of Public Instruction English and curriculum advisors, a religious studies representative, the local school's Assistant Superintendent for Instruction, the local school's English coordinator, and the Associate Dean for Continuing Education from the University's College of Education.

The third level of project organization involved scholar specialists in the Hebrew Bible, New Testament, Apocalyptics and Rabbinics, and the Qur'an. These persons participated individually in providing reading list suggestions and professional criticism to the authorship team, both by correspondence and in personal conferences.

The fourth order of project organization consisted of the Advisory Panel. These were scholarly experts, generally not professional consultants to the project. They have met twice in day-long conferences, once near the beginning of the Western course development to criticize its prospects and once after the completion of the first draft and the teacher's institute to criticize the first year's results. They were invited to participate by the Pennsylvania Superintendent of Public Instruction after consultation with the

Project Director, initially the head of the Department of Religious Studies and subsequently the author-administrator by his appointment. By category, the membership of the Advisory Panel included Department of Public Instruction representatives, public school administrators, and classroom teachers, plus prominent university professors in the fields of English literature, religion, education and anthropology.

A fifth and ultimate order of functional involvement comprised the Department of Public Instruction and the University as signatories to the contract to carry out the intent of the mandating law. Any collapse of the project would leave the University responsible as contractor to the Department of Public Instruction, and the Department of Public Instruction responsible to the State Board of Education for providing an explanation. On the other hand, general credit for success in the undertaking likewise would redound to these ultimately responsible corporate parties.

V

An outline of the sequence of events in the program indicates the time requirements of the development thus far and in prospect, stated in broad terms.

Spring and Summer 1966:

1. Preliminary conversations.

Autumn 1966, Winter and Spring 1967

1. Strategic contract planning.
2. Consultations with scholar experts in the literature.
3. First Advisory Panel conference.
4. Selection of passages to include in the course.
5. Writing the Student's Guide draft.
6. Experimental employment of the drafted course material.
7. Weekly Working Committee meetings.
8. Selection of the field test schools and teachers.
9. Arrangement for the teachers' institute facilities.

10. Negotiations with prospective visiting occasional lecturers at the teachers' institute.
11. Contract negotiations with the Department of Public Instruction for financing.
    (a) Teachers' institute for the Western course.
    (b) 1967-68 field test and revision of the Western course.
    (c) Research and outline for the Eastern course.

Summer 1967:

1. Completion of the Student's Guide draft.
2. The teachers' institute.
3. The second Advisory Panel conference.
4. Continuing contract negotiations.
5. Writing the Teacher's Guide draft.
6. Planning with the field test teachers.
7. Formulation of the field test design.

Autumn 1967:

1. Inauguration of the field test program.
2. Conclusion of contract negotiations for the field test and revision of the Western course.
3. Inauguration of the Eastern course project.
4. Initial steps in the Western course revision.

Winter and Spring 1968 (prospective):

1. Completion of the field test and revision of the Western course.
2. Completion of the detailed, annotated outline of the Eastern course.
3. Contract negotiations for writing the Eastern course, and for an Eastern course teachers' institute in the summer of 1969.
4. Planning a regular University course beginning in the summer of 1968 in teaching the Western course in the secondary schools, plus a course in the influence of the course literature on subsequent secular writings.

Summer 1968:

    1. The summer term courses for teacher preparation.

Autumn and Winter 1968-69:

    1. Writing the Guides for the Eastern course.
    2. Second and final field test year for the Western course.

Spring and Summer 1969:

    1. Plans for the Eastern course teachers' institute.
    2. The teachers' institute (Eastern course).

Autumn 1969, Winter and Spring 1970:

    1. Field test of the Eastern course.
    2. Any necessary revision of the Eastern course.

VI

One scarcely can overestimate the significance of contract negotiations in the experience of those involved in the Pennsylvania project. Thus far, two contracts have been signed and two are ready for signature by the two institutions.

The extensive negotiations behind the contracts, related especially to the Western course, are a function of two general elements in the situation that need to be understood. The first element is the psychometric problem inherent in the fact that the negotiations have taken place between two large bureaucratic institutions. Each has its own ways of doing things and its customary image to maintain vis-à-vis any and all other institutions. The second pervading element is the fact that at the point where money is involved all the erstwhile gloss evaporates from around the grist and grits that either must be separated now or else ground and baked together into the loaf. Often what is grist for one man's mill is grits in another. All the issues of divergent interests must find their resolutions under the general heading of contract stipulations. The number and detail of the stipulations varies in inverse proportion to the volume of mutual trust in any particular contract. Thus a contract finally signed both by the University and by the Department of Public Instruction represents long months invested in the psychometric problem of articulating the customary mind of one hierarchy to that of another in such a way that the resulting contract is as brief and simple as possible. Equally important here is the diplomatic problem of reconciling in the medium of a single product not only the subjective interests within the contracting institutions but also those outside with which both together must deal.

With respect to these elements, experience reveals to the accountable negotiator certain written and unwritten rubrics of conduct within both institutions which, when observed, tend to remove certain personal perplexities and to smooth the way of progress. These principles all have to do with how people respect each other subjectively while dealing with each other objectively. One learns to revere these political rubrics religiously. The shadow of humor that hangs over the following listing should not obscure the subjective wisdom involved in them.

1. *The Principle of Proper Channels:* When moving a pending decision inward toward strategic headquarters from the periphery of inter-institutional contact, or upward from the base of the administrative pyramid toward the executive apex, one never skips an intervening command post or executive sub-apex.

(a) *First Sub-Principle:* One talks an issue in and up before writing it in and up. What is written should be but the record of the spoken word. Nobody likes to be surprised by a challenge in writing.

(b) *Second Sub-Principle:* One uses the telephone for discussing issues, but only for conveying information and requesting it. One doesn't ask a man then and there for a decision. Nobody likes to be surprised by a challenge over the phone. One asks rather that he think about it and call back. This may mean a decision in weeks instead of seconds, but it's worth it in the long run —which is the only run there is in viable religio-political acadeplomacy.

2. *The Principle of Cognate Peers:* A large part of effective negotiation rests on one's appreciation of his privilege of social

affinity with respect to his corresponding executive peer in the other institution. Executive persons (those with a staff of two or more working for them) always have such a cognate peer. Institutional tables of organization never duplicate each other, but nevertheless they always resemble each other, and an alert man can discover his corresponding peer in a relatively short period of time. In doing this, he often simultaneously discovers a warm personal friend. Staff persons, however, functioning as the roots and branches of the executive vine, never have cognate peers and hence never discover such friends in their own right. At group negotiation conferences, peers may walk arm in arm from place to place, graciously gesticulating with their cigars as they chat. Staff persons, however, walk along behind, puffing cigarettes and impersonally exchanging data. Executive peers call each other by their first names after the first day of their friendship.

3. *The Principle of Ascending Issues:* When two lower or peripheral executives cannot resolve an issue between themselves, it is transferred to the next higher pair. Each lower executive explains the problem to his superior, the superior then telephoning his cognate peer. The initial ploy then consists of noting good-humoredly that well-meaning nameless subordinates seem to have struck a snag. Then a date is set for a luncheon meeting to iron the thing out. In the event of a really difficult issue, the process continues several times over until the issue finds equilibrium or release somewhere up the line. Ideally each issue ascends as smoothly and sweetly as an air bubble in a jar of maple syrup.

4. *The Principle of Higher Anonymity:* If in intra-institutional discussions of a particular issue, the word has to be passed down and over to the other institution that someone in and up stands adamant on a point, that higher executive is only identified to the more humble executive and in turn to his cognate peer as "the University" or "the Department." Thus if a contract negotiation flags or fails it never comes as the result of any piquing decision by an individual executive. Instead, it reveals only the perduring burden of self-restraint that must be exercised by the balking institution in the interests of justice and responsibility to precedent. This burden is borne in sorrow by the responsible executives and in frustration by the accountable staff. Happily, however, the

warm personal friendships between the cognate peers continue. Affairs move on to reveal the arena of the next succeeding contract proposal. This usually occurs as a new beginning for the old negotiation, since executives don't like to be sad, staff persons don't like to be frustrated, and nobody likes to flag or fail.

In general, contract negotiation involves an intuitive subjective exercise closely related to the ancient practice of covenanting. It issues in the production and reproduction of express normative statements mutually acceptable to parties holding diverging views of their functional significance.

VII

We come finally to the task of listing a short miscellany of insights germane to the experience we are treating. The systematic evaluation of these insights can only result from further experience of those in the project, and from wider experience of those who are reading this.

1. Throughout the project thus far the doubts most frequently expressed about the prospects of the courses have centered on the teachers. The people generally most dubious about the ability of secondary school teachers to present religious literature in terms of good scholarship and balanced viewpoint have been the university specialists in religion and English literature. Yet field test returns thus far indicate that the training the teachers received in the institute has served well as a start in enabling them to recognize with sympathy, and to balance with informed scholarship, their own and their students' tendencies to speak without reflection from their own ethnological presuppositions.

2. The treatment of three related tradition literatures rather than only two appears to make comparative elements in student discussion more open and enlightening, less guarded and apologetic.

3. It appears that the public school classroom constitutes a micro-community of people in which expressly divergent views of the meaning of religious literature do not threaten to polarize the participants into alienated groups. As a matter of teacher report,

differences in religious background appear to enhance classroom discussion. The student seems to feel responsible to the class for clearly expressing not only his own personal and traditional understandings, but also his interest in the understanding of the other students.

4. There appears to be a tendency on the part of special interest consultants (theologians, literati, educators) to pick up banners other than their own in advising the authorship team. Theologians have emphasized the importance of cultural-historical context, thus sounding like social scientists. Educators have pressed the importance of open discussion of various religious views, sounding like religionists. The literati have pushed persistently the point of view of humanistic existentialism, expressed in promoting "a personal approach to the literature as an individual experience for the student," thus sounding like philosophers.

5. As yet, nobody has reported any local community protests against the appearance of the course. Professional and religious organizations have expressed continuing interest and remarkable patience with the project's reticence to release detailed information about the content of the course until after the field test and revision year.

VIII

Throughout the project thus far the persons involved have kept in mind the people of the Commonwealth whose influences through the legislature have provided the necessary conditions for the project. The legalities and legalisms have been respected, but not worshiped. The subterranean fusions of religion and politics under the ostensible separations of Church and State have not been ignored. One finds that the negotiator needs a Boy Scout law of his own: Be confident, honest, patient, persistent, informed, and work for the best interests of all parties. The context of the project is loaded with the tensions between the communities of theistic religion and those of humanistic politics. They remain for everyone very personal and oddly similar realities, each making its own ultimate claims on the teleology of the work.

One can predict that the courses will turn out to be the product of what both religion and politics can do without either one succumbing to the other, or to a professional scholarship proposing to mediate all issues between them by defining objectivity according to its own subjective point of view.

9 The First Year with Religious Literature in Pennsylvania High Schools

JOHN R. WHITNEY *

In the March-April 1968 issue of *Religious Education,* an article appeared entitled "Introducing Religious Literature in Pennsylvania Secondary Schools." It described the warrant and working organization for a first-year course then in progress in that state. That year now has been completed. The first year served as a pilot year for the course teachers in the field and as a revision year for the course authors as they worked modifications into the course in light of the teachers' experience.

In order to expose the accumulated work of that year to the benefit of criticism, we offer this second report. It provides (a) some historical information concerning the first-year experience, (b) some comments touching on the initial rationale and content of the course, (c) an account of the classroom reactions of teach-

* Reprinted from the March/April 1969 issue of *Religious Education,* by permission of the publisher, The Religious Education Association, 545 West 111th St., New York, N.Y. 10025.

ers and students involved in the pilot course, (d) a description of the structure and content of the revised Student's Guide, (e) some observations regarding public school teacher training where religious literature is the study matter involved, and, finally, (f) some concluding reflections on the significance of the course and its prospects.

I
SOME BRIEF HISTORY

As elaborated formerly,[1] and recalled briefly now, the specific history of the Pennsylvania course development in religious literature began in 1965. In late December of that year, Governor Scranton signed a bill into law that provided for the development of "courses in the literature of the Bible and other religious writings. . . ." Courses of this nature, said the statute, "may be introduced and studied as regular courses in the literature branch of education by all pupils in the secondary public schools. Such courses shall be elective only . . . and shall be prepared and adopted according to age levels by the Department of Public Instruction. . . ." [2] Consequently, the DPI, using Commonwealth and Federal funds, contracted with the Department of Religious Studies at The Pennsylvania State University to produce a first course, "Religious Literature of the West." [3]

In the thirty-one selected schools in which the pilot course was offered, almost 700 students were involved. Class sizes ranged from seven to forty students, the more usual range falling between 15 and 25. The course usually was offered in the pilot schools for juniors and seniors. During a current second year, 43 schools are involved in a continued field test of the course, with nearly 1,500 students participating.

The amount of time allotted to the course has varied considerably from one local school district to another. The following are two polar examples. In one school last year, the course occupied one classroom session a week. It took place as a kind of exotic enclave on Friday afternoons in one of the regular English courses. In another school, one found it operating as an autonomous course that met five class sessions a week for two semesters. This range of variation scarcely reflected what the DPI had desired or recommended, but it did reveal the truth of a persevering local autonomy over course scheduling among Pennsylvania public school districts.

The teachers chosen to introduce the course ranged generally in age from the late twenties to around sixty years. The age of most of them fell in the late thirties through the forties. All had three years or more of certified experience as teachers of English in secondary schools. Roughly one-third were men. From what one dared discern about the teachers' cultic loyalties, they appeared to present a broad array of the sorts and conditions of *homo religiosus Americanus* one would expect Pennsylvania to produce. As one commentator was rumored to have put it, "They seem to represent everybody—Protestants, Christians, and Jews." (*Sic!*) With a half-dozen punctual exceptions, the teachers administered and returned their field-test forms after varying periods of good-natured procrastination. On the other hand, every teacher arrived on time, and was well informed, at the two regional afternoon meetings and the one general overnight conference that DPI provided for them during the school year. At those conferences the teachers shared their experiences in working with the course. They exchanged classroom method suggestions, evaluated various aspects of the Guide material, and reported patterns of the interest and performance among their students.

Four of the participating teachers met twice during the year with the course's Advisory Panel. The latter consisted of university specialists in religion, English literature, education, and anthropology, plus public school administrators, DPI officials, DPI English advisors, and the authors of the course Guides. The four teachers attached to the Advisory Panel turned out to be influential participants in the discussions.

Throughout the first year, inquiries concerning the course continued to arrive at the Project Director's office at Penn State and at the DPI. They usually requested copies of the experimental Guides, which we generally were unable to supply. They asked about prospects and requirements for teaching the course, and about how to produce or introduce such courses in their local schools. Most of these inquiries appeared to come from groups and individuals interested more in religion than in English literature.

In these same months, we met on several occasions with religious leadership groups to clarify our development and construction of the course's goals and orientation. Almost all reaction to those discussions seemed enthusiastically favorable to the course. As of the fall of 1968, no party has sued to have the course excluded from the public curriculum, although one tentative threat has been made in that direction.

Back at the Department of Religious Studies, our activity during 1967-68 consisted primarily in analyzing reports from the classrooms and in constructing the Student's Guide and the Teacher's Guide in their revised forms for use during the current year of 1968-69.

II
COMMENTS ON THE PILOT COURSE'S CONTENT AND RATIONALE

Our primary interest in this report lies in the revised material for the 1968-69 year now in progress. Nevertheless, a few elements in the first year's initial material merit attention the better to understand our rationale for the revisions.

In the first place, we somewhat boldly decided early in the project to produce promptly an initial corpus of reading and commentary. We resolved to get material into the hands of teachers and students as soon as possible. This would give us experience to work with, and an actual product on which revisions could begin. We considered this to be a more promising though risky move. The alternative would have been to work more slowly, with much closer continuing counsel by experts, toward the goal of generating a finished, final, and adequate product on the first attempt. One factor weighing heavily in this decision was the tendency among experts of equal stature and often similar specialties to disagree among themselves as to just what the right form and content of the course should be. All in all, we can say that the first-year material for teachers and students amounted to a rush job, carefully done. We paid attention much more to weighing the prospective *content* to be included in the course than to refining the *form* in which the material would be presented.

As a result, we did not construct the pilot course in units, nor did we include ancillary material such as maps and charts. We did not know how much time in the classroom it might take to treat a given increment of scriptural assignment. Neither did we know what our pilot year experience would indicate to be the optimum number of classroom periods that the course should occupy, although we made some tentative assumptions.

The situation was still more complicated by our initial decision that it would be a better course if classroom emphasis lay in discussion rather than reading and writing. As it turned out, our interest in providing enough scripture and commentary for a relatively full course resulted in our overwriting the Student's Guide. This tended to conflict with another set of interests, that is, the encouragement of aesthetic-inductive reading and classroom discussion. Later criticism also convinced us that the commentaries paralleled the scriptural readings without providing contextual or critical resources for the student.

We found the pilot year experience invaluable in providing us with first insights touching on some of the above factors, and on others such as the following. For example, the teachers were not as convinced in light of their classroom experience that discussion could bear as much of the load as we had hoped. Classroom experience also exposed in the Student's Guide certain systematic biases of the commentary authors as well as some similar biases on the part of experts who had influenced the commentaries. Furthermore, in our studied opinion, the pilot experience emphasized the positive value of thoroughgoing group conferences with teachers as a means for getting helpful information about classroom performance and attitude.

Our pilot year experience justified for us the theory which in the first place had encouraged our going ahead immediately with the course production on a working-paper basis. The general approach had borne the presupposition that, in a project such as this, literature and religion would commingle in a novel intellectual and emotional experience both for the teachers and for the students, issuing in an unusual and hence unpredictable classroom climate. We had assumed that we would gain as much by producing something before our thinking was complete as we would by conceiving the complete course before producing anything for actual use. In other words, we had chosen to construct the course as a *simultaneous* hypothesis, involving the interaction of plan and product. This differed from the alternative, which would have been to construct a *predictive* hypothesis wherein the plan, as a fully formed conceptual structure symbolized on paper, would quite dominate what the first and only actual product would be. By the adopted method, we learned not only how to *produce* the course by thinking, but also how to *conceive* the course by doing, as we worked to keep in touch with (and hopefully on top of) the interesting commixture of cognitive and affective factors which were involved in the pilot year.

III
SOME TEACHER AND STUDENT REACTIONS
TO THE PILOT COURSE

The participating teachers generally expressed enthusiasm for the course and for the scriptures selected. With some exceptions, they found the Hebrew Bible the easiest to teach and the Rabbinic selections the most difficult. Most of them thought that the commentary was well written in style and grammar, yet considerably over-written in detail and somewhat above the *average* twelfth grade level of reading comprehension. They noted the lack of unit structure and graphic material. They felt that the commentaries were unbiased, implying the reality of "objectivity" as a bias in itself.

A large number of students seemed to share these views, according to teacher reports and field-test forms. Some complained at the apparent lack of commitment to any of the traditions on the part of the authors, asking for a recognizable point of view with which they could agree or disagree. The teachers reported that student reaction to specific scriptural and commentary passages varied widely from class to class. In many instances the same passage would evoke strong rejection from some classes matched equally by approval from others. Most students and teachers reported that this course produced *more classroom discussion between students* than any other course during the year.

Our study of teacher comments in the conferences and of written field-test forms indicated to us that several of the teachers, regardless of previous warnings in their summer preparation course, approached their teaching with strong traces of vocation to teach "moral and spiritual values," with homiletical overtones. Others showed signs of having stressed perhaps too much their social science interest in religion at the expense of their interest in the writings as literary expressions of the experience of the communities that produced them. Overt tradition-bias did not appear to be a factor worthy of concern. Some teachers expressed a reticence to give grades "in a course like this." This attitude appeared to correlate very little with the particular religious background of the teacher expressing it. We noted, however, one apparent instance of teacher cynicism regarding the value of religious literature. This was strong enough to show up in a large number of the student field-test forms from that teacher's classroom, on which identical cynical comments appeared—the only case of such a phenomenon.

The great majority of teachers, regardless of religious background, appeared to act both imaginatively and effectively to provide a lively experience for their students in understanding and appreciating the literary quality and human significance of the tradition-writing contained in the course. They related the scriptural readings to many works in contemporary and other literature. They encouraged students to appreciate the universality of human concern for the meaning of existence and other similar problems with religious significance. At the same time, they largely succeeded in avoiding the substitution of sentimentality for scholarship. Several produced excellent examples of individual student projects such as collages, reports, and contemporary parallels of scriptural situations. Not the least important positive quality in the pilot year experience, we thought, was the fact that in the face of material for the most part new to everybody, the teachers could enjoy being both teachers and fellow learners with their students.

IV
REFINEMENTS IN THE REVISED STUDENT'S GUIDE

The revised Student's Guide divides the course into three principal Sections: (I) The Hebrew Bible, (II) Apocryphal, Rabbinic, and New Testament writings, and (III) the Qur'an. Section I contains eight Units of from one to eight Parts each, 30 Parts in all. Section II contains five Units (one Apocrypha, one Rabbinic, three New Testament) of from two to six Parts each, 21 in all. Section III contains two Units, each with five Parts. At the beginning of each Section stands an orientational Unit introducing the whole Section.

Each Part begins with a short Introduction that briefly refers to the literary and historical setting of the assigned scripture in relation to what has gone before in the course reading. Related to each such Introduction, where appropriate, one finds simple graphic representations locating the action in time and place. These occur in the form of Time Cues (time-lines) and Space Cues (sketch maps).

Following the Introduction to the Part comes a list of words and phrases called Search Cues. Some of these are quotations from the scriptural passage and some of them are not, but each is meant to reflect a meaningful person, object, event, or quality in the passage on which the reader would do well to concentrate his attention. These Search Cues avoid taking the grammatical form of either statements or questions, as examples later on in this paper will show.

Next comes an announcement of the scriptural passage or passages to be read, or else the printed passages themselves appear in cases where they are not easily available to all the students. The latter applies to Apocryphal, Rabbinical, and Qur'anic passages.

Following the scriptural passage or announcement is a body of Commentary varying in length. The course plan provides for the student to read the Commentary following his reading of the scriptural passage. It serves as a supplementary clarification after the student has read the scripture first as an aesthetic-inductive literary experience. Nevertheless, the plan presupposes that the reader will review the scripture passage after he reads the Commentary.

Finally, each Part concludes with several Reflection Questions. These serve primarily to raise issues of meaning useful for initiating class discussion. In no way are they meant to prescribe the precise forms and directions of discussion. Teachers and students, working with any particular passage, may find other points for discussion much more relevant to their own experience and interests. We have tried, however, to make these Reflection Questions dramatic enough at least to challenge the readers to use them or else discover better ones for themselves. Appendices in the Student Guide include a pertinent survey of Near East history plus an explanation of Graf-Wellhausen as an example of documentary theory used in scriptural studies.

Typically in each Part one expects the student to become involved in this following sequence: (1) he reads the Introduction, (2) he surveys the Search Cues for impressions to carry into his scriptural reading, (3) he reads the scriptural passage, (4) he reads the Commentary, and (5) he reviews his reading and considers the Reflection Questions in anticipation of class discussion. This is the model. Obviously, one expects students to vary in their response to it.

The following is an example of one of the Parts. The entire Part is included as it appears in the revised Student's Guide. The Commentary for this Part is considerably shorter than most. This example is Part 5 of Unit Three in Section I, Hebrew Bible. The Unit Three title is *The Emergence of the Kingdom.*

* * * * * * * * *

Part 5: King David Loses a Beloved and Rebellious Son

Introduction

When David was in the prime of his life as king, his handsome son, Absalom, grew embittered by tragedies within the family and inflamed by ambition to take the throne. He plotted a wholesale revolt against the power and pride of his father.

Thus the father and the son, who loved each other, found themselves opposed in a life and death struggle for control of Israel. It was a struggle marked by personal intrigue and military violence. The friends of each promoted plots and rumors calculated to feed the ambitions and suspicions of the king and prince against each other, and to bring to a climax the issue of power that stood between them.

The tragic stage was set as Absalom, having driven David from Jerusalem in flight across the Jordan, gathered his forces in the forests of Ephraim, while David mustered his army at Mahanaim, ready for the fatal battle.

Search Cues
1. why the king stayed in the city
2. his orders to his departing generals
3. the victory of David's army
4. the way Absalom died
5. the plan to tell the king
6. the father's question
7. the king's grief
NOW READ:
II SAMUEL 18:1-19:8

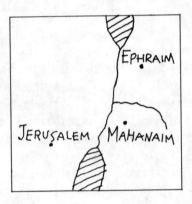

Commentary

Historic Tragedy
Research indicates that this story was written probably by one of David's court historians. In this account of the tragic rebellion of Absalom against his father's pride and power, the overwhelming burden of the writing occurs as a dramatically straightforward chronicle of facts. Apparently no attempt was made by the historian to soften the tragedy, or to make either David or Absalom a better or worse man than the plain facts might indicate. Instead, the historian wrote down his observations of the people and their deeds in a fashion foreshadowing modern documentary reporting. He let the drama and the tragedy of events cry out through his realistic account of the events themselves.

Reflection Questions

1. What unmentioned reason might have restrained King David from leading his army into the field?

2. How does the conduct of Joab and the "certain man" at the oak of Absalom dramatize the moral issues involved in their own careers as professional men of power?
3. What might have been the thoughts of Absalom at the time, assuming he could hear their conversation prior to his death?
4. Do you think David meant what he said as he wept in the chamber over the gate? Make a case for your answer.
5. In the circumstances of this story, in what sense does tragedy consist in a man's not being able to change his mind?
6. Explain the significance of the announcement to the people, "Behold, the king is sitting in the gate."
7. After reading and considering the David-Absalom story, look back to Unit Three, Part 4, and specifically to Nathan's prophetic utterance in II Samuel 12:10. In relation to this, what do you think of the statement, "no history is presented without didactic purposes"?

*   *   *   *   *   *   *   *   *

To conclude this section on the Student's Guide content, I shall refer to certain elements and principles that have informed our production of the revision thus far.

(1) At the very beginning of our work on the course, we debated the relative threat and promise of excluding in the commentaries some treatment of the literary-theological concept of myth. We decided to include it, comparing the positive concept with related positive concepts such as those of legend and history. In contrast, we also compared it with the popular negative uses of the term.

(2) To provide initial experiences with the writings of Judaism, Christianity, or Islam, we have pointed first to the tradition's original identifying event. In the case of the Hebrew Bible we moved from the later vantage point of the Joshuan invasion and the assembly at Shechem directly back to Moses and the Exodus. We began the New Testament readings with accounts of the Resurrection. As for the Qur'an, we emphasized in the Introduction the paramount significance of the revelations to Muhammad as the seal of the prophets.

(3) We focused attention from the outset on the integrating theme of this religious literature as a written expression of Jewish,

Christian, and Muslim responses to God. The readings express, with answers both historical and literary, such universal human questions as: "Who are we?" "What's really happening?" "What does it all mean?"

(4) We tacitly have approved the scholarly use of documentary theory, describing and using Graf-Wellhausen as an example. At the same time, we have recognized a widespread adherence to the principle of God's literal inspiration of sacred writings on the part of many students of the Bible and Qur'an.

(5) A careful discipline has prevailed throughout the Guide-writing to structure the commentaries and other materials in such a way that the literature of each tradition may be read and appreciated in terms of its own mind and inspiration. We have tried, for example, to encourage the student to understand Second Isaiah primarily as a Jew of the Exile might understand it, to read the Gospel of John primarily as a Christian at the turn of the first century A.D. might read it, and to regard the Qur'an primarily as a Muslim of the seventh century A.D. might regard it.

(6) The Guide accents the many related themes and motifs common to the literature, and distinguishes between such types in religious literature as *didactics, prophecy,* and *wisdom.*

(7) We have attempted to be candid in the commentaries about sexually related facts that teachers might otherwise gloss or avoid. These include *circumcision* (many high school students don't know precisely what it is), *"to know,"* in the sense of sexual intercourse, *sodomy* as the sin of the men of Sodom, and *incest* in the story of Lot and his daughters. We also have tried to treat openly and objectively certain politically sensitive elements often avoided as sources of possible contention and embarrassment, such as Israelite *cherem,* Muslim *jihad,* and Christian *polemic.*

(8) We have attempted to make the Commentaries as systematic and non-evaluative as possible, and also have strained to avoid pietisms and moralisms without devaluing religious faith and responsible morality. At the same time, we have worked knowing our own inability to transcend our particular personalities in all this. We also have assumed that the student's active approach to the course content will be more experiential and gestaltic than formal and systematic.

V
SOME ESSENTIALS IN TEACHER TRAINING

Space does not permit me to include in this article an adequate consideration of the critically important problem of how to prepare teachers intellectually and emotionally for conducting such courses as "Religious Literature of the West." I am convinced, however, that *they need both prior and continuing academic study,* not necessarily rigorous, in the literature of religion. At the same time, *they need a continuing emotional orientation* relative to this particular task in order to avoid compulsion moving them to dominate rather than to mediate student discussions, to suppress emotional responses from students instead of guiding students toward a clarification of the issues that have arisen to provoke them. To provide for these needs will insure, I believe, an adequate program of instruction and a good supply of teachers affectively and intellectually adequate to do the job. Their abiding task appears to be to guide young men and women in learning how to search out the universal questions of human experience that literature generally poses, and to appreciate the answers these scriptures specifically reflect.

My own experience in this kind of teacher training convinces me that to ignore these needs would be to court among the teachers facing classes in religious literature an anxious pattern of escapist retreat into related secular literature, that is, into a flight toward *the security of things neutral, eclectic, and well known.* It also would directly produce, I believe, a marked regression in classroom discussion toward a sifting of meaningless moral minutiae. Such a reductionist neglect of the theocentric significance of the readings might reduce the *literature* involved in the course from something highly substantial to something merely accidental, and the religion involved in the course from something highly meaningful to something merely mean.

VI
SOME CONCLUDING REFLECTIONS

People interested in a sound religious literacy among our

American citizenry owe a debt of gratitude to the Pennsylvania Legislature, the Department of Public Instruction, and the participating local districts for their development of this first course. Whether or not the course now being tried turns out well, a chance has been provided, at no mean expense, to build one, try one, and evaluate the results. Each state has its own peculiar *sitz im leben.* Each can learn much from what others have done, but finally each must develop its prevailing insights from its own investment in course-building programs for its own teachers and students. The Pennsylvania experience demonstrates at least that such course-building opportunities capture the imaginations of teachers and enlist a healthy enrollment on the part of students.

The other side of the coin concerns what Christian, Jewish, Muslim, and other religious communities propose to do through their leadership regarding such courses as these—courses which their own members are producing. *Will they see in these courses an educational reality valuable as a complement to their own programs of traditional nourishment?* Certainly no religious tradition will find in such courses in the public schools all that its young people should know about it. Each religious group will see elements to add or correct in light of its own genius and authority. If a tradition sees such public school courses as quite contrary to its interests, then it may choose to resist the first course. If it sees them as a positive support to its interests, then it may choose to uphold the first one. Many of us simply see these courses as a school opportunity for young men and women to read and discuss some great literature that reflects *individual, communal,* and *universal* meaning in human experience. Each religion, through its literature, offers itself as a way that provides a unifying integrity to these living modes of experience.

NOTES

1. John R. Whitney, "Introducing Religious Literature in Pennsylvania Secondary Schools," *Religious Education,* Vol. LXIII, No. 2, March-April 1968.

2. Henceforth herein, DPI.

3. Scriptural content comprising selections from the Hebrew Bible, Apocrypha, Rabbinics, New Testament, and Qur'an. We use *scripture* and *scriptural* to refer to passages used from the literature itself, whether regarded as canonical or not.

10 Further Issues on Religious Literature in Pennsylvania

DAVID E. ENGEL *

In the spring of 1968 John Whitney of the Department of Religious Studies at The Pennsylvania State University reported on the development of curriculum materials on "The Religious Literature of the West" being made available for use within that state.[1] At that time, response from both the general public within Pennsylvania and the academic community was inconclusive. Accordingly, no generalizations about response to this curriculum could be made.

Now, however, the issue has been more sharply joined, especially as a result of the criticism of two Jewish scholars. In addition the American Civil Liberties Union in the Commonwealth of Pennsylvania has discussed the situation and raised some doubts whether any such materials may be introduced into public schools. As it now stands, the emerging discussion and maneuvers about this curriculum have begun to pose some questions about religious instruction that need sustained examination. My purpose here is to raise such questions for religious educators.

* Reprinted from the March/April 1969 issue of *Religious Education,* by permission of the publisher, The Religious Education Association, 545 West 111th St., New York, N.Y. 10025.

I

It should be recalled that in 1965 the Pennsylvania Legislature amended the School Code of the Commonwealth to allow for the development of materials to be used in "courses in the literature of the Bible and other religious writings." Such materials were to be developed under the supervision of the Commonwealth's Department of Public Instruction and were to be utilized in elective courses in the secondary English curriculum when local school districts chose to institute such offerings.

The materials subsequently were prepared by the Department of Religious Studies at Penn State on contract with the Department of Public Instruction. Currently a second unit entitled "Religious Literature of the East" is being developed. The first unit on "Religious Literature of the West" has been undergoing field tests in 31 selected school districts since the autumn of 1967. Both the materials and the field-test feedback have been discussed by an Advisory Panel which has been considering possible revisions and further utilization of the curriculum, including teacher training.

II

At its spring meeting in 1968 the Advisory Panel became aware of a number of positive and negative reactions to the curriculum. By and large, the response from communities where the field tests were being conducted ranged from interest to enthusiasm. At that time, however, there were a few criticisms from scholars which suggested the consideration of revisions of the materials by the panel. The strongest came from Dr. Sidney B. Hoenig of Yeshiva University who claimed that the materials were opposed to his views and those of other orthodox Jewish scholars. He felt that treating Biblical and Talmudic materials according to the methods of literary criticism and higher textual criticism constituted a denigration of them. He was of the opinion that the exposition of passages from the Hebrew Bible relied too heavily on the Graf-Wellhausen documentary hypothesis. He was later joined in this criticism by Dr. Moshe Greenberg of the University of Pennsylvania, ironically one of the original consultants for the compilation of the materials in question and a former member of the Advisory Panel.

The Advisory Panel came to the conclusion that the revisions already in process by the Penn State group under John Whitney's direction were sufficient and should proceed. Then in August the ACLU in its house organ, *Civil Liberties Record*, reported its discussion and recommendations about the evolving issues.

Several positions apparently were represented in the ACLU discussions. Some felt that "no course in religion can satisfy the First Amendment." [2] Others, while critical of some aspects of the curriculum, came to the conclusion that with some alterations the course could be satisfactory in a Constitutional sense. In general the Union's church-state committee and board members united on two propositions:

1. A course in religious literature is not objectionable *per se,* but any proposed course is bound to give rise to objections from religious and other sources. The Commonwealth has an obligation to assess such objections and act in accordance with its assessments.

2. In view of the responsible criticism of the present course, the Commonwealth should add supplementary material to add balance. [3]

III

The questions arising from these propositions are still to be considered within Pennsylvania. But for religious educators as well as the general public there is an underlying issue of considerable import.

In light of developments in education since the 1963 *Schempp-Murray* decision and the Pennsylvania ACLU 1968 conclusions, two dimensions of the issue can be identified. First, in public education any curriculum dealing with religion must be objective. In this connection, despite the frequent reference to such need for objectivity in legal opinion and among educators, the specifications of what could constitute objectivity are far from clear. Operationally the Pennsylvania Department of Public Instruction and its Advisory Panel on the Curriculum have tended to view the matter pragmatically. That is, where there is known variety in the interpretation of biblical materials, such variety should be represented to the learner. Objectivity, thus, is viewed as a matter of fullness and fairness of scholarship.

Second, a curriculum in public education should not be offensive to the learner. Here, there is no clarity with respect to what is offensive and what is not. Obviously, some would hold that any ideological position contrary to their own is offensive. Others would be more open and less threatened by variant opinion and theory. In the discussions in the ACLU some little emphasis was placed on that group's objective of keeping offensive materials out of the schools.

The question being posed here—and it may be a central question for anyone dealing with instruction in or about religion—is whether any curriculum can satisfy the criteria implicit in both propositions. That is, is it possible for a curriculum at once to do justice to diverse opinion and scholarship and also be inoffensive? In addition, it may well be questioned from an educational viewpoint whether a curriculum should attempt to be inoffensive at all. Being inoffensive may merely mean that the proposed study is dull.

For the religious educator or the educator concerned with religious studies, still another matter needs attention. Such persons need to consider the very nature of education with respect to religion. Is learning in religion to reinforce the mindset one has before he engages in study? Or is it to assist him in the evaluation of his cognitive stance as a result of such study? These questions are becoming important in the Pennsylvania situation. They may be of paramount importance for religious instruction in any situation.

NOTES

1. See John Whitney, "Introducing Religious Literature in Pennsyl-

vania Secondary Schools," *Religious Education,* Vol. LXIII, March-April 1968, No. 2.

2. *Civil Liberties Record,* American Civil Liberties Union of Pennsylvania, August, 1968, p. 2.

3. *Ibid.*

11 A New Shape for Religion and Public Education in Changing Times

ROBERT A. SPIVEY *

The title of Bob Dylan's folk song, "The Times They Are A-Changing," suggests not only obvious changes in our society, such as technological advance, environmental crisis, black power, women's liberation, and peace movements but also the current situation of public education. Formerly, public education in the United States had to create a unity out of a great diversity of immigrant peoples; America was a great melting pot and public education enabled assimilation. But now that our nation has, at least in some sense, "arrived," its citizens face the formidable task of deciding where and how to go from here. We have to make difficult, delicate judgments and decisions about political, economic, and ethical matters. The times are a-changing in that today the public schools, instead of having to nurture a consensus of values, are having to create a context for value formation. This observation is not the whole story, but it is

* Reprinted with permission of the publisher from *Journal of Church and State*, Vol. 14, No. 3, Autumn 1972, pp. 441-456.

partially the context for the Supreme Court's clear, emphatic decisions in 1962 and 1963—public education should be concerned not with the *practice of religion,* blessing the values of American society, but with the *study of religion,* inquiring about sources of values in mankind's religious heritage. Moreover, this gradual shift of focus in education is one cause of growing public confusion and mistrust toward education in general.

In 1965 the State Department of Education of Florida created a State Committee on Study about Religion in the Public Schools which set out to explore creative possibilities for the relationship of religion and education. In 1968 an initial three year pilot program, focusing on curriculum development and teacher education for religion-social studies at the secondary level, was conceived and funded for Florida State University by a grant of $146,000 from the Danforth Foundation.[1]

Curriculum efforts produced thirty study units entitled "Religious Issues in the Social Studies," ten units dealing with religious issues in American culture, ten with issues in Western civilization, and ten with world cultures.[2] The titles of the units are as follows:

Issues in Religion for Students of American Culture

1. WHY GO TO THE NEW WORLD?: Man's Motives
2. PENNSYLVANIA: Diversity or Conformity?
3. THE AMERICAN REVOLUTION: A Religious War?
4. THE CHURCHES: Subsidy or Separation?
5. THE ROLE OF THE CHURCH ON THE FRONTIER
6. THE BLACK CHURCH
7. RELIGION: Personal and Social
8. WAYS OF UNDERSTANDING: Science and Religion
9. LOYALTY: Conscience or Constitution?
10. AMERICA: Protestant or Pluralist?

Issues in Religion for Students of Western Civilization

1. BABYLONIAN RELIGION: Order and the Threat of Chaos
2. GRAECO-ROMAN RELIGION: Philosophy or Festival?
3. JUDAISM: Religious Community and National State

4. THE CHRISTIAN IN THE ROMAN EMPIRE: Loyal Citizen or Traitor?
5. THE CRUSADES: War and Peace in Christian Perspective
6. CHRISTIANITY IN MEDIEVAL LIFE: The Pursuit of Unity and Meaning
7. THE REFORMATION: The Christian as Passive Sufferer or Active Rebel?
8. The ENLIGHTENMENT: Reason and Religion
9. THE ECUMENICAL MOVEMENT: The Quest for Unity or Cooperation?
10. SOUTH AFRICA: Christian Responses to Multi-Racial Conditions

Issues in Religion for Students of World Cultures

1. WHAT IS RELIGION: Superstition or Truth?
2. ISLAM: Conquest and Compassion
3. FOLK RELIGION AND GOVERNMENT IN EGYPT
4. HINDUISM: Religion and Nation-Building in India
5. HAS CHINA CHANGED TEACHERS: Confucius and Mao Tse-tung
6. BUDDHISM IN SOUTHEAST ASIA: Tradition and the Modern World
7. SHINTO: Religion and Urban-Industrial Development in Japan
8. THE U.S.S.R.: Religious Freedom or Religious Toleration?
9. THE CHURCH IN LATIN AMERICA: Christian Responses to Social Revolution
10. TAOISM: Man, Nature, and the Way

The studies or lessons, including both a student manual and a teacher's guide, are designed for existing social studies courses as supplemental units which give a richer treatment of religion than that normally provided by either the textbook or the teacher's academic preparation in religion. Each lesson utilizes primary sources as the main focus for study and also includes motivational devices and the usual study aids; moreover, each lesson, varying in length from one to two weeks, is intended to be self-contained.

I

THE FLORIDA EXPERIENCE AS A MODEL

Although no single approach represents the way in this delicate undertaking of religion-study in the public schools, the following ten general observations about the Florida experience highlight what we have learned, through trial and error, about a proper way to proceed in religion-study for the public schools. They are offered as something of a model if it is recognized that the introduction of religion-study will in each case have also to take account of the particular local circumstances.

1. *Auspices of the State Department of Education.* The committee and the curriculum project have worked under the auspices and direction of the State Department of Education. Unfortunately, some efforts to introduce study about religion in public schools are sponsored by religious organizations or by religious individuals. Consequently, there is justifiable fear, both by non-religious folk and by religious minorities, that the introduction of religion-study is only a disguised effort to indoctrinate or reinstate the old values, particularly the Protestant ethos. Religion-study, like any other learning activity in the public schools, has to be responsible to educational authorities.

2. *A Representative Advisory Committee.* Although the actual work of curriculum development and teacher education belongs to trained scholars and competent educators, the critical advice of a broadly conceived advisory committee, including representatives from major religious traditions, parents, teachers, and administrators, is necessary because the public study of religion is new, explosive, and controversial. There are political and practical, as well as educational considerations. Yet caution is needed, for every criticism cannot be fully inculcated; suggestions should

be heard, weighed, and respected as far as possible by curriculum developers.

3. *Unequivocal Support for the Supreme Court Decisions.* Efforts to get prayer back into the public schools or to circumvent the Supreme Court decisions which declared religious practices sponsored by public school authorities unconstitutional are not a legitimate part of the program to further the study of religion in public schools. If the advocates of religion-study do not support the Supreme Court decisions, the study of religion may become subverted into a disguised form of the practice of religion. Opposition to attempts to bring back religious practices into the public schools may thereby incur the wrath of its religious proponents; however, this risk cannot be unduly avoided.

4. *Curriculum Development and Teacher Education Emphasis.* The key to learning about religion in the public schools is adequate curriculum materials and provision for competent teacher education. It is unsatisfactory to leave major efforts at curriculum development to the occasional efforts and inspiration of well-meaning persons. Because there are at present few fully satisfactory models for religion curriculum in the public schools, scholars and educators should be provided with the time and resources to plan and execute imaginative and comprehensive curriculum. Moreover, pragmatically and politically it makes sense to include consultation with scholars from various religious traditions. In regard to teacher education, at least for the time being, it is essential that teachers be regular public school teachers who are graduates of the schools and colleges of education. The ready accessibility of clergymen or dedicated laymen should not be used as an excuse in the hiring of religion teachers. In the initial stages, if there has to be a deficiency, then it should be in the area of knowledge about religion, rather than in knowledge about education. This emphasis guards against the making of the public school into an instrument of religion propaganda.

5. *Religion and Education.* In the Florida work scholars from the area of religion and from social studies education have

collaborated. The former are needed because of religious illiteracy both in the public school and in teacher education; the latter are needed because religion scholars are primarily in higher education and have little knowledge or competence in learning theory and practice at the public school level.

6. *The Advantages of the Existing Curriculum.* The decision to enrich the regular social studies curriculum rather than to create an elective course in religion has the distinct advantage, as an initial thrust, of making use of regular teachers. Furthermore, the total student body, rather than a self-selective cadre of religious or anti-religious students, learns about religion. The defense for religion in the schools is, and can only be, an educational one.

7. *Use of Primary Sources.* Each study utilizes primary sources as the basic reading. Thereby students are brought directly into contact with men and women who feel strongly about religion; they learn from those who were themselves involved, committed, earnest, courageous, penitent, caring, and persuasive. This approach helps to avoid the danger of reductionism, i.e., treating religion as if it consisted simply of dates, names, and places.

8. *An Inquiry Approach.* The curriculum materials seek student involvement through stress on inquiry and discovery. In other words, the student *learns about religion,* rather than is *taught about religion.* The lecture-method, which can easily descend from education into mere information or at worst biased indoctrination, is minimized; instead inquiry, discussion, analysis, and role playing are maximized in order that teacher and student may jointly participate.

9. *Value Education.* The materials include naturally and inevitably not only religious subject matter but also value education in the broadest sense. While studying about religion, students confront human beings wrestling with questions of moral principle, conscience, freedom, responsibility, and justice. Students are helped to weigh values, to foresee consequences, and to realize the significance of human actions. In the process their own values

are tested by new, and often more probing, views of reality which are both challenging and educational.

10. *Pilot Testing for Critical Evaluation and Revision.* The effect of religion-study in the public schools cannot be known apart from the classroom. Curriculum materials and teaching methods should be subjected to systematic observation, continuing feedback, and critical evaluation for revision. Such procedures are expensive and time consuming, but the need for superior, comprehensive, and challenging study of religion warrants such care.

The Florida experience in curriculum development and teacher education does present a viable model for future efforts to improve study about religion in public schools. Yet there are serious problems and questions ahead. The large, overriding practical question concerning the materials is whether they will be used. These are supplementary materials for already existing textbooks; consequently, it is difficult to forecast how many teachers will be attracted to use the study lessons and how many will have access to the additional financial resources necessary to supply students with these materials. In theory, the religion-social studies curriculum is designed to reach all public school students, whereas an elective course approach only affects the relatively few students who opt for a religion course, but in actual practice the impact of our more comprehensive effort may be less far-reaching.[3]

Possibly the most serious problem confronting the study of religion in public education has to do with student attitudes about religion. After learning from the religious issues series it seems the case that students generally move from having strong opinions about religion, either for or against, to the category of undecided. As they gather more information, or data, they become less sure of their convictions. Preliminary investigations into the attitudes of university students' taking courses in religion seem to indicate this same trend.[4] A further and related criticism of the religious issues curriculum is that its focus upon conflict thereby neglects religion in its more positive manifestations for those aspects of religion which relate to issues, crises, and controversies in society.

The crucial question, though, is whether academic study about religion produces students who are undecided, uncommitted, and unresponsive to religion. This problem is a matter of concern for higher, as well as secondary, education. As such it can only be treated by a brief examination of the shape of academic religion-study in the American college and university. It is in higher education that part of the future of religion-study at the lower levels is being formed.

II

A NEW SHAPE FOR THE STUDY OF RELIGION

Two prefatory concerns regarding higher education are in order before presenting a review of developments in patterns for the academic study of religion. Much higher education has a deadening effect, what might be labeled the tired blood syndrome. Students enter the university fresh, eager, expectant, only to be turned off and end by going through the motions to get the degree. David Hauser put the problem boldly and succinctly: "It is highly unlikely that any data study of violence on the campus could make room for a definition of violence perceived as the repression of the student in the classroom by boredom which is supported and maintained by large, punitive powers of the institution." [5] *The* problem of higher education is not riots, but boredom.

The other concern has to do with the crisis of value in our society and the role that the university is playing and will play in that crisis. I know of no major student protest or demonstration which was not directed at moral ambiguity in the American situation. Black student protest, such as that of Cornell, was the most obvious example. However, the others are just as striking: protest at Columbia was directed at the university's indifference to the inner city; vigils at Florida State were directed at adult hypocrisy about four-letter words. The following proposal for a future shape of religion-study in public education is in part informed by these two underlying realities: student boredom and the value crisis in society.

1. *Formal Patterns of Religion-Study in Higher Education.*
The formal patterns of religion-study in higher education are five
in number, listed in ascending order of preference. The basic
criterion used for judging their respective worth is whether the pattern helps facilitate learning in the college or university.

The first pattern, the *Department of Christianity,* rarely appears under that title. It can just as easily be labeled Department
of Bible, Department of Religion, or Department of Divinity. In
essence this undergraduate department type exists to defend the
Christian faith. Its model is usually derived from the seminary
from which its teachers and professors have graduated and to
which they aspire to send the brightest and ablest students. Most
often this department is located in a small denominational college
which epitomizes the philosophy of *in loco parentis.* The parents'
religion is to be faithfully explicated and inculcated. Usually the
college requires that most if not all teachers, especially those in
crucial areas such as religion, philosophy, and biology, should be
confessing members of a particular brand of Christian denomina-
tionalism. By and large the denomination assumes that society
threatens; therefore, the faculty strives to protect students from
the "acids of modernity." The limitations for scholarship of an
apologetic and student-oriented atmosphere are self-evident. Faculty appointments and promotions favor the pious, well-meaning
adherent of the faith over a critical scholar with superior academic
training.

The second pattern, the *School of Religion,* seeks to function
more positively in regard to the general culture by taking account
of various religious options. On the one hand, the School of
Religion often focuses upon teaching the Bible because this holy
scripture serves as the common denominator of all major American
religious traditions. Moreover, such teaching will help improve
the moral and spiritual values of students. On the other hand,
the School brings together representatives of major religious traditions to teach courses as religious specimens of the prevailing
religious traditions. These "school of religion" arrangements, when
connected with state universities, are often financed by those
church traditions which are willing and able to be included in the
zoo. Moreover, the university frequently places restrictions on the

number of courses which may be counted toward the university's academic degree. At least the school takes cognizance of the pluralism of American society.

The third pattern, the *Department of Philosophy and Religion,* gives to the study of religion greater academic respectability than either of the former approaches. Here philosophers and theologians engage one another in critical conversation through philosophy of religion. Organized, institutionalized religion or religious life gets short shrift because the natural focus is upon religious thought. In these traditional courses, study of the Western heritage includes the thought of Plato, Augustine, Aquinas, Descartes, Hegel, and others with little attention to the total religious context of each thinker. Faculty are regular faculty, not local imported ministers. But in most cases, the major emphasis, both in terms of appointments and courses, is philosophy rather than religion.

The fourth, and in some ways the most alluring, pattern for the study of religion in higher education is the *Interdepartmental Program.* This approach locates a religion specialist in the several departments of the college or university where religion naturally and appropriately arises as a subject matter, for example, art, anthropology, history, English, philosophy, sociology, psychology, classics, and Asian studies. The rationale for such an interdepartmental program may arise from the most exalted claims for religion—as the depth dimension of every discipline, religion should be studied within that discipline. Or advocacy of the interdepartmental program may arise from the assertion that religion-study does not have a method of its own and hence must be located where the established methods of study (philosophical, historical, and literary) are already at work. Pragmatically, this approach has the appeal of not siphoning funds from already existing departments to establish a new department. An obvious weakness is the difficulty of bringing together these scattered scholars of religion who employ different methodologies to converse and stimulate one another about a common subject matter, religion. Such a company of scholars operates most effectively only in a department.

The fifth and climactic pattern is the *Department of Religious Studies,* located in a college of arts and sciences and operating in the same manner as other departments. There is a subject matter religion. There are religions. People need to be brought together who have trained competence to investigate, study, and teach about this subject matter.

There are three goals toward which such a department is working in its teaching and scholarly work. First of all, the study of religion has to be as *comprehensive* as possible. The department cannot afford to ignore primitive religion or to exclude non-Western religions. A second goal of study in the department is the *avoiding of reductionism* in understanding religion. Most approaches to religion, for example, psychology of religion, reduce the phenomenon of religion to something else, in this case, to psychology. Religion study must not settle for something other than religion or for simply a part of the phenomenon. The third goal for the department's study of religion is *discipline*. Scholarly rigor and patience prevent the study of religion from degenerating into sloppy bull-session popularity. Real concern and compassion for the student offer more than warm sentimentality.

2. *An Informal Pattern of Religion-Study in Higher Education.* Whether or not education is committed to formal discourse about religion by its academic program, informal learning about religion will occur. There are legions of professors or students who advocate a "religious" viewpoint: pragmatism, ethical idealism, scientism, Marxism, capitalism, existentialism, individualism. "The university is the veritable cockpit of value conflicts in the world at the moment." [6] No other institution (family, government, church, or business) shows so clearly the conflict of values which marks our time. The question is not whether the university experiences value conflicts, but whether faculty and students have yet acknowledged that the university is *the cockpit* of value conflicts in America today.

Surely then the informal value discussions which take place in the university in seeking to help people think more adequately about religion are indirectly asking for more formal disciplined thinking about those informal theologies that are put forth as accepted fact. Promethean illusions about modern man which usually end with a whimper could be exposed early and easily with proper understanding of any number of religious postures. Although everyone acknowledges that there is good and bad religion, the problem arises in determining which is good and which bad. Surely the university must help people to understand their religious past and that of others so that the educated man is not victim of the first thing that comes along. Moreover, it is a good thing for a student to see his own religious tradition clearly, even if it means seeing deficiences and weaknesses, because thereby one is more liberally educated, more aware of his own imperfections, and therefore able to understand better those of others. To think more adequately about religion may also cause one to realize potentialities in one's own faith not yet known.

The crisis in higher education is not with informal religion-study as such, but rather with the failure to realize that such agonizing conflicts in values are the very stuff of the university. Increasing professionalization and specialization in higher education minimize nasty questions like why this research is being undertaken or what good will result for humanity from this vocational choice. Scholarship for its own sake is but another variation of vocational pragmatism. "Instead of increasing wisdom and ennobling the human spirit, academic professionalization may be breeding a corrupting careerism, the professor entrepreneur whose purpose is worldly success, not intellectual service: just another working man." [7] Religion-study at its best could help the university acknowledge its role as the cockpit of value conflict in American life, if religion scholars do not betray their own subject matter. A note of warning is appropriate here because the religion scholar does not offer the answer of religion or a religion. He offers theologies from religions as possible competing ways of understanding the nature of the good and what man shall do with himself.

3. *A Future Pattern of Religion-Study.* The curious anomaly for religion-study is that just at the time when the university is becoming the place for value conflicts (student protests on the one hand and a disenchantment with the image of the scientific scholar on the other) much religion scholarship represents a retreat from the conflict and a search for security in past victories.

Before attempting to suggest a corrective to the overextension of scholarly objectivity and professional specialization, I want to assert that the shape for the future of religion-study will not deny the past but learn from its truths and errors. No one can afford to despise his past, but we may quarrel with its emphases, its balance, its sensitivity. The study of religion should include scientific, academic objectivity but at the same time the dominant way of sensing religious reality must become humanistic. The following pointers to a new shape for the study of religion fall under three sets of observations: introductory study, the relation of arts and sciences, and the post-Christendom era. These suggestions should be distinguished from superficial, facile attempts to move beyond scholarly objectivity by homiletic, moral exhortation or sensitivity training disguised as effective education. The new shape must be integral to the field and nature of religion itself not an ecclesiastical or psychological import.

Introductory Study. In the past the introductory study of religion has been viewed as a means for establishing literacy for the student in the Biblical tradition. Who? When? Where? What? To Whom? How? Why? The Christian faith is assumed; knowledge about that tradition is lacking. But such an exposure fails to take account of the situation of most modern, secular students. For them the Thomistic model is stood on its head; faith and relevation do not stand above reason and experience; the reverse is true. And it is their own religious tradition which they find most difficult to appreciate critically because earlier exposure has inculcated a scientific, literal, factual view of the Biblical events. As a consequence my recommendation calls either for abandoning the Biblical introductory content and substituting a complex of religious traditions, some of which are necessarily less close at hand for the student, or concentrating upon helping students view the Biblical material as story, as myth, as a particular way of viewing reality.

At present introductory study usually serves to introduce the student to a major, a specialization, a technical terminology. The scientific model of building a cumulative body of knowledge dominates as the student is initiated into the power of a discipline. The student thus introduced into scholarly rigor and theological terminology *gains control* over the object of study for clean, precise analysis and dissection. By contrast, undergraduate students could be initiated into a critical appreciation of several religious traditions including at least one non-traditional religion such as scientism, Marxism, or behaviorism. Because several religious expressions would be presented, the faculty would have to teach out-of-field and hence be less subject to lapsing into technical jargon. The aim would be to teach and learn by use of human, non-specialized language and analogies so that the ways of viewing life could be communicated to other students and faculty besides those in religion courses. Moreover, students would be encouraged to think imaginatively and critically about their own stories, their own views of reality.

The Relation of Arts and Sciences. Our departments of religion are primarily in colleges of arts and sciences and that name "arts and sciences" is no accident. Underlying our educational coherence is a serious division [8] which I shall caricature in order to make the point clear. Science begins with the desire simply to learn what is the case, but science soon moves into the desire to control or to master nature. That is the reason why it is difficult, if not impossible, to separate science and technology. Science swallows reality. By contrast, the arts seek to appreciate, enjoy, encounter, and participate in reality. The division is imaged by thinking about the scientific professional: competent, cool, in control, precise, objective. The other image, that of the artist, is quite different: sensitive, temperamental, open, passionate, involved. The dimension of the artist's appreciation of reality has been lost in the academic world, and this dimension is in danger of being lost in the academic study of religion. What I am suggesting almost sounds heretical in *academic* circles, but the thrust of old style courses in art, music, and literature appreciation, should be made available in university courses of religious appreciation.

A practical difficulty involved with such learning is measurement of achievement, but that again is one problem with modern education which is more interested in measuring success or failure than in learning. To understand religion as one of the arts, a subject matter to be approached in appreciation and inviting participation, is another contribution to a future pattern.

This point may be illustrated by asking how one is to study

a sacred text of a religious tradition. Although these texts preserve original experiences of the sacred, this dimension of meaning often gets overlooked in the thirst for precise, neat facts or answers. Countless questions arise about the text, and the answers to these relatively scientific questions (what is the original text? how are the words to be translated? what is the historical situation to which the writing is directed?) are neither easy nor unimportant. But the "meaning" question—how does one know when he has caught the spirit of the text or, better still, how can a student feel his way into a different view of reality, a standpoint different from one's own?—is the primary one. Moreover, the text cannot be raped and hence made dispensable as one prevailing view of cumulative knowledge suggests. Is not the role of the learner more like that of the lover who meditates upon, enjoys, wonders in the reality of the other? The lover returns again and again to the beloved. He does not consume and then pass on. Although the black marks on the page are profane, the way of living and meeting that the text preserves is sacred; the student's way of meeting is through the text itself.[9]

The Post-Christendom Era. The third point starts from the observation that we are now in an age which is neither post-Christian (contrary to Cox) nor post-religious (contrary to Bonhoeffer) but one which is post-Christendom.[10] Since the fourth-century embrace of Constantine, Christianity has been captivated by the vision of becoming the world-wide, all-embracing religion. Much anxious energy of Christian folk, particularly in the United States, has been directed toward extending the umbrella of Christendom. Christian vitality has been measured in terms of converts rather than the quality of Christian life. Even in that unique Protestant institution for Christian nurture, the Sunday School, study was directed most frequently to saving the lost and winning souls. Liberal Christianity also was permeated by an image of bringing the kingdom of God to earth, of changing the social and ethical structures of the world so that God's Kingdom, i.e., Christendom, would be realized. In other words, Christianity was guilty of a naive progressive historicism (an inevitable accompaniment of scientism) that pictured the Christianization of the world either through *conversion* or *ethical effort*. Today as Christians are forced by historical and technological realities into greater familiarity with the world, this dream of *Christendom* is slowly, and at times painfully, being abandoned.

The ghosts are difficult, however, to exorcise. It is not without significance that scholars of religion, particularly theologians, busy themselves with all kinds of compensatory activities in order "to make a difference." Pastoral counseling, social activism, administration, faddishness are possible symptoms of the disease of viewing life under the pseudo-scientific, cumulative, kingdom-is-coming perspective. But this thirst for literal, tangible signs of progress may be waning and if so then professors and students are once more on the verge of a passion and wonder at the world of religion. This plea for "passionate scholarliness," or "involved disinterestedness," or "intelligent subjectivity," or "critical appreciation" can serve as the corrective to an academic objectivity which realized its human subjectivity in peripheral and sometimes harmful ways.[11]

A subsidiary observation, suggested by Flannery O'Connor's phrase, the South as "Christ Haunted, not Christ centered," is that a time may come in which scholars and students of religion will no longer be haunted by their past. Many faculty members, both within and without departments of religion, who call themselves Christians are Christ-haunted, not Christ-centered. Many have exorcised this lingering demon by studying about the Christian religion in order to control. Future faculty of religion need to be concerned for religion rather than to be rid of its effects. Faculty are to be existential guides for students who want not only examples in reflection about religion, but also paradigms in commitment to particular religious postures. Just as the university offers *doers* as well as *critics* of the arts, so it should present doers as well as critics of religion—Christian as well as Buddhist, Muslim, Jew, atheist.

This new shape for religion-study in the university is also a pattern for study of religion in the public schools. In actual fact, the public schools may be more creative and responsive to this new situation for religion-study. There are all sorts of problems in "religious appreciation," yet the new media which are by and large being explored only in the public schools offer the means to bring life into classroom study of religion. The times are a-changing, and both citizens and scholars need to be concerned about the future shape of religion in public education.

> Then (we'd) better start swimming
> Or (we'll) sink like a stone
> For the times they are a-changing.

NOTES

1. For descriptions of the work of the State Committee and fuller detail on the initial project and its rationale, see Robert A. Spivey, "Religion and Public School Education: A Plan for the Future," *Journal of Church and State* 10 (Spring 1968), pp. 193-205, and Edwin S. Gaustad, "Teaching About Religion in the Public Schools: New Ventures in Public Education," *Journal of Church and State* 10 (Spring 1969), pp. 265-276.

2. To be published in three volumes beginning in July 1972 by Addison-Wesley Publishing Co. of Menlo Park, California.

3. A recent, significant statement on religious education by a governmental committee in the Province of Ontario in Canada concludes with recommendations strikingly similar to those contained in the Florida model; see Gregory Baum, "The Mackey Report," *The Ecumenist* 7 (June 1969), pp. 57-61.

4. Part of the reason for such an "undecided" move by students is that they are experiencing a critical, disciplined study of religion for the first time. They have had no opportunity in their formal education to develop a critical appreciation for religious phenomena. Florida State University has just begun a three-year curriculum development and teacher education project, funded by the Stone Foundation and the National Endowment for the Humanities, for the study of religion in the social studies at the elementary level. Future plans also call for the completion of a Religion Biography Series for junior high school students and slow learners. Both projects specifically focus on the development of appreciation for the religious dimension of human life.

5. "Introduction: Toward a New University," *Soundings* 52 (Summer 1969), p. 126.

6. Julian N. Hartt, *Theology and the Church in the University* (Philadelphia: The Westminster Press, 1969), p. 76.

7. John Maguire, "From Teapot to Armageddon," *Soundings* 52 (Summer 1969), p. 236.

8. Hartt, *Theology and the Church in the University,* p. 61.

9. See the brilliant and highly suggestive treatment of the future shape for religious studies by Michael Novak, *Ascent of the Mountain, Flight of*

the Dove: An Invitation to Religious Studies (New York: Harper & Row, 1971), esp. pp. 178-180.

10. Paul Peachy, "New Ethical Possibility: The Task of 'Post-Christendom' Ethics," *New Theology* (New York: Macmillan, 1955) 3, pp. 103-117.

11. See the balanced and perspective discussion by Robert Michaelsen, *Piety in the Public School: Trends and Issues in the Relationship Between Religion and the Public Schools in the United States* (New York: Macmillan Co., 1970), pp. 265ff.

12 Teacher Certification: Michigan's Approach to Teaching about Religion

PAUL J. WILL *

As was true in so many states, teaching about religion in the Michigan K-12 educational system until recently was confined to a few individual pioneering teachers. Several public school districts in Michigan, such as Royal Oak, Oak Park, Southfield, Flushing, and Cherry Hill, offer courses in world religions on the senior high school level, and there are offerings in Bible as literature in other districts. However, most public school districts do not have distinctive courses about religion.

Instead, some schools incorporate units on religion in their regular offerings, like Ann Arbor which includes a six-week unit on religions in their junior high school curriculum. There have even been efforts on the elementary level; for example, reading lessons on Buddhism are utilized in Trenton. Nevertheless, a very small proportion of the state's schools have considered the place of religion in the curriculum. But in the last few years there has

* This essay was originally written for presentation at a consultation at the Public Education Religion Study Center, Dayton, Ohio, June, 1973 and is printed here with permission of the author.

been a series of developments that hold out the promise of a far wider and professional involvement in the academic study of religion.

I

The means for opening and expanding possibilities in this area is the teacher certification process. The Michigan State Board of Education is empowered to authorize colleges and universities to certify teachers in various subject areas. Prior to the 1970's, there was no formal program in the area of religion, but a combination of increased interest and governmental directives is shaping a new response in Michigan. In 1967 Calvin College, a private denominational four-year institution, inquired about the propriety of preparing teachers for certification in the area of religion. In 1969 the college requested the State Board of Education to approve certification of a major and/or minor in religion. This led to a study of constitutional considerations, existing courses in Michigan schools, and practices in other states.

The result was that in 1970 the State Board approved the inclusion of the academic study of religions as a minor certification field in elementary and secondary education and established a set of general standards for the approval of programs in this subject area. Among these criteria are proof that the college is accredited in three other areas, the instructional staff is academically qualified, adequate resources for instruction exist, there are broad, comprehensive course offerings, and the opportunity for student teaching is provided. The Michigan Department of Education, while acknowledging that there will be diversity between college programs, has also given suggestions as to the types of courses that colleges should include in this twenty semester hour teaching minor. There should be a systematic curriculum of required core offerings encompassing introductory courses in the methodology of the discipline and the Asian religions. All world religions are to be represented as well as contemporary religious developments. Electives may be taken from related academic disciplines to supplement regular religion offerings.

162   RELIGION IN PUBLIC EDUCATION

Several schools have applied to the state for certification, and these requests are gradually being acted on after a Committee of Scholars appointed by the Department of Education has reviewed each individual request and made recommendations. This committee is composed of professors from both private and public institutions of higher learning as well as a representative from the Michigan Department of Education. At least one visitation to the campus of the institution seeking approval is part of the committee's standard procedure.

In practice, several years are involved between application and approval. Calvin College's program was approved in 1972. Western Michigan University and Michigan State University were visited by the Committee of Scholars in the same year and have since submitted revised proposals which await further action. Hope College and the University of Detroit have also asked for approval, but no official action has been taken in regard to their requests.

II

During the same period that the certification guidelines were being finalized by the state, a separate organization was established for promoting interchange between various approved schools and the public sector. The Council on the Study of Religion in Public Schools was created as an outcome of the Conference on Religious Studies in State Schools hosted by the University of Michigan on March 21-22, 1972. This meeting was attended by representatives from both private and public colleges and universities involved in teaching about religion. It resulted in the formation in principle of a state-wide council concerned with the academic study of religion on the K-12 level as well as the exchange of ideas on the collegiate level.

The Council will consist of two units plus observers from the State Department of Education. There will be an academic unit consisting of representation from each institution approved by the state to offer a teaching minor in religion. The second unit will be drawn from local school boards, superintendents, principals, teachers, and parent-teacher organizations. Until the actual formation of the Council, its activities are being directed by a steering committee with Dr. David Noel Freedman, Director, Program on Studies in Religion, University of Michigan as chairman and Dr. Robert T. Anderson, Chairman, Department of Religion, Michigan State University as secretary.

The Council is charged to concern itself with the identity of the academic discipline of religion, theoretical problems in the study of religion, criteria for certification of teachers, various curricular structures or models, publicity and outside referrals, funding the academic study of religion, and providing a clearing house for information. So far, twelve institutions have indicated interest in the Council and provided a modest treasury.

III

Thus in Michigan, colleges are applying for and gradually gaining certification in the academic study of religions, and a Council is ready to assist on a state-wide basis when sufficient schools are approved. In addition several universities, for example Western Michigan and Eastern Michigan, are planning in-service training and conference opportunities for teachers interested in teaching about religion. Obviously the thrust of all these efforts is to insure that the teacher who undertakes the academic study of religion is competent in the subject matter and professionally trained for his responsibilities.

13 The Academic Study of Religions in the State of Michigan

STATE OF MICHIGAN
DEPARTMENT OF EDUCATION *

The material in this chapter, as developed by the Department of Education of the State of Michigan, presents the standards for approval of the academic study of religions for the certification of teachers and program development suggestions for a teaching minor in the academic study of religions.

I
STANDARDS FOR APPROVAL OF
THE ACADEMIC STUDY OF RELIGIONS
FOR THE CERTIFICATION OF TEACHERS

The standards which follow are designed to supplement existing policies and procedures for teacher education program review actions.

* Reprinted with permission of the Division of Teacher Preparation and Professional Development, Department of Education, State of Michigan, Lansing, Michigan 48902.

164

DEFINITION OF THE AREA

Religion as an academic discipline describes, interprets and compares sacred writings, creeds, theologies, mythologies and cultic practices of a culture or cultures. It is one key to the understanding of a culture and the value orientation of individuals. To protect the integrity of the discipline and assure its maximum benefit in the elementary and secondary schools, the following standards are proposed for the training of persons to teach religion in the elementary and secondary schools.

I. INSTITUTIONAL ELIGIBILITY

Any institution undertaking to provide a minor in the academic study of religions for the certification of teachers for elementary and secondary schools should be approved by the State Board of Education for the preparation of teachers, accredited by the North Central Association, and approved for the training of teachers in at least three other certification areas.

Questions:

What evidence demonstrates accreditation?

What evidence demonstrates that this institution is approved for training teachers? (Specify three other areas in which the institution now certifies teachers.)

II. QUALIFICATIONS OF INSTRUCTIONAL STAFF

Each instructor responsible for the training of teachers of religions shall have earned academic degrees appropriate to the level and content of the courses he teaches in the academic study of religions and should be involved in research activities and appropriate professional societies.

Questions:

What evidence demonstrates that instructors in this academic area have earned academic degrees?

What evidence demonstrates that instructors in this academic area have degrees appropriate to the level of the courses they are teaching?

What evidence demonstrates that instructors in this academic area have degrees in the fields in which they are teaching?

What evidence demonstrates that instructors in this academic area are involved in research (e.g., publications and scholarly papers)?

What evidence demonstrates that instructors in this academic area are involved in professional learned societies?

III. PROGRAM COMPONENTS

An institution preparing teachers of religions should offer a comprehensive curriculum in the academic study of religions. The instructors of such courses should have some direct involvement in the field where the teachers will be working.

Questions:

What evidence demonstrates that the curriculum provides exposure to the breadth of cultures represented and extent of courses in both the structure and the history of religions?

What evidence demonstrates that the curriculum is comprehensible (i.e., what is the rationale)?

What evidence demonstrates that instructors are involved on a continuing basis with elementary and secondary schools offering such programs?

What evidence demonstrates the availability of complementary courses in other departments (e.g., anthropology, philosophy, psychology, etc.)?

What evidence demonstrates institutional plans to incorporate in the professional education component experiences (including plans for student teaching) appropriate to the academic study of religions?

IV. RESOURCES FOR INSTRUCTION

An institution preparing a person to teach religions should have adequate library and staff resources both in the field of religion and such cognate fields as anthropology, philosophy, psychology, history and languages.

Questions:

What evidence demonstrates the adequacy of the library (approximate number of volumes and key journals in each field)?

What evidence demonstrates the adequacy of the related faculty resources?

What evidence demonstrates the availability of instructional materials appropriate to teaching the academic study of religions?

II
PROGRAM DEVELOPMENT SUGGESTIONS FOR TEACHING MINOR IN THE ACADEMIC STUDY OF RELIGIONS

Standards have been developed for State Board approval of institutional requests in the Academic Study of Religions for the certification of teachers. The suggestions below are intended to supplement these standards to assist institutions in preparing requests for the Committee of Scholars' review and State Board action.

1. The program should have a systematic design which reflects its intention—the academic study of religions. It should not be simply a collection of courses.

2. The program should include offerings representative of all of the great religions of the world. It should not reflect a particular religious orientation.
3. The program of study should be distinct and be designated in institutional catalogs and bulletins.
4. A program administrator should be designated, responsible for management, development and evaluation.
5. Staff assigned to the program should be cosmopolitan in training and experience, with backgrounds appropriate for the nature of the offerings.
6. At least one-half of the proposed minor should be composed of basic or core courses required of all but exceptional candidates.
7. Courses should include offerings in Eastern, non-Judeo-Christian religions and these should be a part of the required core. The program should include an introductory course which provides a common orientation for students concerning methodology and ontology which is relevant to the academic study of religions.
8. Courses for this program drawn from related and supporting disciplines should be double-titled and double-numbered in order to specifically identify their attachment to the academic study of religions and as a legitimate part of this minor.
9. It is suggested that institutions give serious consideration to offering a course which focuses on the contemporary American religious situation.
10. Teaching and curriculum materials appropriate for use in the public and private schools should be provided and specific provision made for the development of student familiarity with these materials to enable them to develop programs and teach this field in schools in which they will be employed.
11. Library and instructional holdings should be reviewed to insure that these are representative and inclusive of the range of religious offerings incorporated in the program.
12. The institutional budget should provide adequate and visible resources for the development of this program. The level of support in the early years of program development should reflect an institutional commitment to the acquisition of ap-

propriate resource levels. These will be staff, library holdings and instructional materials.

13. A system for periodic and orderly review on this program should be devised by the institution to insure that appropriate changes are made where necessary. Provision for review should be included in the early planning for program development.

14 Teacher Certification for Religion Studies in Wisconsin

FRANK L. STEEVES *

On November 21, 1972, the Department of Public Instruction of the State of Wisconsin granted approval to a teaching major and a teaching minor at Marquette University in religious studies. These programs lead to certification for teaching in the public schools of Wisconsin in religious studies. State approval followed a two-year effort by the Department of Theology and the School of Education at Marquette to agree on the nature and essential content of a program in religious studies that could and would result in teacher-certification. The characteristics and requirements of the Marquette major/minor are as follows:

An Interdisciplinary Program: Courses from departments other than theology are required as part of the core requirement for the religious studies major and minor; courses from other departments are electives applicable to the major. The interdis-

* Reprinted with permission of the author. This report was originally given at a consultation sponsored by the Public Education Religion Studies Center, Wright State University, Dayton, Ohio, June 15-16, 1973.

ciplinary character of the program enables the student easily to develop related minors in such fields as social studies, literature, or history. The student can construct a unified undergraduate program and at the same time improve his job opportunities in an era when interdisciplinary competence and skill is being sought by hiring agencies.

Content of the Program: The Marquette Theology Department and the School of Education want the teacher of religious studies in a contemporary American school to have a knowledge of religion as a phenomenon of man, and as a culturally and historically significant factor in man's interpretation of reality. This means knowing the basic human situations out of which religious experience arises. It means knowing the major ideas that have arisen in the history of religions, and acquaintance with the history and literature of the world's major religions. The teacher of religious studies should know the religious attitudes, values, and symbols which have most influenced the evolution of Western and American culture as well as the relationship between religion and non-theistic humanism. The teacher should be able to handle the distinction between the study of religion and the practice of religion, so that teaching will deal with inquiry into religious thought and not the propagation of a religion. The teacher should be able to relate religious thought to other disciplines which interpret reality and human experience (the empirical and social sciences, literature and the arts), so that students can locate their own experience of religion, positive or negative, in a larger cultural and social context. To this end the specific requirements are as follows:

Requirements for the Teaching Major: A total of 34 upper-division hours are required. The core requirements are the following:

A. *Foundations of Religious Study.* Two of these courses: Theo 130 (Contemporary Atheism and Theism), 135 (Theology and Man), 137 (Religious Language).

B. *History of Religions.* All three of these courses: Theo 120

(History of Religions), 195 or 196 (Eastern Religions), Hist 115 or 116 (History of Religion in America).

C. *Religion and Society.* Two of these courses: Theo 143 (Religion and Culture), Anth 112 (Anthropology of Religion), Soci 144 (Sociology of Religion).

In addition to these requirements, one course is required from Biblical Theology, one course from Historical Theology or Theological Themes, and one course from Theology and Society. The requirement for Historical Theology or Theological Themes may include Phil 103 (Philosophy of God); the requirement for Theology and Society may include Soci 145 (Religious Institutions) or Soci 146 (Social Psychology of Religion). These courses, if applied to the religious studies major, do not apply to a minor in the fields of those departments.

Students wishing state certification also need the regular teacher education sequence: 18 hours, including a special methods course and student teaching.

Requirements for the Teaching Minor: A total of 22 upper-division hours is required. This must include the core requirements for the teaching major (A, B, C, as described above).

Other Wisconsin Approved Programs. A similar major/minor program was approved at Edgewood College, Madison, by the Department of Public Instruction on July 1, 1971.

First of its kind in Wisconsin to be given state approval was the religious studies minor at the University of Wisconsin-Whitewater. The 22 credit minor at Whitewater includes at least three credits in religious thought, three credits in world religions, and three credits in religious literature. Established in 1966, the program was granted approval in March 1971 by the Department of Public Instruction.

Other State Programs. Shortly after the Marquette program was granted state approval in November 1972, the office of the Dean of the School of Education attempted to locate other state-approved curricula in religious studies throughout the nation. To this end, an inquiry was addressed to every state department of education and, ultimately, replies were received from all 50 states. In addition to the three programs in Wisconsin three other state-approved programs in religious studies leading to certification as teachers in this field were identified.

The University of California, Santa Barbara, has an academic major in religious studies approved by the California State Board of Education on June 9, 1972. The UCSB Department of Religious Studies offers programs leading to a B.A., M.A., and Ph.D. in Religious Studies.

The California State University, Northridge, has an academic major in religious studies approved by the California State Board of Education during the summer of 1972. Started as an experimental program in the fall of 1968 with one instructor and two courses with a total enrollment of 51 students, by 1972-73 the Department of Religious Studies at Northridge included 12 full-time faculty members, a number of part-time faculty, 60-70 undergraduate courses, more than 20 graduate courses, and an enrollment of at least 1,500 students. The Department offers B.A., M.A. and Ph.D. programs.

In April, 1972, the Michigan State Board of Education granted provisional approval for an initial five-year period to Calvin College, Grand Rapids, for a certifiable minor program in the Academic Study of Religions.

Beyond This. The six programs identified in the preceding pages of this report are all that this investigator was able to locate. An official of each of the remaining 47 state departments of education responded that there are no state-approved teacher-education curricula in religious studies leading to certification in his state. It is understood, of course, that extensive programs in religious studies and theology exist in every state. However, the inquiry was intended only to identify those programs leading to teacher-certification.

IV
ISSUES AND PROBLEMS FOR THE FUTURE

Introduction

The material contained in this section is of two kinds. The first two essays propose to look at the traditional questions in reversed order. That is, instead of asking what gain religious institutions can get out of education (or insert in the curriculum), the authors of both pieces are concerned to see what the religiously aware and sensitive person may contribute to the education of the public.

Lynn says: "It is time . . . to go beyond the conventional Protestant stand on the teaching of religion in public schools." Quite in line with the criticism of the teaching *about*/teaching *of* religion distinction developed earlier (see Part II, Chapter 6, "Toward a Theory of Religion in General Education"), Lynn doubts the value in differentiating normative from objective teaching. The problem, he says, is the absence of "intelligent dissent" in the schools which leads to a "leveling-out process" among learners.

Speaking as a Protestant, Lynn suggests that his concerns—and he would hope other Protestants might share his view—are not only religious but educational. Accordingly, the churchman or religious educator needs to address the broad range of issues confronting the public with respect to educational development and policy.

My article begins with Lynn's suggestion that Protestants be concerned with "sustaining . . . public ventures in education," and relates how several national Protestant bodies have developed a program for implementing concerns about public education policy and reform.

The remaining four chapters in this section include a variety of readings on the basis of values and education. The reader will recall that Phenix' essay (Part II, Chapter 5) makes two points in connection with values. First, he asserts that the basic problem in contemporary education is a moral one. What education adds up to and what meaning can be discerned in existence through education are the kinds of issues which need serious on-going consideration by people in education. Second, Phenix notes a fairly well-known research phenomenon: "There is no evidence of a positive correlation . . . between religious profession and moral strength." Yet he also suggests (and here he is commenting on an *objective* study of religion) that "real understanding of the kinds of life commitments people make will make a difference also in what they do in relation to other persons."

The four readings on valuation in this section provide alternate, though not mutually exclusive, ways for approaching values in education. My article attempts to describe some of the theoretical questions and practical problems that need to be confronted, especially if schools are to be a vehicle for clarifying the value stance of learners. Although it is not explicitly stated in the article, the author would suggest that one of the ways such clarification can proceed is through an "objective" understanding of the individual's religious stance alongside an understanding of the religious stance of other individuals.

The ground-breaking work in value clarification has been done by Raths, Harmin and Simon. Since the publication in 1966 of their book *Values and Teaching,* there has been much interest in this possibility. Two excerpts from their work are reprinted here. The first constitutes their perception of the contemporary context within which values are formed. The second excerpt describes their process for approaching value clarification.

The essay by Lawrence Kohlberg is an exposition of his attempt to view valuational-moral matters against the background of developmental psychology. Although this is one of Kohlberg's earlier pieces on this topic, his analysis of six stages of moral development has not changed in its central thrust. And here he explicitly relates morality to the phenomenon of religion and studies about religion. Somewhat comparable to Piaget and Erikson in his developmental outlook, Kohlberg has provoked many to rethink their understanding of morality in light of contemporary psychological research.

John Rawls' work is of a different character. Although Kohlberg is not unconcerned with philosophical matters, Rawls has

developed a comprehensive theory of justice since the 1958 publication of his seminal paper on "Justice as Fairness." In his approach, Rawls posits a hypothetical circumstance, which he calls
the original position, in which all relationships among individuals
are equal. No one knows or presumably cares about his status or
class. Hence individuals can agree on principles of justice for their
interaction which are essentially fair. As such, Rawls' position is a
version of social contract theory and in some opposition to widely
accepted utilitarian views by virtue of his emphasis on the principle of justice as fairness.

For the purposes of this book, selections from Rawls have
been included here as an example of a distinctly rational approach
to matters related to values and valuation. In my article on "Some
Issues in Teaching Values," it is pointed out that values are formed
in significant degree in social settings. Rawls' work provides a
theoretical analysis of a central social value (or set of values)—
justice.

Although Rawls makes no mention of the relation between
religion and justice, it can certainly be said that religion is an
important social phenomenon and could well be one ingredient
in an understanding of matters pertaining to the social equilibrium.
The full scope of Rawls' theory is not presented here and the
reader may well wish to refer to his book *A Theory of Justice*.
Still it is possible to get a sense of his rational approach and determine the degree to which this kind of outlook may be incorporated in studies which have moral implications.

The selections in this section are by no means exhaustive.
And it is not suggested here that these are the only issues or
problems that are to be associated with religion in public education. Certainly there are problems pertaining to curriculum development and teacher education. Likewise legal matters and social dynamics are open to constant change; hence such topics
need constant review. But it can be said that the two areas the
readings in this chapter explore are still relatively undeveloped
and therefore deserve attention.

15 Some Unfinished Business

ROBERT W. LYNN *

Where are the "enemies" of Protestantism's understanding of education?
There is an ominous silence on this topic nowadays. (Here is another impressive bit of evidence of marginality.) Almost twenty-five years ago H. Shelton Smith wrote that "the present situation calls less for construction than for unsparing criticism." [1] His work *Faith and Nurture* was a remarkable beginning in that direction. Yet in the succeeding years church educators largely ignored the critical task. Consequently, their "constructive" theories of nurture were blighted by what James D. Smart has properly called "the sterility that seems to afflict the so-called 'new theological era' in religious education." [2]

It is now time to renew the work of "unsparing criticism." And so, in these . . . comments, I shall suggest several lines of inquiry for prospective critics. The following suggestions point in one direction—the responsibility of Protestantism in sustaining the public ventures in education. My emphasis here represents a deliberate reversal of the order of treatment usually accorded the topics of church and public education. Since the turn of the cen-

* Reprinted with permission of the publisher from *Protestant Strategies in Education*. New York: Association Press, 1964, pp. 74-82.

tury, Protestant church educators have tended to begin and end with reform of church education. In offering an alternative point of departure, I do not mean to imply an either/or choice, but instead, a corrective of our "natural" inclinations.

An Inadequate Lens

How can American Protestantism help in sustaining the public ventures in education?

This question rates a high priority on the agenda of any critic in the future. In the past Protestants have not seriously pressed this question because they believed the answer was already within their grasp. That assumption should be tested in the days ahead.

Earlier, I described the common Protestant preoccupation with church-state problems in education. Our tendency is to make this single interest into a lens for viewing the whole enterprise of public education. At its worst, this procedure amounts to a kind of narcissistic folly. But, even at its best, it provides a poor set of spectacles for looking at educational policy. The resulting perceptions are inadequate and subject to distortion.

The importance of the church-state issue becomes vastly exaggerated. This tendency can be seen in the thinking of both the religionizers—those who hanker after the frayed practices of school piety—and the de-religionizers who want to make the public schools antiseptically free of all traces of religious language and worship activities.

Both camps need to consider the potentially divisive effects of their efforts upon the politics of education. Recently the editors of *The New Republic* cautioned the de-religionizers:

We need desperately to multiply our schools, to disperse homogeneous neighborhood groups through the systems, and to draw those who are leaving back into the public schools. Is this the time, then, to ventilate the issue of religion in the sort of absolute terms that are certain to alienate many of those whose support is needed because they possess the means to seek in alternative? [3]

It is time now to go beyond the conventional Protestant stand on the teaching of religion in the public schools. The present thinking of most Protestants on this matter varies little from the formulation developed in the 1930's, that is, such instruction is permissible if it is "objective." George R. LaNoue's statement is representative of other contributions along this line:

> Public school teaching, as is stated in the teacher manuals of any public system, must strive toward a balanced neutral presentation of religious questions. Descriptive or empirical teaching about religion is acceptable, but teaching supported by public funds must avoid normative teaching or teaching for commitment.[10]

No one could quarrel with this judgment if it were simply a plea for integrity in curricula materials and fairness in the presentation of diverse points of view. But, obviously enough, it involves more than that. The sharp emphasis upon an absolute distinction between normative and objective teaching is a dubious contribution to good educational policy.

What if the same argument were applied to other areas of controversy, such as politics, economics, or history? It would make education into a dull process of acquiring marketable skills and neutral information. There are already enough schoolmen who prefer the safe, "public relations" approach to lively issues. Why encourage their timidity in exploring the depths and heights of contemporary life? This flatlander version of education misses the point. The critical problem—I would submit—is not the presence of "normative teaching," but rather the absence of the freedom of intelligent dissent by both teacher and student. The health and vitality of any school depends upon its ability to deal with controversy without fear of reprisal.

On this score there is reason for pessimism. By and large the American public school is timid and anxious in its approach to controversial matters. "When a specific conflict arises," according to Edgar Z. Friedenberg, "the school almost automatically seeks to *mediate* rather than to clarify. It assesses the power of the conflicting interests, works out a compromise among them, and keeps its name out of the papers." [11] This leveling-out process is particularly evident in the school personnel's treatment of the humanities. Mr. Friedenberg's further comments on this point are most instructive, since the study of religion poses comparable problems—and temptations:

> They [the school personnel] fear that students will find passages too difficult, and assume that it is the artist's job to say no more than can be easily understood. They fear that the American Legion, or a Catholic action group will object to the implication of other passages, and they also fear that they themselves will be called censors; so rather than suppress a work, they set up committees to edit it and forestall any possible objections.[12]

Such are the exigencies of developing a "balanced, neutral presentation."

In this setting the prospects for a lively teaching about religious convictions and institutions are not favorable. But at least Protestant churchmen should reflect on how their appeal for "objective" instruction might be heard in this context. Hopefully, they will venture even further. I would propose the following test for any Protestant action in this area: Do our attitudes and recommendations strengthen the resolve of the school to deal with controversy *wherever it may be found?* The study of religion in the public schools will become competent only when the educator is free and willing to exercise his rightful independence from community pressure. Our first intent, therefore, is to help the school be a school and not the frightened shadow of American society. And our first need, therefore, is for informed critics who can demonstrate the intricate relationships between academic freedom, the development of a true profession among public school educators, and the ability to handle explosive issues in the classroom.

Now comes the most troublesome question of all. Should the comprehensive concern of the Protestant for the public venture in education include the Catholic parochial school? Here the burden of the past weighs as heavily upon Protestants as it does upon Catholics. Despite all the words written and said on the subject,

there has been very little honest conversation about it. Dean M.
Kelley's report of an exchange between Protestant and Catholic
leaders nicely symbolizes the ineffectiveness of the ecumenical dialogue at this point:

> Many Roman Catholics insist that parochial schools—at least
> insofar as they concern the public—are primarily and essen-
> tially *educational* institutions, and that their educational func-
> tion can be viewed as distinct from their religious function.
> "This is an educational issue, not a religious issue," insisted
> one Roman Catholic leader, to which a Protestant spokesman
> responded, "For us, it is a religious issue, not an educational
> issue." [13]

Surely both claims are misleading.

For the Protestant it is an educational issue as well as a religious one. The Catholic Church in America has taken on the
responsibility for educating a sizable number of the population.[14]
Up until now American Protestants have been inclined to view this
fact as a threat, an all too visible reminder of Catholic power.

But do Protestants have any responsibility toward these schools
and their students? I believe that we have the responsibility to re-
consider—seriously and without premature polemic dismissal—
the following questions proposed by Rabbi Arthur Gilbert:

> Are we prepared to write off 12 percent of our children as
> excluded from our concern? Can America afford such a waste?
> Is it not possible, therefore, to provide educational services for
> *all* children without regard to the school they attend; or train
> all teachers without regard to the uniform they wear; or pro-
> vide laboratories and workshops, testing facilities as well as
> health and medical benefits and textbooks and transportation
> for all children without involving the Government in direct aid
> to one religion over another? [15]

To this list, I could add some further questions. How can
Protestant congregations properly express their interest in the local
Catholic schools? By offering to cooperate in the production of
curricular materials in Christian education? By working alongside

Catholics in the political struggles that inevitably accompany responsible experimentation with shared time? By lending an empty Sunday school building to a crowded parochial school? (Even if the Sunday school does not represent "the most wasted hour of the week," [16] nevertheless the Sunday school building is probably the most wasted building space in America.)

Daniel Callahan, in speaking for the editors of *Commonweal,* said:

> More than once have we wished that the N.C.W.C. would devote some of its energy to these public school matters; that the diocesan papers, which manage to find considerable space for the "Catholic case," would dramatize the plight of the public school; that the bishops, pastors, and lay organizations would put their minds to work on some of these American educational problems which do not directly concern Catholics.[17]

By the same token, a Protestant might say: "Even though the parochial school and public school are not comparable in their importance to the common good, I wish that the National Council of Churches would devote some of its energy to the questions stated above; that the denominational magazines which manage to find considerable space for the case against the Catholic schools would dramatize the plight of these schools; that pastors and laymen would put their minds to work on some of these American educational problems which do not directly concern Protestants." [18]

These are only a few of the possible lines for any future critic. But when considered together, these suggestions do indicate something of the enormity and excitement of the task now facing American Protestantism. That task, as I interpret it, is to acknowledge the presentness of the past as it is manifest in the "typical Protestant parallelism," to gain our freedom from its legacy in and through renewed historical self-understanding, and then to work toward a new understanding of the relation of public and church education.

NOTES

1. H. Shelton Smith, *Faith and Nurture* (New York: Charles Scribner's Sons, 1942), p. ix.

2. James D. Smart, *The Creed in Christian Teaching* (Philadelphia: The Westminster Press, 1962), p. 8.

3. "Shall We Pray?" *The New Republic*, CXLVIII (June 29, 1963), p. 5.

4. Lawrence T. Cremin, *The Transformation of the School* (New York: Alfred A. Knopf, Inc., 1961), p. 350.

5. The proponents of shared time are inclined to press the advantages of this scheme without thinking clearly about its consequences as an educational policy. There are countless questions that come to mind once one sees shared time in relation to other issues. How would its enactment affect the process of desegregation? Would it reinforce the power of the neighborhood school? These questions need to be asked, lest shared time—now viewed as a possible resolution of a church-state matter—be used by local communities as a way of disguising other motives that are not so well-intentioned.

6. "A court is not qualified to order large-scale busing to distant areas: it is not qualified to decide that the neighborhood system should be abandoned, or that the so-called Princeton plan of consolidating several grades from a number of neighborhoods in one school can be suitably applied; it is not qualified to estimate the tipping point at which a desegregated school will resegregate—and such judgments will not, and ought not, be accepted from a court"—Alexander M. Bickel, "Beyond Tokenism: The Civil Rights Task That Looms Ahead," *The New Republic*, CL (Jan. 4, 1964), p. 14.

7. Harlem Youth Opportunities, Inc., *Youth in the Ghetto: A Study of the Consequences of Powerlessness and a Blueprint for Change* (New York: HARYOU, 1964), p. 426.

8. William Lee Miller, "Aid to Education: A Better Deal," *The Reporter*, XXX (Apr. 23, 1964), p. 20.

9. There is evidence that this search has already commenced. One hopeful sign of change is indicated in the testimony of a spokesman for mainline Protestantism before a Congressional committee in January 1965. After years of hesitation and opposition Protestant leaders are now clearly moving toward accepting a wider range of federal benefits for the child in the parochial school. Such a willingness to venture beyond previous positions may mark the beginning of a new chapter in the history of the Protestant-Catholic debate over aid to education. For further information see Robert W. Lynn, "New Opportunity in Education," *Christianity and Crisis*, XXV (March 8, 1965), pp. 30-31.

10. George R. LaNoue, *Public Funds for Parochial Schools?* (New York: Dept. of Religious Liberty, National Council of Churches, 1963), p. 36.

11. Edgar Z. Friedenberg, *The Vanishing Adolescent* (New York: Dell Publishing Co., 1959), p. 80.

12. *Ibid.*, p. 88.

13. Dean M. Kelley, "Protestants and Parochial Schools," *Commonweal*, LXXIX (Jan. 31, 1964), pp. 522-523.

14. "In ten states with a concentrated Catholic population, Catholic schools now educate between 20 and 25 percent of the total school enrollment. These schools take an even larger share of the school-going population

in certain eastern and midwestern cities: in Dubuque, 61 percent; in Manchester, 52 percent; in Pittsburgh, 42 percent; in Philadelphia, 39 percent; in Buffalo, 38 percent; in New Orleans, Milwaukee, and Chicago, 33 percent; in Cleveland, and New York, 26 percent; in St. Louis, 25 percent; and in Detroit, 23 percent"–Neil Gerard McCluskey, S. J., *Catholic Education in America: A Documentary History* (New York: Bureau of Publications, Teachers College, Columbia University, 1964), pp. 1-2.

15. Arthur Gilbert, "American Public Education and the Challenge of Religious Pluralism" (a talk at an Institute on Religion and the Public Schools, Lafayette, Ind., Oct. 6-9, 1963; mimeographed), p. 10.

16. Wesley Shrader, "Our Troubled Sunday Schools," *Life,* XLII (Feb. 11, 1957), pp. 110-114.

17. Daniel Callahan, "Into the Briar Patch," *Commonweal,* LXXIX (Jan. 31, 1964), p. 503.

18. A hopeful beginning in this direction is indicated in the pronouncement "Federal Aid to Education: The Shared-Time Concept," a statement adopted by the 176th General Assembly of the United Presbyterian Church in the United States of America, Oklahoma City, Okla., May 26, 1964.

16 A New Perspective in Religion and Education

DAVID E. ENGEL *

T raditionally religious educators have been concerned with programs geared to religious or moral instruction. In terms of institutional focus this concern has been expressed primarily through religious bodies or schools. In those cases where agencies of public education have been involved in religious instruction (courses in the objective study of religion, released time and shared time programs) the religious educator has looked to the public school for the service it may render to religious interests.

Only in isolated instances have other concerns emerged among religious educators. Robert Lynn, at the conclusion of his analysis of *Protestant Strategies in Education,* suggested "a deliberate reversal of the order of treatment usually accorded the topics of

* Reprinted from the November/December 1972 issue of *Religious Education,* by permission of the publisher, The Religious Education Association, 545 West 111th Street, New York, N.Y. 10025.

church and public education." [1] In Lynn's view, instead of trying to get something religious into or out of public education, it is more important to ask how "American Protestantism can help in sustaining the public ventures in education." [2]

Since Lynn raised his question there has arisen much debate over the purpose and character of institutions of public education, especially in light of the several critiques published in the last ten years. The wide readership of books and articles critical of public schools is well known. The development of alternate school programs is a clear manifestation of such critiques.

Although most religious educators have read the books and have had some limited involvement in innovations in general education, what Lynn was suggesting almost ten years ago has scarcely become a priority in the religious education field. Religious educators are still by and large concerned with explicitly religious instruction in religious institutions.

There has emerged, however, one agency supported by religious bodies with another perspective. It is called United Ministries in Public Education and originally was created by four Protestant denominations. [3] As these groups first articulated their stance, they stated that the church "must accept its accountability for education as a major dimension of public life." In turn, this meant that the church's worldly service with respect to education was working as "an agent to support the public educational system where it is contributing to the humane development of persons." Support, however, was not understood in an uncritical way. The Approach and Intent document which initially mapped out the possible role of United Ministries in Public Education also called for a "re-evaluation of the [public education] system where needed," and saw the need or "reform in educational policy and practice" as well as the support of "new educational ventures."

Among the goals established by the church bodies constituting UMPE were:

1. preparing "persons to assume responsibility for *public life*";

2. developing "an *internationalization of our understanding of citizenship*";

3. encouraging *"the liberation and nurture of individual capacities, interests, objectives, and sense of worth";*

4. assisting in *"the discovery and effective use of the best instructional theories, techniques and materials";*

5. developing *"policy . . . and administration open to effective participation by affected groups";*

6. encouraging "life-long innovation and adaptive capacity";

7. promoting *"access for all persons and groups to an educational experience that equips them for a life of public responsibility and individual achievement";*

8. working for *"financial support adequate to attract competent teachers and administrators and provide an optimum learning environment for every child."*

Although such extensive goals are difficult to realize, their significance may be found apart from their breadth. What is noteworthy about them, especially for the religious educator, is their dissimilarity from both traditional objectives of religious bodies and the operating focus of most religious instructional programming. In general they constitute a response to Lynn's concern that religious education be reconceived, in part, and redirected to "help in sustaining the public ventures in education." . . .

Religious instruction in churches and synagogues and the objective study about religion in public schools continue to be valid concerns for the effective education of the public in his outlook and his responsibility.

United Ministries in Public Education represents a model by which the system for public education might be engaged and affected by persons with religious concerns. The field, however, is not overcrowded. Approaches similar to UMPE's may be developed by educational ministries and concerned congregations in their locale. In this way, a new perspective in religion and education can become more widely manifest.

NOTES

1. Robert W. Lynn, *Protestant Strategies in Education* (New York: Association Press, 1964), p. 74.

2. *Ibid.*, p. 75.

3. The national church bodies supporting UMPE include: the Episcopal Church, the Presbyterian Church in the U.S., the United Church of Christ, the United Methodist Church, the United Presbyterian Church U.S.A., and the Division of Christian Life and Mission of the National Council of Churches.

17 Some Issues in Teaching Values

DAVID E. ENGEL *

Of all the concerns which educators share, one of the most difficult to implement is the teaching of values. From the time of the rise of the common school movement, through the progressive period to the present moment when many educators feel the need for having some effect upon the nation's crisis, the teaching of values seems to have been a paramount matter. Yet there has been no consensus about the values that might be taught or reinforced by the schools. Some have favored the treatment of democratic ideals as an integral part of citizenship training. Some have spoken of "moral and spiritual values" without detailing to any great extent precisely what these might be.

Horace Mann in his last annual report to the Massachusetts Board of Public Education asserted that common schools "shall create a more far-seeing intelligence and a purer morality than has ever existed among communities of men." Lawrence Cremin has summarized the hope for social and moral betterment through education inherent in the common school movement: "There was

* Reprinted from the January/February 1970 issue of *Religious Education,* by permission of the publisher, The Religious Education Association, 545 West 111th Street, New York, N.Y. 10025.

no social evil which could not be attacked by their [the schools'] beneficent influence." [1] The purer morality which Mann hoped for, however, has not become a reality either in school or society.

In a more critical vein, John Dewey saw that "all the aims and values which are desirable in education are themselves moral." [2] To separate morals from education was artificial and unnatural. As Dewey put it: "Education is not a mere means to such a life. Education is such a life. To maintain the capacity for such education is the essence of morals." [3]

Despite the persistent concern for the school to be a moral as well as an intellectual instrument, the teaching of values in schools has not ordinarily been approached in a systematic or even a conscious fashion. Educators have focused on the general need without specifying either what they mean or investigating in any great detail how specific values might best be communicated in the classroom. As a result, the whole area is both vague and problematic.

I

Theodore Brameld has related an incident which is germane to such considerations. He observed a classroom in which there were 50 boys and girls. The boys were wearing navy blue uniforms with brass buttons. The girls were wearing middy blouses and blue skirts. They were seated in small groups around several tables. Each group had a student leader. A male teacher was moving from table to table helping to clarify questions and to stimulate discussion. Brameld was so impressed with the incident that he took a flash picture of the classroom. At that moment, something surprising occurred! Neither the teacher nor the students looked up when the flash bulb went off. Apparently they were so involved in what they were doing that they never noticed he was there.

It is interesting to speculate whether any of us have ever been in a learning environment where such undivided attention was exhibited. While the uniformed students did seem to indicate an authority-oriented school system, the activity of the teacher and the involvement of the students in open conversation around the tables would indicate otherwise. They were so wrapped up in what they were doing that a diversion was entirely unnoticed. It was their activity—reinforced, not directed, by the teacher—that so engaged them.

What Brameld observed was not a classroom in the United States, but a discussion of values in a Japanese school. It should be noted in passing that Japan requires moral instruction in its schools. The program has been widely debated and has been the cause for considerable teacher unrest. It is feared that such a program could be so standardized by a conservative government as to allow only the indoctrination of values congenial to that political point of view.

According to Brameld, however, at least in the one instance reported, the program appeared to be distinctly contrary to a normative approach to the inculcation of values. As he saw it, the students were "encouraged freely to examine their ethical judgments rather than to accept preconceived judgments of those in authority." [4]

Two aspects of this illustration are noteworthy. The first is the obvious difference between this Japanese classroom and the majority of learning environments in the United States. A high premium was placed upon the student's autonomy in developing his own value concepts and standards. The second aspect of the situation that is striking is the contrast between value clarification and value inculcation. Inculcation suggests that the learner has limited control and hence limited responsibility in the development of his own values. He needs to be told what values are or what he should value. Value clarification, on the other hand, suggests that the student with appropriate aids and reinforcement is responsible to discern what he thinks and how he feels and then to make some decisions on that basis. That is, he should be responsible for developing his own values.

The proposition I would examine here is that value clarification, not value inculcation, is the appropriate course to be followed in any educational context. This is not to suggest, however, that nothing is ever inculcated. As a matter of fact, in order to clarify values, at least one principle needs to be adopted by all concerned. Perhaps the only way the principle can be adopted is through some procedure which might best be termed inculcation. That principle might be stated as follows: In the consideration of values there is no single correct answer. More specifically it might be said that the adequate posture both for students and teachers in clarifying values is openness.

Of course, such a principle could be dangerously misunderstood if one interpreted it to mean that no general values were important. That need not be the meaning of the principle, however. A freer interpretation would be to say that it is of utmost importance that educators recognize the centrality of being clear about whatever values one holds. In short, then, in education the one supreme value is understanding. G. K. Chesterton in another context stated this in a negative fashion with considerable power. He said: "There is a thought which stops thought. That is the only thought which ought to be stopped."

Once this principle becomes the rule for any valuing process in education, then the clarification of all other values is possible. What this is to suggest, in turn, is that one enters the affective domain through the cognitive. It is important to notice the limits and the focus of such an approach. Instead of analyzing emotive-unconscious matters utilizing the insights and procedures of depth psychology, one is making conscious probes into the way in which ordinary attitudes and actions seem to reflect some central values an individual holds.

A number of strategies have been devised by which this kind of value clarification might be attempted. Raths, Harmin, and Simon in their book *Values and Teaching* [5] have suggested a number of devices which can be employed to clarify the value structure one might encounter in any learning environment. But whatever procedures one might adopt he would be making several assumptions which need to be spelled out. If these assumptions are warranted, then the value clarification approach might also be justified.

II

The first assumption is that while men may not be entirely rational, they are rational enough to develop objective means for analyzing their own value systems. This suggests that it is possible for persons to recognize that they do have criteria by which they establish their own values. If one asserts, for example, that it is a good thing to love or show respect for his neighbor, value clarification would necessitate that one examine the basis or personal justification for such a value. At the same time, it would be required that the individual determine whether or not he actually operates according to the value. In other words, clarification of values requires that the individual know both the basis of a value judgment and its relation to practice. The fact that one can examine a specific value, its criteria and its functional effect suggests that men do possess sufficient cognitive skills to make useful probes into the domain of values.

Second, while values may be personally examined, it is also assumed that many general and specific values are held by virtue of group or social consensus. Such a notion as the value of love or respect for one's neighbor is not purely an individual judgment. It is constantly reinforced or threatened by one's corporate involvements. Hence, at significant points in experience men show respect for their neighbors where there is a social reason to do so. But it is equally true that in other incidents men show a lack of respect for their neighbors.

An illustration of this phenomenon is seen in the situation of war. War makes it difficult for one to show respect for the enemy. Although there may be dramatic exceptions to this rule, armies in wartime would seriously founder if they did not commonly operate on the assumption that the enemy was not worthy of respect. At the same time, one's respect for others with whom he is fighting is markedly enhanced. It would be less surprising to us if we saw a white supremacist from Mississippi engage in some sacrificial act for a black man in the United States Army than if we saw the same act carried out between members of opposing armies. Thus, it might be said at this point that while values are personally held, they are also socially qualified and expressed.

Further, this suggests that value clarification can be a means for reflection on an important dimension of socialization. Values personally held result from one's social involvement in the family and larger associations. Reflection about such involvements legitimately is part of the dynamics of education generally.

The third assumption recognizes that while an individual may have many unconscious core values (what Milton Rokeach in his research on belief systems calls primitive beliefs),[6] nevertheless deliberate teaching and learning of values can occur on a conscious level employing cognitive means. It may be entirely possible for a depth psychologist to bring into consciousness material that has always been unconscious or consistently suppressed in the past. Such a process, however, is aimed at alleviating pathological behaviors and achieving some psychological balance for the individual. While such therapy is not unconcerned with the client's values, that is not the prime objective. At the same time, to expect education to be therapeutic is in most cases a misplaced presumption. In contrast, value clarification in education need not be therapy. One may begin to understand his values without engaging in psychotherapy. He may, for example, come to realize significant disjunctions between attitude and act. In a process of value clarification such a realization would be extremely important. If one does not act according to his professed values, then there is doubt that he really holds them. Although he may give lip service to a set of values, the disparity between attitude and act suggests he actually holds some other values. Recognizing the disparity thus becomes a step toward clarifying the values one actually holds.

III

These three assumptions form the basis for the development of an hypothesis about the teaching of values. The hypothesis might be stated in some such fashion as: Values are learned only insofar as they are clarified. In order to establish such a hypothesis a number of questions need to be examined.

First, is such a notion culturally conditioned? In this connection it needs to be discerned whether one can talk about value clarification at all in intercultural situations. For example, among persons with divergent world-views in Western culture there is considerable consensus about values. For such polar individuals as Bertrand Russell with a fundamentally secular orientation and the late Martin Luther King with a fundamentally religious viewpoint, there can be a good degree of agreement about specific values because they have shared a tradition which relies on a residue of Judeo-Christian teaching, and the Enlightenment has provided an atmosphere in which such investigations are acceptable. Perhaps one of the difficulties of communication between the Western and non-Western world or in such negotiating sessions as the Paris peace talks is that there are no clear common denominators in the value realm. Hence one may be forced to see that value clarification can only be undertaken within the confines of one culture or even one sub-culture.

The Kerner report states that America is moving toward two separate societies, one white and one black. It may be that a severe limitation in the communication between these two growing sub-cultures is the lack of similarity in their value systems. Hope for resolving racial tension may thus be linked with the possibility of finding values that are shared in both segments of our segregated society. Black power may well be the most viable means for establishing economic freedom and authentic identity for a significant minority of this society. But it seems probable that cooperation among differing racial groups in one society will be achieved only insofar as they can establish some compatible value systems.

The second question has to do with educational resources. If values are to be clarified primarily on the individual level, do educators have the means to provide instruction that is sufficiently individualized to reinforce personal autonomy? One major consideration here is whether teachers and administrators themselves are secure enough to allow differing student values to be expressed and operative. Can administrators reconcile the different value sets on either side of the generation gap? How can a college president, for example, remain responsive both to the pressures of the student left and the Board of Trustees?

But more than this, it must be questioned whether educational environments can be developed in which concentration on the individual's values is possible. Most formal learning situations are corporate in character. They are concerned with a common body of subject matter. Although there is some concern of late for individualized instruction, actual instances of it are few and far between. Is it possible on the procedural level to concentrate on the clarification of the individual's values instead of the inculcation of general norms?

Accordingly, it would be necessary to investigate what changes in institutional policy and instructional procedures would be necessary if value clarification were to become an explicit educational objective. Some teachers assume the pose that their teaching does not depend upon any personal values. In such areas as the natural sciences it may be possible to function with only a minimum of moral commitments. But even here one would have to be committed to empirical procedures. And such a commitment has the status of a central value. For others who would be willing to express their values, there is sometimes pressure to remain blandly neutral, academic freedom to the contrary notwithstanding. Especially two, three and four years ago, for instance, many teachers felt they could not express a "dove" position with respect to the Vietnam War without seriously jeopardizing their jobs. Shibboleths about the need for neutrality in schools are roundly criticized in some quarters, but they still form the basis for a popular image of teaching.

In this connection, therefore, it would be appropriate to ask whether teachers themselves can tolerate an educational environment where there are no such myths of neutrality behind which they might hide. At the same time, it would be necessary to determine whether administrators and boards of trustees and boards of education can provide and secure a climate where the free expression and examination of values can occur without threat to individuals.

IV

It may seem apparent that one of the central jobs of education is to help people understand what they actually value. Procedures to expedite this task, however, should not be adopted until we have honestly assessed our resources and developed a theory of education that clearly and coherently warrants value clarification.

NOTES

1. Lawrence Cremin, ed., *The Republic and the School: Horace Mann on the Education of Free Men* (New York: Bureau of Publications, Teachers College, Columbia University, 1957), p. 8.

2. John Dewey, *Democracy and Education* (New York: The Macmillan Co., 1916), p. 360.

3. *Ibid.*, pp. 360-361.

4. Theodore Brameld, *Education as Power* (New York: Holt, Rinehart and Winston, Inc., 1965), p. 88.

5. Louis E. Raths *et al., Values and Teaching* (Columbus, Ohio: C. E. Merrill Books, 1966).

6. See Milton Rokeach, *The Open and Closed Mind* (New York: Basic Books, 1960).

18 Developing Values

Louis E. Raths, Merrill Harmin,
and Sidney B. Simon *

Modern life in the United States is rich with choices and opportunities, but it is also very, very confusing for a child to comprehend. Although few of us would willingly return to the simple and more austere life of earlier days, we must recognize the penalty we pay for the complexities of the present. One of those penalties deals with values. It is certainly much more difficult today than it was at the turn of the century for a child to develop clear values.

Look at the family, for example. Many persons believe that values develop in and around the family. But the changes in the family from more stable days are dramatic if not frightening. According to recent figures, one out of every three mothers is working. It is estimated that in one out of every five families the mother is not home when children return from school.

Recent estimates suggest that one out of every five families represents a broken home. In this context the word *broken* means that one of the parents is dead, the parents are divorced or separated, or one of them is institutionalized. As in the case with

* Reprinted with permission of the publisher from *Values and Teaching,* by Raths, Harmin, and Simon (Columbus, Ohio: Charles E. Merrill Books, 1966), pp. 15-26 and 38-48. For information about current values clarification material or a series of nation-wide training workshops, contact Values Associates, Box 43, Amherst, Mass. 01002.

working mothers, the result is a decrease in the amount of contact which a child might have with either parent.

The character of the father's job and its relation to family life has changed considerably. It is almost universally true today that the children really do not know very much about what the father does to earn a living. They do not see him at his work and they are not informed enough about it to enter into meaningful discussions about the nature of his career, its problems, and its successes. In other words, a major part of the father's life is almost beyond the possibilities of communication with his children.

It is said that one out of every five American families moves every year. Think of what this means for the stability of the life of children. Friendship patterns are often destroyed. There are new children and new teachers to meet. There is the requirement of becoming oriented to new communities, new neighbors, new congregations, and perhaps to new and different patterns of living. This very high geographical mobility is something quite unique in our history. Even so, it is becoming an expected part of family life; and today it can be said that parents are not very much upset when it becomes necessary or desirable to take the children and move to a new community.

There is some little truth in the saying that the family has become a refuge from the world. Father, mother, and children go there to hide from the pressures of life outside. Very often fathers commute several hours daily. They leave the house too early in the morning to have intelligent conversations with children. They come home late at night, tired out, not only from their work, but from the travel. They would like the home to be quiet. They wish that the children would be still. Before long it is time for the children to go to bed, and another opportunity is lost for discussing the meanings of the day's activities, whatever they may have been.

In recent years tremendously potent new means of communication have been introduced into standard family life rituals. In the early days of the century the telephone was brought into more and more families. Then, in the second decade, radio came into being; almost immediately children began to listen; those in charge of programming began to develop programs which they thought would be interesting to children. (Not much attention was paid to the question: What programs would be *good* for children?) Just previous to the advent of radio, the motion picture began to have a great impact upon life in the United States. And then, after World War II, television arrived and with great rapidity captured vast adult and child audiences.

If values represent a way of life, if values give direction to life, if values are those things which make a difference in living, one might expect that, in our concern for developing values among children, there might be a focus upon one or two ways of life which might give stability to the child. Yet the rapid incursion of these new media of communication meant the presentation to the child of many, many *different* ways of life. The output was vast on radio, in the movies, and on the television screen. He saw numerous things and heard many views, which in the ordinary run of life would never have been presented to him as a part of family living. Inanity, crime, violence were hour-by-hour occurrences. Acts that can truly be called depraved were committed by people who were seemingly well-educated, while people watched, listened, and took it in. Surely children must have imbibed some ideas from all of this.

There is another possible inference: being exposed to so many different alternatives, perhaps the child was left with *no* ideas, but instead absorbed just the confusion. It is possible that the biggest contribution these media made was to baffle the child's nascent understanding of what is right and what is wrong, what is true and what is false, what is good and what is bad, what is just and what is unjust, what is beautiful and what is ugly.

Radio, movies, and TV were not the only forces at work. In the same period of time, new and cheaper ways of distributing printed materials were discovered. The comics came into being, and there were publishers who saw great riches in the children's market. "Comic" books became another purveyor of crime stories, horror stories, and all sorts of strange ways of life. They found a market, for children bought these books, and bought them in large quantity.

At about the same time, the family newspapers changed greatly. More crime stories, more sex stories, more corruption were reported; more suggestive pictures were printed; and our children read them along with the comics.

We are not suggesting here that the alternatives which life offers should be blacked out. Nor are we suggesting that the children cannot learn something from all of this exposure. We are suggesting, however, that by themselves children cannot profit greatly from exposure to this myriad of choices. If the family as a *unit* had been exposed to all these choices, if the family as a *unit* could discuss the reasonableness or unreasonableness of what had been presented, every child might have learned something of the meaning of these new ways of living. But, as has been suggested, with the mother working, with more homes broken, with the father away all day, there was even less family sharing. The consequence, we submit, has been a growing confusion in the life of children as to what is good and what is bad, what is right and what is wrong, and what is just and what is unjust.

In addition to all of these other technological innovations, one must not lose sight of the impact of the automobile. At the beginning of the century it was probably quite unusual for a family or children to have traveled very much. In general, the family stayed home except for short excursions on trolley cars, if it were lucky enough to live near one, or on trains. With the advent of the automobile, it became the usual custom to travel quite a bit. The family car moved from luxury to necessity; and under these circumstances, one met new people more often. One was in more frequent contact with customs of another town or another region. One saw other children doing things which perhaps were un-thought of in one's own community.

Out of this welter of traveling and communication, there came not only confusion and uncertainty but also the idea that perhaps anything was all right, nothing really mattered, that while many people were different, there was nothing particularly signifi-cant in the differences. One way of life was as good as another. Nobody really was an example of what was the right way to be.

Another factor operated in the life of children which may or may not be significant for our discussion of values. At the turn of the century the teacher in her local classroom was almost always a local girl. She knew the ways of the community, and she most often knew each child's family. There was a local standard of life, and she was familiar with it. The policemen were often known personally. The storekeepers were often known by name, and the man who ran the store knew a child's parents and they knew him. As a child lived in such a world, he was aware that he was noticed. His behavior was personal in the sense that he was a member of a family and this family was known by the teacher, by the minister, priest, or rabbi, by the storekeeper, by the neighbors. All of this acted as a kind of brake on innovations in behavior. The child was more likely to absorb the mores of the community. There was a kind of common understanding of what behavior was good and what was bad, of which attitudes and aspirations were appropriate and which were inappropriate. In other words, it was easier for a child at that time to come to understand what society expected of him now and would expect of him later as an adult.

It is commonplace to point out that in the early years of this century the church also seemed to have a much greater influence on the growing child than it does today. Father and mother, grandfather and grandmother had an attitude toward the church and its teachings which was forcefully conveyed to the children of the family. As the family changed, and as new influences came into the family, the impact of the church began to wane. The way of life represented by a long religious tradition began to be neglected. It would be too much to say that the church was opposed. It wasn't opposition that began to appear. It was, first of all, a weaning or separation. With all this moving around, with so many new stimuli coming into the family, there was a gradual but continuing separation of family life from frequent church and Sunday school participation. This meant a decrease in the quantity and quality of contact with religious traditions and their emphasis upon values. This should not be underestimated as a factor in today's world of confusion and apathy. As this separation from frequent contact with the church continued, clergymen were seen more frequently as people who merely officiated at baptisms, deaths, weddings, and the rites associated with the idea of confirmation.

World events also had an incalculable effect upon family life. In the first forty years of this century, there were two terrible world wars; and in the past twenty years, the newspapers have shouted almost continual news of cold wars and hot wars. Under these circumstances it must be very difficult for children to believe in nonviolence and in peace as a reality. Atomic bombs have been developed by educated men and have been used on human populations. Even now they are held as a threat to slaughter millions of people.

During these same years, there have been disastrous famines at a time when, in other places, large amounts of excess food overflowed storage bins. In the last world war, millions of human beings were exterminated by a country which had been regarded as one of the most civilized and educated in the world. Children are now being told that the Communists are "ahead" in education—whatever that means—and are also told that these educated Communists want to capture the world, to crush liberty everywhere, and to make human beings the slaves of the party or the state. Under these circumstances, isn't it natural for children to come to believe that education has very little to do with what is good and what is bad, what is right and what is wrong, what is just and what is unjust?

Out of this uncertainty and confusion, it has come to pass that our schools can hardly stand for a single set of values. For example, there was a time when the schools celebrated the Christian holidays, Christmas and Easter. Groups other than Christian called this practice into question and suggested that the school should not represent one religion any more than another, and it wasn't long before the celebration of Christmas was very different from what it had been. The schools used to put an emphasis upon a daily prayer, but the rulings of the Supreme Court of the land have decided that a common prayer may not be demanded of all children in the schools. As it is with religious matters, so it is with other matters of deep concern. If someone was for something, someone else was against it; and to avoid controversy, schools began to stand for nothing.

Teachers turned toward "teaching the facts." If controversy was to be troublesome, one should stay away from it. Administrators tended to prefer teachers who did not raise issues. In communities of strangers living together, people who did not know one another well, people with many different backgrounds, it became easier to have schools which themselves represented an absence of consensus. Moral, ethical, aesthetic values were quietly abandoned as integral parts of the curriculum. Thus the gap widened between what we *said* the schools were to foster and what was actually taught. Children saw this gap between reality and something perhaps more promising. They saw many other gaps, too. A child who asks his parents to buy a gadget advertised on television and who quotes its supposed good qualities is very often told that you cannot believe what the television says. When he repeats to his mother what the clerk in the store has said about a product, his mother lets him know that you cannot believe what clerks say. As he attempts to accept some of the things that appear in newspapers and magazines, he is again told to be suspicious. What can one believe? Is it true that most people in the adult world regularly lie, and, in general, lie for money? Why isn't something done about this?

The child sees pretty much the same thing when it comes to most serious matters. He is surrounded by repetitive statements pledging a dedication to peace, and all around him are signs of war. He is told that we must be militarily strong; might is at least as important as right. In school and out of school, our country is held up to him as a model of equal rights before the law. He also receives reports over and over again that Negroes in our culture do not receive equal rights. But he is so accustomed to duplicity that he very often does not wonder how this can be so.

In school and out, he is told that to co-operate is not only excellent but is practically a necessity in our world. At the same time, he is told that everybody should look out for himself, that if you don't look out for yourself nobody else will. You are to get yours and everyone else is to get his. He is told that women are the equal of men, and as he grows up he sees that in many situations they are not. In school he learns a romanticized version of the vigilantes in California history. He comes to believe that they were fine people. And at the same time he is supposed to pledge loyalty to a society that is ruled by law. He learns about some of the great patriots who initiated our revolution, people who stood up and spoke their minds; and while he is learning these things, people close to him advise him to be careful of what he says, not get into any trouble, go along with the authorities, and make the best of whatever the situation is.

He learns a lot of verbalisms about religion; and as he grows up, he also learns that one should not let religion interfere with making money. He is told again and again that education is a fine thing and that it helps to enrich life; but he is apt to learn that it is the certificate, the diploma, or the degree which is really significant. It is not education itself which is so important, but the accepted symbols of education that open up the door to success. While he is told that knowledge is power and that skill is to be respected, he is also told that it is not what you know but who you know that really counts.

Many more of these kinds of conflicts could be added but enough have been listed to suggest that the child's world is indeed a confused one. It must not be easy to grow in a society characterized by these conflicts.

Does this suggest that human beings are more inconsistent now than ever before in the history of mankind? Probably not. What it does suggest is that with the development of all these new means of mass communication, with the increased travel, with the increased moving around of people, *more children are exposed to more of these inconsistencies*. This means that it is probably increasingly difficult for the growing child to develop clear values of his own. There is so much confusion surrounding him and so little attention paid to the child's dilemma, so few persons with the time and patience to listen to him and to help him untangle some of the confusion, that he simply remains without sufficient clarity of beliefs or purpose.

One way of summing up what has been said is to indicate that the child of today confronts many more choices than the child of yesterday. He has so many more alternatives. In one sense, this makes him less provincial and more sophisticated. In another sense, the complex array of choices makes the act of choosing more difficult. How can one size up all of the available alternatives? How can one examine the grounds on which each rests, and how can one anticipate the consequences toward which each one points? In short, how does one know what to believe? The job seems so staggering that one is tempted to throw up his hands at the outset.

Just take this matter of choosing: think of the alternatives which confront the child in the world of products. There are all these different automobiles with their presumed uniqueness. Think of the toothpastes, the soaps, the toys, and the clothes which are offered. How do you choose? Is it true that one thing is as good as another and that discrimination is fairly useless? Is it not possible that in situations like this a kind of apathy about choice develops, and one begins to think that almost nothing makes a difference?

On the international scene, TV, radio, newspapers, and magazines bring to children news of violence and conflicts and disaster from all over the world. It assails the eyes and ears of our children; and in some vague, unknown way, the idea is communicated that we should all be concerned about these happenings. Concerned in what way? Will someone help us to relate these particular happenings to some general notions of value, of what is good and just?

There is yet another factor. It is widely proclaimed that there has been a significant shift in social class relationships, that many people have emerged from the working class and are now to be regarded as middle class. In a sense this means that the kind of work the parents are doing has changed. Probably the parents have joined the march to the suburbs. It almost certainly means that the parents have become more dedicated to schooling and education for their children. It is apt to mean, too, that parents are beginning a longer range type of planning, that they are not consuming their total earnings week by week or month by month. There may well be some plan for the future of the children, perhaps college. More money is spent on insurance. The house, even with its mortgage, is seen as an asset which will increase in value with the years. In other words, children are growing up in families where there is an emphasis upon security, and there is a minimizing of the value of taking risks. Parallel to the literature of daring and adventure, running beside a national emphasis on exploration of space and trips to the moon, there is a family atmosphere of "Don't stick out your neck," "Don't take a chance," "Play it safe."

The new social class alignments also tend to raise some new kind of insecurity on the part of parents. Parents are not yet accustomed to the new roles they have chosen to play. In these new suburbs they do not know their neighbors very well, and they do not know the standards which their neighbors have or do not have. In this absence of knowing there is a tendency to withdraw; and as the months go by, very little knowledge about each other's ways of living is exchanged. If a child comes home from high school and wants to stay up for the late news and argues that other children in his class do so, his parents are quite apt to accede reluctantly to his request, and they do this without knowing in fact whether such a practice is common in other homes. If this kind of situation is repeated often enough, it may be one of the bases for saying the children now have too much to say about their own conduct. As a matter of fact, they probably say so much because no one else is in a position to say very much at all. It suggests a weakening of the authority of parents with no substitute authority to fill the vacuum beyond the temporal standards of the boys and girls themselves.

These standards do not always work. We do know that there is much more delinquent behavior *reported* now than fifty years ago. We hear of many more cases of children using various kinds of narcotics. We know that there are large numbers of babies born out of wedlock, and we know that there are tens of thousands of abortions each year. We know that rates of criminality have increased. We have reports that ever so many children have ulcers, and we know that the rate of suicide amongst children is growing. Increasingly we are recognizing that there are many children who are in need of psychological assistance of a very specialized kind.

We know, too, that along with the growing emphasis upon commodities as symbols of status, there has been great unemployment, that the number of the *very poor* has changed hardly at all in the past sixty years, and that those who are poor today tend to be even poorer in relation to the other social classes. In many classrooms poverty is a very great problem. Interestingly, while this condition persists, the very children who are poor hear about national and local efforts to help the poor in Africa and in Asia and in Central America. Many of them must wonder deeply why the poor here at home are not receiving the attention which they deserve. How does one know what is right under these circumstances? Is poverty the problem, really, or is it an image of the United States which is to be created in the eyes of a world split between communism and noncommunism? What will these young people in our schools come to believe about our attitudes toward poverty, toward segregation, toward civil rights, toward law, toward freedom and liberty?

Although many more things might be suggested which make it difficult for a child to develop values, only one more will be added to the list: the standardized role which seems to be played by most adults when they are in the presence of children. Somehow or

We are not suggesting here that the alternatives which life offers should be blacked out. Nor are we suggesting that the children cannot learn something from all of this exposure. We are suggesting, however, that by themselves children cannot profit greatly from exposure to this myriad of choices. If the family as a *unit* had been exposed to all these choices, if the family as a *unit* could discuss the reasonableness or unreasonableness of what had been presented, every child might have learned something of the meaning of these new ways of living. But, as has been suggested, with the mother working, with more homes broken, with the father away all day, there was even less family sharing. The consequence, we submit, has been a growing confusion in the life of children as to what is good and what is bad, what is right and what is wrong, and what is just and what is unjust.

In addition to all of these other technological innovations, one must not lose sight of the impact of the automobile. At the beginning of the century it was probably quite unusual for a family or children to have traveled very much. In general, the family stayed home except for short excursions on trolley cars, if it were lucky enough to live near one, or on trains. With the advent of the automobile, it became the usual custom to travel quite a bit. The family car moved from luxury to necessity; and under these circumstances, one met new people more often. One was in more frequent contact with customs of another town or another region. One saw other children doing things which perhaps were unthought of in one's own community.

Out of this welter of traveling and communication, there came not only confusion and uncertainty but also the idea that perhaps anything was all right, nothing really mattered, that while many people were different, there was nothing particularly significant in the differences. One way of life was as good as another. Nobody really was an example of what was the right way to be.

Another factor operated in the life of children which may or may not be significant for our discussion of values. At the turn of the century the teacher in her local classroom was almost always a local girl. She knew the ways of the community, and she most often knew each child's family. There was a local standard of life, and she was familiar with it. The policemen were often known personally. The storekeepers were often known by name, and the to the question: What programs would be *good* for children?) Just previous to the advent of radio, the motion picture began to have a great impact upon life in the United States. And then, after World War II, television arrived and with great rapidity captured vast adult and child audiences.

If values represent a way of life, if values give direction to life, if values are those things which make a difference in living, one might expect that, in our concern for developing values among children, there might be a focus upon one or two ways of life which might give stability to the child. Yet the rapid incursion of these new media of communication meant the presentation to the child of many, many *different* ways of life. The output was vast on radio, in the movies, and on the television screen. He saw numerous things and heard many views, which in the ordinary run of life would never have been presented to him as a part of family living. Inanity, crime, violence were hour-by-hour occurrences. Acts that can truly be called depraved were committed by people who were seemingly well-educated, while people watched, listened, and took it in. Surely children must have imbibed some ideas from all of this.

There is another possible inference: being exposed to so many different alternatives, perhaps the child was left with *no* ideas, but instead absorbed just the confusion. It is possible that the biggest contribution these media made was to baffle the child's nascent understanding of what is right and what is wrong, what is true and what is false, what is good and what is bad, what is just and what is unjust, what is beautiful and what is ugly.

Radio, movies, and TV were not the only forces at work. In the same period of time, new and cheaper ways of distributing printed materials were discovered. The comics came into being, and there were publishers who saw great riches in the children's market. "Comic" books became another purveyor of crime stories, horror stories, and all sorts of strange ways of life. They found a market, for children bought these books, and bought them in large quantity.

At about the same time, the family newspapers changed greatly. More crime stories, more sex stories, more corruption were reported; more suggestive pictures were printed; and our children read them along with the comics.

another the idea is held by adults that their chief function—in relationship to children—is to *tell* them things; to tell them what to do, when to do it, where to do it, how to do it, how often to do it, and when to stop doing it. If the child resists, he is apt to be characterized as disobedient, impertinent, unstable, or rebellious. In other words, typically, the adult only *adds* to the array of directives already urged upon the child by TV, radio, movies, newspapers, magazines, textbooks, teachers, other children, etc. The real problem is that almost no one sees the necessity for helping a child to make some order out of the confusion which has been created inside his head. Almost no one sees the necessity for questioning a child, to help him sort out and examine all those confusing ideas.

In one sense, the adult is led to believe that children are not people. Children are to follow the proposals of adults. They are to follow the aspirations which adults have for them. Children are to have the same feelings as adults, *without,* by the way, having had the same experiences as those adults. Children should have the "right" attitudes, and the "right" attitudes are those which correspond to those held by the adults who have control over them at the moment. Notwithstanding the tremendous amount of new knowledge which has accumulated in recent decades, and assuming that beliefs are related to knowledge, there is nevertheless a tendency on the part of grownups to assume that adult beliefs should persevere unmodified, that children should have the beliefs of their elders.

And when, as is frequently the case, children do not have the same beliefs as adults say they should have, grownups become frustrated and sometimes angry. They begin again to tell the child what he is to believe. They push more ideas into his confused mind. They pressure him, bribe him, sometimes frighten him. This manipulation only further confuses many children. One person will tell the child one thing. His father insists something different. The child's friends are certain of something else. Successful people all around demonstrate yet other notions. What is one to believe? How is one to know? Who is to help the child unravel this bewildering array of ideas? Would it help for a teacher to sit the child down and add another lecture or reasoned argument to the turmoil? How *is* the child to know what to believe?

This distressing and not totally unfamiliar survey of what

problems and dilemmas confront a young person growing up in this culture need not go on any longer. We do not wish to return to a simpler and less rich life, but we do wish to develop methods for helping children deal with the complexities of modern living. The important thing is that we agree that it is indeed a confusing and complex world into which we welcome our youth. We must now ask, how does all of this affect the behavior of children? In what ways does it show up in how they think, how they react, how they plan, and how they dream? Just what does it mean for teachers?

For a long time now teachers have been able to identify children who do not hear very well or who do not see very well. We have finely developed tests to reveal those students who are not reading up to grade level and whose mathematical skills will most likely require special tutoring. Now, are there signs to indicate a child who has had serious trouble in coping with the development of values? It is one of the principal contentions of this book that there are such signs.

We believe that we have the means for identifying many of the children who are having difficulty in forming values and, having identified them, we have found that teachers can do a great deal about the problem. It need not plague the child throughout his life. On many occasions we are going to need help from the family, from other teachers, and perhaps from a counselor, but—as is outlined below—the main burden in this confused and confusing world can be borne by the classroom teachers of America. . . .

Teaching for Value Clarity

Earlier we noted some of the uncertain and confusing aspects of society and speculated upon the difficulties children have in making sense of it all. We also said that we use the term "value" to denote those beliefs, purposes, attitudes, and so on that are chosen freely and thoughtfully, prized, and acted upon. We suggested, further, that since the development of society and the people in it is best seen as dynamic, it is perhaps wiser to focus upon the process of *valuing* than upon any particular values themselves.

Now let us be a bit more explicit about that process. What,

according to the theory that we propose, does one *do* if one wants to take on the problem of helping children develop values? Briefly, one assists children in using the process of valuing. The process flows naturally from the definition of values presented earlier. That is, an adult who would help children develop values would be advised to:

1. Encourage children to make choices, and to make them freely.
2. Help them discover and examine available alternatives when faced with choices.
3. Help children weigh alternatives thoughtfully, reflecting on the consequences of each.
4. Encourage children to consider what it is that they prize and cherish.
5. Give them opportunities to make public affirmations of their choices.
6. Encourage them to act, behave, live in accordance with their choices.
7. Help them to examine repeated behaviors or patterns in their life.

In this way, the adult encourages the process of valuing. The intent of this process is to help children (although it is equally applicable to adults) clarify for themselves what they value. This is very different from trying to persuade children to accept some predetermined set of values. It is based on a conception of democracy that says persons can learn to make their own decisions. It is also based on a conception of humanity that says human beings hold the possibility of being thoughtful and wise and that the most appropriate values will come when persons use their intelligence freely and reflectively to define their relationships with each other and with an ever-changing world. Furthermore, it is based on the idea that values are personal things if they exist at all, that they cannot be personal until they are freely accepted, and that they cannot be of much significance if they do not penetrate the living of the person who holds them.

The next section of this book describes the value clarifying process in much more detail and gives many examples of how it might be used by teachers at many grade levels and in many subject areas. At this point it might be useful to contrast the value clarifying approach with more traditional approaches to values.

Traditional Approaches to Values

Here are some ways that have often been advocated for helping children develop values.

1. *Setting an example* either directly, by the way adults behave, or indirectly, by pointing to good models in the past or present, such as Washington's honesty or the patience of Ulysses' wife.

2. *Persuading and convincing* by presenting arguments and reasons for this or that set of values and by pointing to the fallacies and pitfalls of other sets of values.

3. *Limiting choices* by giving children choices only among values "we" accept, such as asking children to choose between helping wash the dishes or helping clean the floor, or by giving children choices between a value we accept and one no one is likely to accept, such as asking children to choose between telling the truth and never speaking to anyone again.

4. *Inspiring* by dramatic or emotional pleas for certain values, often accompanied by models of behavior associated with the value.

5. *Rules and regulations* intended to contain and mold behavior until it is unthinkingly accepted as "right," as through the use of rewards and punishments to reinforce certain behavior.

6. *Cultural or religious dogma* presented as unquestioned wisdom or principle, such as saying that something should be believed because "our people have always done it this way."

7. *Appeals to conscience,* appeals to the still, small voice that we assume is within the heart of everyone, with the arousing of feelings of guilt if one's conscience doesn't suggest the "right" way, such as telling a child that he should know better or that he shamed his parents.

We have no doubt that such methods as those listed, and there are others that could be listed, have in the past controlled behavior and even formed beliefs and attitudes, but we assert that they have not *and cannot* lead to values in the sense that we are concerned with them—values that represent the free and thoughtful choice of intelligent humans interacting with complex and changing environments.

In fact, those methods do not seem to have resulted in deep commitments of any sort. The values that are supposedly being promoted by those methods in our society—honor, courage, devotion, self-control, craftsmanship, thrift, love, etc.—seem less than ever to be the values that guide the behavior of citizens. On the pragmatic test of effectiveness alone, the approaches listed above must receive a low grade. They just do not seem to work very well. This alone would suggest that we try a new approach.

We emphasize that these methods are not without some useful effect. It is certainly useful, for example, for adults to set examples for the kinds of behaviors that they say they support. Also, most of us have had our lives stirred and enriched by inspiring words and deeds. And many have found that religion is able to nourish virtue and hope, even in an otherwise desperate and dark life. Our main point, then, is not that the above approaches to values have been without use, but that they have not worked as well as we might have hoped and that we now have some understanding of why this might have been.

The reader will note that with each of the above approaches there is the idea of persuasion. The "right" values are predetermined and it is one method or another of selling, pushing, urging those values upon others. All the methods have the air of indoctrination, with some merely more subtle than others. The idea of free inquiry, thoughtfulness, reason seems to be lost. The approach seems not to be how to help the child develop a valuing process but, rather, how to persuade the child to adopt the "right" values.

When we ask persons why such persuasive approaches are employed, why there is little effort to have the child think through issues and freely choose what *he* prizes, we tend to receive certain answers.

1. "Children are not old enough or experienced enough or wise enough to choose values for themselves. We are responsible for starting them off on the right track. We have to drill values into children now; later they will learn to value for themselves."

The assumption here is that one does not have to practice valuing for oneself at an early age and that after twenty years or so of indoctrination one can readily break the habit of conforming to the values of others.

2. "It takes too much time to help children figure out their own values. It's faster and simpler to merely show them the best way."

There are probably assumptions here about what is most important for a limited amount of time and energy, with an implication that something other than values is most important. Also implied is the assumption that everyone can get values from being shown "the best way," even as we note that a child is exposed to many varied models of what are touted as "best ways." Note also the implication that the best ways are already defined in such a form as to be generally applicable.

3. "You can't really trust children to choose the values that would serve them best. Both their inexperience and some tendency to obstinacy may lead them to poor choices. We may have disastrous results, and most certainly we will have many regrettable results."

This view assumes that one would have children choose in all areas, whether they understood the alternatives or not and whether the choice could lead to disaster or not. It also reflects some limited faith in the intelligence and good will of children.

4. "Think of the problems that will develop from wrong choices! Time wasted, unnecessary hurt and pain, and perhaps even irreparable human damage. Besides, how can adults contain themselves when they see children going astray? What, after all, are adults for if they do not point the way to wisdom and righteousness?"

There are two separate sets of assumptions here. One set has to do with the problem of "poor" choices, which assumes that children cannot learn from such choices, that the consequences of such choices are not educational, and, in fact, that children can learn about values *without* making some poor choices. There is the idea that one is helping if he prevents a child from making a mistake.

The second set of assumptions, more by implication, seems to say that adults will feel some loss of function, perhaps of power, if they do not intervene in the decisions of children. One almost imagines an adult looking back at a long childhood of being manipulated at the whimsy of the surrounding adults and hoping that his turn to assert himself will not be denied.

5. "Look, what can I do? Everyone else tries to give values to children. My children will think I'm crazy if I do otherwise, and certainly other adults will look at me and wonder at my laxness."

This says quite plainly that many adults feel pressure from others to conform in some way. It would be unwise to underestimate the strength behind that pressure, but it tends to assume that adults under pressure have not the wherewithal to assert whatever values they hold. For some, this may be true. But it may be a result of an adult's own lack of values. One might assume that if a person didn't have a clear set of values in a certain area, he would be likely to look around and see what others are doing. Thus, some conformity is not the result of a desire to conform, but represents a desire to do what is best in circumstances which are unclear. Perhaps, then, clarity here as elsewhere is what is needed.

6. "I really do not want to get too deeply into examinations of values. It is too confusing and I do not understand it well enough myself. Maybe professionals can do it, but it is much easier to let things be and direct my attention to other things."

The assumption that is clearest here is that an adult should not work with children in areas in which he is not expert, that it would be too threatening to do so. There may also be an implication that some adults do not want to recognize how ineffective their own valuing process has been.

7. "It is a matter of will power. If one wants to do something, all he needs is the will to do it."

This assumes, of course, that one does want to do something, that purposes are clear, that something is blocking the achievement of personal goals. It does not seem to take in the possibility that purposes are not clear and that ambivalence is in control.

8. "Frankly, children are more difficult to handle if they are deciding too many things for themselves. If children expect to learn what they should believe and value from us, it is easier all around. There will be fewer discipline problems."

The assumption here is that children who are tractable are

more valuable than children who have values. There is the additional assumption that the indoctrination of values does lead to more obedient children and fewer behavior problems.

9. "Children appreciate being told what to do and what to believe. It gives them security. Freedom is frightening to many of them."

The assumption here would seem to deal with the cause of insecurity that arises when duties cease to direct children. Are children insecure only because they now would have free time and free choice, or are they insecure because they have had no help in acquiring real values to direct their use of that freedom? Is the answer to keep children under pressure, keep them busy, keep them under control? Or is the answer to help them to develop values so that they can be responsibly self-directing in an ever-changing world?

Now these reasons for wanting to persuade children to take on certain values seem to us to be based on questionable assumptions, although some of the assumptions seem more temptingly tenable than others and some are probably reasonable for some situations and not for others. There is at least one additional reason for adults trying to impose their values on children, and it is perhaps the overriding reason: *no other alternative that is clear and testable has been provided.* Not being aware of another choice, who can blame adults for doing what they think best? The observation that many children and adults do not, in fact, seem to have many clear values may have raised questions about the efficiency of trying to sell adult beliefs to children, but what alternative choice is there? This book, of course, hopes to offer one.

Why a New Approach?

There is widespread concern that youth, and adults in some cases, do not seem to live by any consistent set of values. They act impetuously, erratically, and sometimes with malice. Many children find nothing enjoyable to do with their free time. Even in school many seem purposeless and listless, motivated only—but not always consistently—by outside pressures. Our population is becoming other-directed, it is asserted; we guide our lives not by what we believe is right and proper, but by what others do or say. Does this not suggest that many persons have unclear values?

We note the wide discrepancy between what people do and what they say. Many political leaders, business executives, military leaders, workers of all sorts, and even professional people are known to *do* things that are inconsistent with what they *say* are their values. Corruption is not an unusual occurrence. So many people can be "bought." Does this not suggest that the approaches to values that have been so widely used in the past have been less than effective?

Adults have been trying to set examples for years. They have tried often with ingenious manipulation to persuade children to accept certain values. They have carefully limited choices given to children. They have attempted to inspire identification with particular values. They have made rules and insisted on certain patterns of behavior. They have relied upon religion and cultural truisms. They have appealed to the consciences of young people. But even a casual look at the results of these approaches is discouraging. They just do not seem to have worked.

In the past we have told children, children who have been exposed to so many different and confusing stimuli, that they should believe in one thing or another. We have said this in many ways: by our example, our rules, our arguments, and so on. But as we spoke, they were surrounded by other examples and arguments which stood for different values; and when a child indicated by a lack of purpose or a disregard of purpose that he was confused by all this, we insisted, punished, pleaded, and otherwise campaigned even harder for one of the many values that we were convinced he must adopt. More than likely this only further confused many children and made them less able to decide in what to believe. Consequently, many children pretend to believe. Or if they do believe, they try not to do it very keenly. Or they deal with the dilemma by taking whatever belief is popular and convenient at the moment, switching frequently.

Why must teachers see their role only as putting things into the mind of the child? Why can't a role be defined that would help a child take all the confusion that already exists in his mind, remove it, look at it, examine it, turn it around, and make some order out of it? Why can't teachers learn to spend some of their time helping a child understand what the bewildering array of beliefs and attitudes that saturate our modern life are all about and which suits him best? Is this not the road to values, to *clear* and *personal* values?

We believe it is. We believe that as children are helped to use what we call the valuing process, they will move toward value clarity in a more sensible and dramatic way than ever before. Peck and Havighurst (1960, p. 191) put it succinctly:

> It is temptingly easy and insidiously gratifying to "mold" children, or to "whip them into line" by exercising one's superior status and authority as an adult. It is often personally inconvenient to allow children time to debate alternatives, and it may be personally frustrating if their choice contradicts one's own preferences. If there is any selfish, sensitive "pride" at stake, it is very hard for most adults to refrain from controlling children in an autocratic manner. Then, too, like any dictatorship, it looks "more efficient"—to the dictator, at least. However, the effect on character is to arrest the development of rational judgment and to create such resentments as prevent the growth of genuine altruistic impulses. For thousands of years, the long-term effects have been ignored and sacrificed to short-term adult advantages, most of the time. Probably it is no accident that there are relatively few people who are, or ever will become, psychologically and ethically mature.

Summary of Part Two

So far we have presented a view of the concept of value that is based on a particular notion of human potential, one which emphasizes man's capacity for intelligent, self-directed behavior. We have said that it would be well to reserve the term "value" for those individual beliefs, attitudes, activities, or feelings that satisfy the criteria of (1) having been freely chosen, (2) having been chosen from among alternatives, (3) having been chosen after due reflection, (4) having been prized and cherished, (5) having been publicly affirmed, (6) having been incorporated into actual be-havior, and (7) having been repeated in one's life. In different words, we might say that something will not qualify as a value if *any* of the following conditions apply.

1. It has not been *freely* chosen (no room in this theory for values that are imposed upon one by outside pressures).

2. It is without one or more available alternatives (a real choice must exist, not a spurious choice).

3. It has been chosen without thoughtful consideration (this excludes impulse or highly emotional choices from the category of values).

4. It is not prized or cherished (we exclude from the level of values those things which we have or do of which we are not proud and would rather not have or do—as when one chooses the least objectionable of several undesirable alternatives).

5. It is denied upon public confrontation (to be ashamed or unduly fearful of something is to indicate that one does not value it highly).

6. It is not in some way reflected in one's actual behavior (one who chooses democracy and never does anything to put that choice into practice may be said to have an attitude or belief about democracy but not a value).

7. It is a passing fancy and lacks any persistence over time (a one-shot effort at pottery-making, for example, would not qualify as a value).

The meaning here for schools and, more particularly, the busy classroom teacher is implicit in the definition. If one wishes to help children develop clearer values, one must help children use the process of valuing. That is, one must help children: (1) make free choices whenever possible, (2) search for alternatives in choice-making situations, (3) weigh the consequences of each available alternative, (4) consider what they prize and cherish, (5) affirm the things they value, (6) do something about their choices, and (7) consider and strengthen patterns in their lives. It is as simple, and complex, as that. As the teacher helps students use these proc-esses, he helps them find values.

It should be increasingly clear that the adult does not force his own pet values upon children. What he does is create conditions that aid children in finding values *if* they choose to do so. When

operating with this value theory, it is entirely possible that children will choose not to develop values. It is the teacher's responsibility to support this choice also, while at the same time realizing
that value development is likely to be one of the goals of the school
and, if so, it should be encouraged by providing regular experiences that will help raise to the value level the beliefs, feelings,
interests, and activities children bring with them.

The next section of the book details procedures that teachers
can use to do this. Procedures are presented that teachers can use
without taking time away from on-going programs or activities.
Also outlined are techniques for relating value lessons to the
familiar subject matter.

The teacher who activates the value theory in some of the ways
suggested in those chapters can expect that children will have
more values, be more aware of the values that they have, have
values that are more consistent with one another, and, especially, be
ready to use the valuing process as they continue to grow and learn.

But there are also purposes that are more concrete, more relevant to the typical school task, and more readily measurable that
seem to be promoted by the valuing process. For example, research
(discussed more fully in Chapter 11) shows that when the valuing
process was promoted with children who were very apathetic, over-
conforming, flighty, and likely to act in a variety of poses or
"phony" roles, this type of behavior became noticeably less acute
and less frequent. There is also evidence that these techniques help
children who are very indecisive, who are very inconsistent, or
who are chronic dissenters. Other research showed the valuing
process to help underachievers improve in the following:

Attitudes toward learning
Raising of questions and alternatives
Initiation and self-direction of classroom activity
Perseverance
Active participation

In general, the research shows that students become more vital
and purposeful when given opportunities to clarify their values.
How, specifically, this may be done is the subject of the chapters
which follow.

19 Moral and Religious Education and the Public Schools: A Developmental View

LAWRENCE KOHLBERG *

The major impetus for this volume is the recent Supreme Court interpretation of the First Amendment. As the previous essay by William Ball indicates, it is possible to interpret the Court's decision as ruling out any form of moral or ethical, as well as religious, instruction in the school. He points out that the recent Court decisions define religion as embracing any articulated credos or value systems including "Ethical Culture" or "Secular Humanism," credos which essentially consist of the moral principles of Western culture. He concludes that the Supreme Court is in effect prohibiting the public school from engaging in moral education since such education is equivalent to the state propagation of the religion of Ethical Culture or Humanism.

My first reaction to the notion that moral education and reli-

* Reprinted with permission of the publisher from *Religion and Public Education,* edited by Theodore R. Sizer (Boston: Houghton Mifflin Co., 1967), pp. 164-183.

gious education are identical in their implications for civil liberties was, like that of most laymen, one of incredulity and shock. This reaction was especially intense because as a psychologist I have attempted to formulate a conception of moral education in the public schools based on research findings, a conception in which a complete separation of moral and religious education is implicit.[1] In this chapter I will try to focus explicitly on both the scientific findings and the philosophical reasoning which leads me to view moral education as completely separable from religion from the point of view of civil liberties.[2]

Justice as the Core of Morality

It appears to me that Ball's interpretation of the Supreme Court's ruling is possible only because of ambiguity and confusion in the Court's definition of ethical values as these relate to public institutions on the one hand and to religion on the other. It is clear that the Constitution and the law of the land compose or imply a "value system" or a body of norms, and it is equally clear that the government's maintenance of the Constitution and the laws does not mean the establishment of a religion. Accordingly, the public school's effort to communicate an understanding of, and intelligent respect for, the law of the land and the underlying conceptions of human rights on which it is based does not constitute the establishment of a religion. The school is no more committed to value neutrality than is the government or the law. The school, like the government, is an institution with a basic function of maintaining and transmitting some, but not all, of the consensual values of society. The most fundamental values of a society are termed moral values, and the major moral values, at least in our society, are the values of justice. According to any interpretation of the Constitution, the rationale for government is the preservation of the rights of individuals, i.e., of justice. The public school is as much committed to the maintenance of justice as is the court. In my opinion, desegregation of the schools is not only a passive recognition of the equal rights of citizens to access to a public facility, like a swimming pool, but an active recognition of the responsibility of the school for "moral education," i.e., for transmission of the values of justice on which our society is founded.

In essence, then, I am arguing that Ball's interpretation of the Supreme Court ruling is possible only if morality or ethics is confused with "value systems" in general, and if it is not recognized that the core of morality is justice.[3] Unless one recognizes the core status of justice, any conscious concern about the school's responsibility for developing the basic values of the society and making citizens as well as scholars will run into difficulties as soon as one tries to define the exact content of these basic values. Obviously the values transmitted by the school should not be the values of an organized minority. Once the school becomes engaged in teaching a particular moral doctrine belonging to a particular group of citizens organized as a religious, political, or ideological body, it may well be accused of the establishment of religion. The principle involved here would be unquestioned if the schools were to impose the moral beliefs of an organized minority upon children, e.g., the doctrine that it is wrong to receive a blood transfusion, or that it is wrong to work on Saturday. It applies equally, however, if the moral belief happens to be that of an organized majority, e.g., the belief of the majority in some southern states that it is wrong for whites and Negroes to mingle socially or to marry. Neither the government, the law, nor the schools represent a vehicle whereby the values of the majority may be imposed upon the minority. Both prayer in school and segregated education were the will of the majority as determined by the Gallup Poll before the Supreme Court decision, yet the Court had no hesitancy in defending the rights of the minority. The basic values of our society are basic not in the sense of representing majority or even unanimous consensus; they are basic in the sense of representing universal values which either the majority or the minority must appeal to in support of their own beliefs.

The problems as to the legitimacy of moral education in the public schools disappear, then, if the proper content of moral education is recognized to be the values of justice which themselves prohibit the imposition of beliefs of one group upon another. The requirement implied by the Bill of Rights that the school recognize the equal rights of individuals in matters of belief or values does not mean that the schools are not to be "value oriented." Recognition of equal rights does not imply value neutrality, i.e., the view that all value systems are equally sound. Because we respect the individual rights of members of foreign cultures or of members of particular groups in our society, it is sometimes believed that we must consider their values as valid as our own. Because we must respect the rights of an Eichmann, however, we need not treat his values as having a cogency equal to that of the values of liberty and justice. Public instruction is committed to maintenance of the rights of individuals and to the transmission of the values of respect for individual rights. This respect should include respect for the right to hold moral beliefs differing from those of the majority. It need not include respect for "moral" beliefs predicated on the denial of the rights of others, whether of the majority or of a minority, such as the beliefs of the American Nazis or the Ku Klux Klan.

I
FORMULATING GOALS IN MORAL EDUCATION

So far, it has been claimed that the schools cannot be "value neutral" but must be engaged in moral education. It has also been claimed that the content of moral education must be defined in terms of justice, rather than in terms of majority consensus, if the civil rights of parents and children are not to be infringed upon by such education. These claims have been made in terms of the political philosophy underlying the school as a public institution.

When we consider the actual workings of the public school, the conclusions become more inescapable. All schools necessarily are involved in moral education. The teacher is constantly and unavoidably moralizing to children, about school rules and values and about his students' behavior toward one another. Since moralizing is unavoidable, it seems logical that it be done in terms of consciously formulated goals of moral development. Liberal teachers do not want to indoctrinate children with their own private moral values. Since the classroom social situation requires moralizing by the teacher, he ordinarily tends to limit his moralizing to the necessities of classroom management, i.e., the immediate and relatively trivial kinds of behavior which are disrupting to him or to the other children. Exposure to the diversity of moral views of teachers is undoubtedly one of the enlightening experiences of growing up; but the present thoughtlessness concerning which of the teacher's moral attitudes or views he communicates to children and which he does not leaves much to be desired. Many teachers would be mortified to know what their students perceive to be their moral concerns. My seven-year-old son told me one day that he was one of the good boys in school but he didn't know whether he really wanted to be. I asked him what the differences between the good and bad boys were and he said the bad boys talked in class and didn't put books away neatly, so they got yelled at. It is highly dubious that his teacher's moralizing was stimulating his or any of the children's moral development, but this type of "moral teaching" is almost inevitable in an educational system in which teachers have no explicit or thought-out conception of the aims and methods of moral education and simply focus upon immediate classroom management in their moralizing.

Ambiguities in "Character Education"

The value problems of moral education, then, do not concern the necessity of engaging in moral education in the school, since this is already being done every day. Value problems arise from the formulation of the aims and content of such education. At an extreme, the formulation of aims suggests a conception of moral education as the imposition of a state-determined set of values, first by the bureaucrats upon the teachers, and then by the teachers upon the children. This is the "character education" employed in Russia, as described by Bronfenbrenner.[4] In Russia the entire classroom process is explicitly defined as "character education"—that is, as making good socialist citizens—and the teacher appears to have a very strong influence upon children's moral standards. This influence rests in part upon the fact that the teacher is perceived as "the priest of society," as the agent of the all-powerful state, and can readily enlist the parents as agents of discipline to enforce school values and demands. In part, however, it rests upon the fact that the teacher systematically uses the peer group as an agent of moral indoctrination and moral sanctions. The classroom is divided into cooperating groups in competition with one another. If a member of one of the groups is guilty of misconduct, the teacher downgrades or penalizes the whole group, and the group in turn punishes the individual miscreant. This is, of course, an extremely effective form of social control if not of moral development.

In contrast to the Russian educators, American educators are not likely to take obedience to, and service to, the state as the ultimate content of moral education. Instead, when they have attempted to formulate some general notions of the content and aims of moral education, they have usually conceived of it as the inculcation of a set of virtues: honesty, responsibility, service, self-control, etc.[5] The implicit rationale for the definition of moral education in terms of virtues or character traits has been that it represents the core of moral agreement in the American community. In fact, however, community consensus on verbal labels like "honesty" conceals a great deal of disagreement about what "honesty" is and when it should be compromised to serve another value or virtue. This is indicated by the results of a recent National Opinion Research Center survey of a representative sample of American adults concerning judgments of right or wrong in situations involving honesty.[6] While in general "dishonest" behavior was said to be wrong, lying, stealing, or cheating was said to be "all right" or not "dishonest" by very sizable proportions of the population in certain specific situations. A majority believe it is right to lie to spare another's feelings, a substantial minority believe it is right to steal to obtain expensive medical treatment for one's wife that is otherwise unobtainable, a considerable minority believe it is all right to take hotel ashtrays and towels, etc. As soon as one leaves vague stereotypical terms like "honesty" and attempts to specify concrete moral actions, then, it becomes very difficult to empirically establish consensus concerning moral values. Does 51 per cent agreement represent moral consensus, does 75 per cent, or does 100 per cent? If the latter, our society has no moral consensus. The problem becomes worse if one considers virtues or character traits other than honesty. The lack of agreement about "moral character" appears when it is recognized that each educator draws up a different list of virtues. Havighurst and Taba [7] include friendliness and moral courage in the list, while Hartshorne and May [8] leave these out and include self-control (persistence). "Religious" virtues (faith, hope, and charity) are hard to distinguish from "civil" virtues. What about "respect for authority"—is that a virtue or not? How about cleanliness—is it next to godliness?

Criticism of Present Content of Moral Education

My criticism of statements of the content of moral education in terms of moral character traits rests on three grounds. First, it is impossible to define the content of moral education in terms of factual majority consensus about good and bad behavior. Though the majority may agree upon the value of cleanliness and proper dress, this does not answer the question of whether it is legitimate "moral education" for a school principal to expel boys whose families allow them to wear long hair. In the second place, even if one were willing to accept a majority opinion as defining moral education, vague character traits or labels do not represent majority consensus, since they conceal a great *lack* of consensus about specific actions and values. A parent will agree with a teacher that "cooperation" is a virtue, but he will not agree that a child's specific "cooperation" is a virtue, but he will not agree that a child's specific failure to obey an "unreasonable" request by the teacher was wrong, even if the teacher calls the act "uncooperative," as teachers are prone to do. In the third place, even if one were willing to ignore the lack of consensus concealed by moral character terms, these terms do not represent objective or observable behavioral outcomes of moral education. Psychologically, there are no such traits as honesty, service, responsibility, etc. Research to date suggests that these words are only varying evaluative labels; they do not stand for separate consistent traits of personality. Insofar as consistencies of personality appear in the moral domain, they are quite different from labels of virtues and vices.[9]

II
THE DEVELOPMENT OF MORAL JUDGMENT

I have so far objected to two conceptions of moral education.

The first is the current thoughtless system of moralizing by individual teachers and principals when children deviate from minor administrative regulations or engage in behavior which is personally annoying to the teacher. The second is the effort to inculcate the majority values, particularly as reflected in vague stereotypes about moral character. I shall now present a third conception of moral education. In this conception, the goal of moral education is the stimulation of the "natural" development of the individual child's own moral judgment and of the capacities allowing him to use his own moral judgment to control his behavior. The attractiveness of defining the goal of moral education as the stimulation of development rather than as teaching fixed virtues is that it means aiding the child to take the next step in a direction toward which he is already tending, rather than imposing an alien pattern upon him. Furthermore, I will claim that the stimulation of natural development as the basis of moral education coincides with my earlier statement that the legitimate moral values that the school may transmit are the values of justice.[10]

Research Findings

This third conception of moral education rests on some recent research findings for its plausibility. These findings suggest that liberty and justice are not the particular values of the American culture but culturally universal moral values which develop regardless of religious membership, education, or belief. This contention is based primarily on my own studies of the development of moral values in hundreds of boys aged nine to twenty-three in various American communities, in a Taiwanese city, in a Malaysian (Atayal) aboriginal village, in a Turkish city and village, in a Mexican city, and in a Mayan Indian village.[11] The boys were interviewed about a variety of standard moral conflict situations and their responses were classified into the system of stages defined in Table 1. Classification was made in terms of placement of each moral idea or judgment of the child in a given stage with regard to one of twenty-five aspects of morality. Table 2 lists these twenty-five aspects, and an example of statements placed in each stage for one of the aspects, "The Basis of Worth of Human Life," is presented in Table 3.

The assertion that the stages of Table 1 are genuine stages implies invariant sequence, i.e., that each individual child must go step by step through each of the kinds of moral judgment outlined. It is, of course, possible for a child to move at varying speeds and to stop (become "fixated") at any level of development, but if he continues to move upward he must move in this stepwise fashion. Although the findings on this issue have not been completely analyzed, a longitudinal study of the same American boys studied at ages ten, thirteen, sixteen, and nineteen suggests that such is the case.

The finding of sequence is extremely important for the assertion that Stages 5 and 6, i.e., stages focusing morality upon principles of justice, are indeed higher stages. In Figure 1 the age trends of the use of each stage of moral judgment for American and Taiwanese boys are presented. In the United States the "higher stages" are still minority stages in the adult American population, even though Stage 5 constitutes the public morality of the Constitution and the Supreme Court. These stages, though they represent the minority, are nonetheless developmentally more advanced because boys in Stage 5 or 6 have gone through the previous stages whereas the boys in the lower stages have not gone through Stage 5 or 6.

The assertion that the stages are culturally universal rests on evidence like that presented in Figure 1. Figure 1 indicates much the same age trends in both the Taiwanese and the American boys. In both groups the first two stages decrease with age, the next two increase until age thirteen and then stabilize, and the last two continue to increase from age thirteen to age sixteen. In general, the cross-cultural studies suggest a similar sequence of development in all cultures, although they suggest that the last two stages of moral thought do not develop clearly in preliterate village or tribal communities.

Questions of the existence of culturally universal moral stages differ somewhat from questions of the dominant public morality of a society. Under certain conditions of social conflict and stress it is possible for the public morality of a society to be formulated by individuals at a lower level of development than the average, as

TABLE 1

Classification of Moral Judgment into Levels
and Stages of Development

Levels	Basis of Moral Judgment	Stages of Development
I	Moral value resides in external, quasi-physical happenings, in bad acts, or in quasi-physical needs rather than in persons and standards.	*Stage 1:* Obedience and punishment orientation. Egocentric deference to superior power or prestige, or a trouble-avoiding set. Objective responsibility.
		Stage 2: Naïvely egoistic orientation. Right action is that instrumentally satisfying the self's needs and occasionally others'. Awareness of relativism of value to each actor's needs and perspective. Naïve egalitarianism and orientation to exchange and reciprocity.
II	Moral value resides in performing good or right roles, in maintaining the conventional order and the expectancies of others.	*Stage 3:* Good-boy orientation. Orientation to approval and to pleasing and helping others. Conformity to stereotypical images of majority or natural role behavior, and judgment by intentions.
		Stage 4: Authority and social-order maintaining orientation. Orientation to "doing duty" and to showing respect for authority and maintaining the given social order for its own sake. Regard for earned expectations of others.
III	Moral value resides in conformity by the self to shared or shareable standards, rights, or duties.	*Stage 5:* Contractual legalistic orientation. Recognition of an arbitrary element or starting point in rules or expectations for the sake of agreement. Duty defined in terms of contract, general avoidance of violation of the will or rights of others, and majority will and welfare.
		Stage 6: Conscience or principle orientation. Orientation not only to actually ordained social rules but to principles of choice involving appeal to logical universality and consistency. Orientation to conscience as a directing agent and to mutual respect and trust.

TABLE 2

Coded Aspects of Developing Moral Judgment

Code	Description	Aspects
I. *Value*	Locus of value—modes of attributing (moral) value to acts, persons, or events. Modes of assessing value consequences in a situation.	1. Considering motives in judging action. 2. Considering consequences in judging action. 3. Subjectivity vs. objectivity of values assessed. 4. Relation of obligation to wish. 5. Identification with actor or victims in judging the action. 6. Status of actor and victim as changing the moral worth of actions.
II. *Choice*	Mechanisms of resolving or denying awareness of conflicts.	7. Limiting actor's responsibility for consequences by shifting responsibility onto others. 8. Reliance on discussion and compromise, mainly unrealistically. 9. Distorting situation so that conforming behavior is seen as always maximizing the interests of the actor or of others involved.
III. *Sanctions and Motives*	The dominant motives and sanctions for moral or deviant action.	10. Punishment or negative reactions. 11. Disruption of an interpersonal relationship. 12. A concern by actor for welfare, for positive state of the other. 13. Self-condemnation.
IV. *Rules*	The ways in which rules are conceptualized, applied, and generalized. The basis of the validity of a rule.	14. Definition of an act as deviant. (Definition of moral rules and norms.) 15. Generality and consistency of rules. 16. Waiving rules for personal relations (particularism).
V. *Rights and Authority*	Basis and limits of control over persons and property.	17. Non-motivational attributes ascribed to authority (knowledge, etc.). (Motivational attributes considered under *III* above.) 18. Extent or scope of authority's rights. Rights of liberty. 19. Rights of possession or property.

TABLE 2 (CONTINUED)

Code	Description	Aspects
VI. *Positive Justice*	Reciprocity and equality.	20. Exchange and reciprocity as a motive for role conformity. 21. Reciprocity as a motive to deviate (e.g., revenge). 22. Distributive justice. Equality and impartiality. 23. Concepts of maintaining partner's expectations as a motive for conformity. Contract and trust.
VII. *Punitive Justice*	Standards and functions of punishment.	24. Punitive tendencies or expectations. (a) Notions of equating punishment and crime. 25. Functions or purpose of punishment.

happened under the Nazis. To indicate this possibility, Table 4 presents a sample of moral statements by Eichmann, almost all scored as Stage 1 and Stage 2 by various raters using a carefully defined rating manual. (Moral statements from Hitler's *Mein Kampf* are different in tone but are also scored mainly as Stage 1 or Stage 2.)

On the whole, however, public morality tends to be expressed or formulated by individuals capable of articulating a more advanced morality than that of the average man. It has been found experimentally [12] that preadolescents will learn or assimilate moral argumentation one level above their own more readily than they will assimilate moral argumentation one level below their own. Furthermore, though they do not learn or assimilate much of moral arguments two or more stages above their own, they choose them as "liked" much more than lower-level arguments. Active members of civil rights movements may often be moved by low-level themes of "black power," but most leaders of the movement, like Martin Luther King, tend to formulate reasons for civil disobedience in Stage 6 terms. It is not surprising, then, that most presidential and Supreme Court utterances are consistent with our definitions of Stage 5 (or Stage 6 in the case of Lincoln and others), even though they are above the majority level of response.

TABLE 3

Classification of Statements on One Aspect of Morality ("The Basis of Worth of Human Life") into Stages in the Development of Moral Judgment

Stages	Statements on "The Basis of Worth of Human Life"
Stage 1: The value of a human life is confused with the value of physical objects and is based on the social status or physical attributes of its possessor.	*Tommy, age ten* (Why should the druggist give the drug to the dying woman when her husband couldn't pay for it?) "If someone important is in a plane and is allergic to heights and the stewardess won't give him medicine because she's only got enough for one and she's got a sick one, a friend, in back, they'd probably put the stewardess in a lady's jail because she didn't help the important one." (Is it better to save the life of one important person or a lot of unimportant people?): "All the people that aren't important because one man just has one house, maybe a lot of furniture, but a whole bunch of people have an awful lot of furniture and some of these poor people might have a lot of money and it doesn't look it."
Stage 2: The value of a human life is seen as instrumental to the satisfaction of the needs of its possessor or of other persons.	*Tommy, age thirteen* (Should the doctor "mercy kill" a fatally ill woman requesting death because of her pain?): "Maybe it would be good to put her out of her pain, she'd be better off that way. But the husband wouldn't want it, it's not like an animal. If a pet dies you can get along without it—it isn't something you really need. Well, you can get a new wife, but it's not really the same."

TABLE 3 (CONTINUED)

Stages	Statements on "The Basis of Worth of Human Life"
Stage 3: The value of a human life is based on the empathy and affection of family members and others toward its possessor.	*Andy, age sixteen* (Should the doctor "mercy kill" a fatally ill woman requesting death because of her pain?): "No, he shouldn't. The husband loves her and wants to see her. He wouldn't want her to die sooner, he loves her too much."
Stage 4: Life is conceived as sacred in terms of its place in a categorical moral or religious order of rights and duties.	*John, age sixteen* (Should the doctor "mercy kill" the woman?): "The doctor wouldn't have the right to take a life, no human has the right. He can't create life, he shouldn't destroy it."
Stage 5: Life is valued both in terms of its relation to community welfare and in terms of being a universal human right.	*Bob, age sixteen* (Should the captain order the soldier on a suicide mission to save the company?): "If nobody wanted to volunteer, I don't think he has the right to make someone go. I don't know if the army rules give him the right not to go, but as a person in the world I think he has the right not to go. But if it would save so many other lives, he really should go. The captain would have to decide to send him if it's necessary to save all their lives."
Stage 6: Belief in the sacredness of human life as representing a universal human value of respect for the individual.	*Steve, age sixteen* (Should the husband steal the expensive drug to save his wife?): "By the law of society he was wrong but by the law of nature or of God the druggist was wrong and the husband was justified. Human life is above financial gain. Regardless of who was dying, if it was a total stranger, man has a duty to save him from dying."

FIGURE 1

*Mean Per Cent of Use of Each of Six Stages
of Moral Judgment*

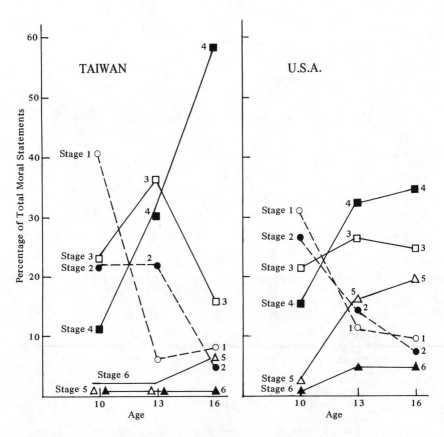

A Universal Definition of Morality

Moral development in terms of these stages is a progressive movement toward basing moral judgment on concepts of justice. To base a moral duty on a concept of justice is to base it on the right of an individual, and to judge an act wrong is to judge it as violating such a right. The concept of a right implies a legitimate

TABLE 4

Scoring of Moral Judgments of Eichmann
for Developmental Stage

Moral Judgments	Score *
In actual fact, I was merely a little cog in the machinery that carried out the directives of the German Reich.	1/7
I am neither a murderer nor a mass-murderer. I am a man of average character, with good qualities and many faults.	3/1
Yet what is there to "admit"? I carried out my orders. It would be pointless to blame me for the whole Final Solution of the Jewish Problem as to blame the official in charge of the railroads over which the Jewish transports traveled.	1/7
Where would we have been if everyone had thought things out in those days? You can do that today in the "new" German army. But with us an order was an order.	1/15
If I had sabotaged the order of the one-time Führer of the German Reich, Adolf Hitler, I would have been not only a scoundrel but a despicable pig like those who broke their military oath to join the ranks of the anti-Hitler criminals in the conspiracy of July 20, 1944.	1/1 1/1
I would like to stress again, however, that my department never gave a single annihilation order. We were responsible only for deportation.	2/7
My interest was only in the number of transport trains I had to provide. Whether they were bank directors or mental cases, the people who were loaded on these trains meant nothing to me. It was really none of my business.	2/3 2/7
But to sum it all up, I must say that I regret nothing. Adolf Hitler may have been wrong all down the line, but one thing is beyond dispute: the man was able to work his way up from lance corporal in the German army to Führer of a people of almost eighty million. I never met him personally, but his success alone proves to me that I should subordinate myself to this man. He was somehow so supremely capable that the people recognized him. And so with that justification I recognized him joyfully, and I still defend him.	1/6 1/17
I must say truthfully, that if we had killed all the ten million Jews that Himmler's statisticians originally listed in 1933, I would say, "Good, we have destroyed an enemy."	2/21
But here I do not mean wiping them out entirely. That would not be proper—and we carried on a proper war.	1/1

* The first code number in this column refers to Stages 1-6 (see Table 1); the second number refers to the aspect of morality involved (see Table 2).

expectancy, a claim which I may expect others to agree I have. Though rights may be grounded on sheer custom or law, there are two general grounds of a right: equality and reciprocity (including exchange, contract, and the reward of merit). At Stages 5 and 6, all the demands of statute or of moral (natural) law are grounded on concepts of justice, i.e., on the agreement, contract, and impartiality of the law and its function in maintaining the rights of individuals. For reasons I have elaborated elsewhere,[13] it is quite reasonable psychologically to expect similar conceptions of justice to develop in every society, whether or not they become the official basis of political morality as they have in the United States.

To a large extent, a conception of moral development in terms of justice coincides with a culturally universal definition of morality. In my view, a culturally universal definition of morality can be arrived at if morality is thought of as the form of moral judgments instead of the content of specific moral beliefs. Although philosophers have been unable to agree upon any single ultimate principle which would define "correct" moral judgments, most philosophers concur on the characteristics which make a judgment a genuine moral judgment.[14]

Moral judgments are judgments about the right and the good of action. Not all judgments of "good" or "right" are moral judgments, however; many are judgments of aesthetic, technological, or prudential goodness or rightness. Unlike judgments of prudence or aesthetics, moral judgments tend to be universal, inclusive, consistent, and to be grounded on objective, impersonal, or ideal grounds. "She's really great! She's beautiful and a good dancer." "The right way to make a Martini is five-to-one." These are statements about the good and right, but they are not moral judgments since they lack the characteristics of the latter. If we say, "Martinis should be made five-to-one," we are making an aesthetic judgment; we are not prepared to say that we want everyone to make them that way, that they are good in terms of some impersonal ideal standard shared by others, and that we and others should make five-to-one Martinis whether we wish to or not.

In similar fashion, when a ten-year-old answers a "moral should" question, "Should Joe tell on his older brother?" in Stage 1 terms of the probabilities of getting beaten up by his father and by his brother, he does not answer with a moral judgment that is universal (applies to all about the situation) or that has any impersonal or ideal grounds. In contrast, Stage 6 statements not only specifically use moral words like "morally right" and "duty" but use them in a moral way: "Regardless of who it was," "By the law of nature or of God," imply universality; "Morally I would do it in spite of fear of punishment" implies impersonality and ideality of obligation, etc. Thus the responses of lower-level subjects to moral judgment matters are not moral responses in somewhat the same sense that the value judgments of high-level subjects about aesthetic or morally neutral matters are not moral. In this sense, we can define a moral judgment as "moral" without considering its content (the action judged) and without considering whether it agrees with our own judgments or standards. It is evident that our stages represent an increasing disentangling or differentiation of moral values and judgments from other types of values and judgments. With regard to the particular aspect, the value of life, defined in Table 2, the moral value of the person at Stage 6 has become progressively disentangled from status and property values (Stage 1), from his instrumental uses to others (Stage 2), from the actual affection of others for him (Stage 3), etc.

A definition of the aim of moral education as the stimulation of natural development appears, then, to be clear-cut in the area of moral judgment, which has considerable regularity of sequence and direction in development in various cultures. Because of this regularity, it is possible to define the maturity of a child's moral judgment without considering its content (the particular action judged) and without considering whether or not it agrees with our own particular moral judgments or values or those of the American middle-class culture as a whole. In fact, the sign of the child's moral maturity is his ability to make moral judgments and formulate moral principles of his own, rather than his ability to conform to moral judgments of the adults around him.

III
MORAL JUDGMENT AND MORAL BEHAVIOR

We have so far talked about the development of moral judgment as an aim of moral education. The sheer capacity to make genuinely moral judgments is only one portion of moral character, however. One must also apply this judgmental capacity to the actual guidance and criticism of action. Thus, in addition to stimulating the development of general moral judgment, a developmental moral education would stimulate the child's application of his own moral judgment (not the teacher's) to his actions. The effort to force a child to agree that an act of cheating is very bad when he does not really believe it will only encourage morally immature tendencies toward expedient outward compliance. In contrast, a more difficult but more valid approach involves getting the child to examine the pros and cons of his conduct in his own terms (as well as introducing more developmentally advanced considerations).

Although we cannot yet be sure that the stimulation of development of moral judgment will result in moral conduct, research indicating considerable correspondence between level of judgment and conduct in children provides some optimism on this score.[15]

IV
MORALITY AND RELIGION

It is clear that the conception of the words "moral" and "moral education" just advanced distinguishes moral judgment and development from other types of value judgment and development, including religious development. In fact, we find remarkably little use of religion in American children's responses to moral dilemmas, regardless of denomination. In less religiously pluralistic societies, like Turkey, more religious concepts are introduced into moral responses, but mostly at lower levels of development (Stages 1 through 4). Preadolescent Turkish boys typically say that one should not steal because "good Moslems don't steal" and because "God would punish you." They also believe it is worse to steal from a fellow Moslem than from a Christian. As they develop further, they elaborate more intrinsically moral or justice-based reasons for not stealing and use less "religious" reasons. At higher levels, religion may be invoked as the ultimate support for universal human values, but moral action is not justified in terms of conformity to God or to the religious community. Because a morality of justice evolves in every society or religious group, then, a morality of justice cannot be said to represent the beliefs of a religious sect like Humanism or Ethical Culture, or even to represent the "Judeo-Christian tradition."

Our evidence of culturally universal moral stages, then, is also direct evidence against the view that the development of moral ideologies depends upon the teachings of particular religious belief systems. No differences in moral development due to religious belief have yet been found. Protestant, Catholic, Moslem, and Buddhist children go through the same stages at much the same rate when social class and village-urban differences are held constant. With regard to the content of moral beliefs, religious differences exist, e.g., differences in views of birth control, divorce, eating pork, etc. When members of given religious groups attempt to support these beliefs, however, they fall back upon the general forms of moral judgment or moral principles described by the stages discussed above, forms which I said develop regardless of religious affiliation. The same distinctions between specific values and basic moral principles must be made in considering sociological studies of religious differences in values. For instance, values of educational and entrepreneurial achievement have been held to be favored by "the Protestant ethic" or the "Jewish ethic" as opposed to the "Catholic ethic." There is considerable evidence of such differential emphases in various religious traditions, but it should not obscure the common moral ideas and principles which seem to develop equally in all. All religious and non-religious belief systems distinguish worldly achievement from conformity to moral principles and stress the latter regardless of different notions of the linkage between the two.

Religious persons may readily accept the idea that moral principles develop regardless of religious belief. Since St. Thomas Aquinas, a great deal of theological doctrine has held that moral principles are grounded on natural reason rather than on revelation. It is more difficult, however, for most religious persons to accept the thought that actual behavioral adherence to moral principles is independent of religious belief or commitment. They feel that their morality and their religion are closely bound together. In a recent nationwide National Opinion Research Center survey, a large majority of Americans stated that their morality was dependent upon their religious beliefs. Subjectively they may be correct. Objectively, however, empirical studies, from Hartshorne and May [16] onward, have found no relation between experimental measures of honesty and type or amount of religious participation or education. Cross-national comparisons suggest the same conclusions as the Hartshorne and May findings. Theft, deceit, and juvenile delinquency are low in some atheistic societies (Soviet Russia, Israeli atheistic kibbutzim) as well as in some Buddhist and Christian societies, while some strongly religious nations have high rates of dishonesty (Islamic Middle Eastern nations, Italy, Mexico, etc.). Although we should not conclude from these and other findings that there is no relation between religious experience and moral character, we can conclude that religion is not a necessary or highly important condition for the development of moral judgment and conduct.[17]

In summarizing findings suggesting the very limited influence of religious education upon moral development, I am not attempting to argue that religious education may not be capable of playing a role in moral development. I am arguing that formal religious education has no specifically important or unique role to play in moral development as opposed to the role of the public school and the family in this area. The primary purpose of religious education in our society is not to develop moral character but rather to develop religious beliefs and sentiments. The teaching of religious beliefs requires a teaching of their moral aspects as well as their theological aspects, since all religions stress an associated moral code. On the whole, however, the mark of success of such teaching is that it helps the child to make his religious and his moral beliefs and sentiments an integrated whole, not that it leads to the formulation of basic moral values not formed elsewhere. Part-time religious education can hardly take as its goal fitting the child for moral citizenship, and is fortunate if it can achieve its primary goal of creating religious meanings in the child's experience.

V

THE CLASSROOM CLIMATE

In contrast to institutions of part-time religious education, the public school is the most important environment of the child outside the home. While the Hartshorne and May findings did not show that specific religious or character education classes had a strong effect on moral conduct, they did demonstrate that the total school or classroom atmosphere had an extremely important influence on such conduct. By and large, basic morality develops "naturally" through a variety of intellectual and social stimulations in the home, the peer group, and the school; it does not require systematic programs of indoctrination. However, recent research suggests that the school may play a positive role in stimulating this development and suggests some lines along which it may be done.[18] Regardless of quantitative findings, the definition of the public school as fitting the child for citizenship and the pervasiveness of moral issues in classroom life and curriculum require explicit educational thought about the moral objectives of education. As an example, recent unpublished work by Grannis at Harvard suggests that teaching comprehension of law in an experimental social studies curriculum for preadolescents entails just the sort of stimulation of upward movement of stages of moral thought one might elaborate if one were concerned with moral education as an explicit school function. It would be unfortunate, then, if the outcome of the recent Supreme Court decision were to inhibit our recognition that an ultimate statement of the social aims and processes of public education must be couched in moral terms.

NOTES

1. L. Kohlberg, "Moral Education in the Schools: A Developmental View," *School Review*, 74:1-30 (1966).

2. My philosophical reasoning as to the relation of the schools to moral education is hardly original. It is largely a restatement of John Dewey (*Moral Principles in Education* [Houghton Mifflin, 1911]) and "The Schools

and Religion" in *Character and Events* (Holt, 1929). A recent statement by the philosopher Michael Scriven (*Primary Philosophy* [McGraw-Hill, 1966]) forcefully develops a basically similar position, except that he advocates direct teaching of rational morality whereas I advocate indirect stimulating of its development.

3. I have attempted elsewhere (L. Kohlberg, *State and Sequence: The Developmental Approach to Moralization* [in preparation]) to define terms like "morality" and "justice" more explicitly and in a fashion which allows study of these concepts in any culture or society.

4. U. Bronfenbrenner, "Soviet Methods of Character Education: Some Implications for Research," *American Psychologist,* 17:550-565 (1962).

5. H. Hartshorne and M. A. May, *Studies in the Nature of Character:* Vol. I, *Studies in Deceit;* Vol. II, *Studies in Self-Control;* Vol. III, *Studies in the Organization of Character* (Macmillan, 1928-1930). V. Jones, *Character and Citizenship Gaining in the Public School* (University of Chicago Press, 1936). R. J. Havighurst and H. Taba, *Adolescent Character and Personality* (Wiley, 1949).

6. Unpublished data, some reported on an NBC television special in January, 1966.

7. Havighurst and Taba, *op. cit.*

8. Hartshorne and May, *op. cit.*

9. L. Kohlberg, "The Development of Moral Character and Ideology," in M. and L. Hoffman (eds.), *Review of Child Development Research* (Russell Sage, 1964).

10. Justice (respect for the rights of others based on considerations of equality and reciprocity) includes the other cardinal American value of liberty. It also partially includes the second major moral value of benevolence (consideration of the welfare of all other individuals).

11. Kohlberg, "Moral Education in the Schools," and *Stage and Sequence: The Developmental Approach to Moralization.*

12. E. Turiel, "An Experimental Analysis of Developmental Stages in the Child's Moral Judgment," *Journal of Personality and Social Psychology,* 1966.

13. Kohlberg, *Stage and Sequence.*

14. R. M. Hare, *The Language of Morals* (New York: Oxford University Press, 1952) and I. Kant, *Fundamental Principles of the Metaphysics of Morals* (New York: Liberal Arts Press, 1949).

15. Kohlberg, "Moral Education in the Schools."

16. Hartshorne and May, *op. cit.*

17. Relations between conduct and religious experience may be more apparent where the given moral behavior depends largely upon specific religious proscriptions than where it is based upon general secular principles of justice. In contrast to findings on honesty, Kinsey (A. C. Kinsey *et al., Sexual Behavior in the Human Female* [W. B. Saunders, 1953]) indicates that both premarital and extramarital sexual behavior is related to religious devoutness and, to a slighter extent, to religious denomination. The suggestion is also that subjective moral attitudes may be related to moral behavior even if the amount of institutional religious exposure is

not. However, we cannot safely draw either of these conclusions because moral attitudes may determine religious ones rather than the reverse. For example, the Kinsey finding may be due to the tendency of young people who fear or condemn sexuality to become religiously devout rather than vice versa.

18. Kohlberg, "Moral Education in the Schools."

20 A Theory of Justice

JOHN RAWLS *

M y aim is to present a conception of justice which generalizes and carries to a higher level of abstraction the familiar theory of the social contract as found, say, in Locke, Rousseau, and Kant.[1] In order to do this we are not to think of the original contract as one to enter a particular society or to set up a particular form of government. Rather, the guiding idea is that the principles of justice for the basic structure of society are the object of the original agreement. They are the principles that free and rational persons concerned to further their own interests would accept in an initial position of equality as defining the fundamental terms of their association. These principles are to regulate all further agreements; they specify the kinds of social cooperation that can be entered into and the forms of government that can be established. This way of regarding the principles of justice I shall call justice as fairness.

Thus we are to imagine that those who engage in social cooperation choose together, in one joint act, the principles which are to assign basic rights and duties and to determine the division

* Reprinted with permission of the publishers from John Rawls, *A Theory of Justice* (Cambridge, Mass.: The Belknap Press of Harvard University Press, and Oxford: The Clarendon Press, Copyright, 1971, by the President and Fellows of Harvard College), pp. 11-17, 46-53, and 577-587.

of social benefits. Men are to decide in advance how they are to
regulate their claims against one another and what is to be the
foundation charter of their society. Just as each person must decide
by rational reflection what constitutes his good, that is, the system
of ends which it is rational for him to pursue, so a group of persons
must decide once and for all what is to count among them as just
and unjust. The choice which rational men would make in this
hypothetical situation of equal liberty, assuming for the present
that this choice problem has a solution, determines the principles
of justice.

In justice as fairness the original position of quality corre-
sponds to the state of nature in the traditional theory of the social
contract. This original position is not, of course, thought of as an
actual historical state of affairs, much less as a primitive condition
of culture. It is understood as a purely hypothetical situation characterized so as to lead to a certain conception of justice.[2] Among
the essential features of this situation is that no one knows his place
in society, his class position or social status, nor does anyone know
his fortune in the distribution of natural assets and abilities, his
intelligence, strength, and the like. I shall even assume that the
parties do not know their conceptions of the good or their special
psychological propensities. The principles of justice are chosen
behind a veil of ignorance. This ensures that no one is advantaged
or disadvantaged in the choice of principles by the outcome of
natural chance or the contingency of social circumstances. Since all
are similarly situated and no one is able to design principles to favor
his particular condition, the principles of justice are the result of a
fair agreement or bargain. For given the circumstances of the
original position, the symmetry of everyone's relations to each other,
this initial situation is fair between individuals as moral persons,
that is, as rational beings with their own ends and capable, I shall
assume, of a sense of justice. The original position is, one might
say, the appropriate initial status quo, and thus the fundamental
agreements reached in it are fair. This explains the propriety of
the name "justice as fairness": it conveys the idea that the principles of justice are agreed to in an initial situation that is fair. The
name does not mean that the concepts of justice and fairness are the

same, any more than the phrase "poetry as metaphor" means that the concepts of poetry and metaphor are the same.

Justice as fairness begins, as I have said, with one of the most general of all choices which persons might make together, namely, with the choice of the first principles of a conception of justice which is to regulate all subsequent criticism and reform of institutions. Then, having chosen a conception of justice, we can suppose that they are to choose a constitution and a legislature to enact laws, and so on, all in accordance with the principles of justice initially agreed upon. Our social situation is just if it is such that by this sequence of hypothetical agreements we would have contracted into the general system of rules which defines it. Moreover, assuming that the original position does determine a set of principles (that is, that a particular conception of justice would be chosen), it will then be true that whenever social institutions satisfy these principles those engaged in them can say to one another that they are cooperating on terms to which they would agree if they were free and equal persons whose relations with respect to one another were fair. They could all view their arrangements as meeting the stipulations which they would acknowledge in an initial situation that embodies widely accepted and reasonable constraints on the choice of principles. The general recognition of this fact would provide the basis for a public acceptance of the corresponding principles of justice. No society can, of course, be a scheme of cooperation which men enter voluntarily in a literal sense; each person finds himself placed at birth in some particular position in some particular society, and the nature of this position materially affects his life prospects. Yet a society satisfying the principles of justice as fairness comes as close as a society can to being a voluntary scheme, for it meets the principles which free and equal persons would assent to under circumstances that are fair. In this sense its members are autonomous and the obligations they recognize self-imposed.

One feature of justice as fairness is to think of the parties in the initial situation as rational and mutually disinterested. This does not mean that the parties are egoists, that is, individuals with only certain kinds of interests, say in wealth, prestige, and domina-

tion. But they are conceived as not taking an interest in one another's interests. They are to presume that even their spiritual aims
may be opposed, in the way that the aims of those of different religions may be opposed. Moreover, the concept of rationality must
be interpreted as far as possible in the narrow sense, standard in
economic theory, of taking the most effective means to given ends.
I shall modify this concept to some extent, as explained later,
but one must try to avoid introducing into it any controversial
ethical elements. The initial situation must be characterized by
stipulations that are widely accepted.

In working out the conception of justice as fairness one main
task clearly is to determine which principles of justice would be
chosen in the original position. To do this we must describe this
situation in some detail and formulate with care the problem of
choice which it presents. . . . It may be observed . . . that once
the principles of justice are thought of as arising from an original agreement in a situation of equality, it is an open question
whether the principle of utility would be acknowledged. Offhand it
hardly seems likely that persons who view themselves as equals,
entitled to press their claims upon one another, would agree to a
principle which may require lesser life prospects for some simply
for the sake of a greater sum of advantages enjoyed by others.
Since each desires to protect his interests, his capacity to advance
his conception of the good, no one has a reason to acquiesce
in an enduring loss for himself in order to bring about a greater net
balance of satisfaction. In the absence of strong and lasting benevo-
lent impulses, a rational man would not accept a basic structure
merely because it maximized the algebraic sum of advantages
irrespective of its permanent effects on his own basic rights and
interests. Thus it seems that the principle of utility is incompatible
with the conception of social cooperation among equals for mutual
advantage. It appears to be inconsistent with the idea of reciprocity
implicit in the notion of a well-ordered society. Or, at any rate, so
I shall argue.

I shall maintain instead that the persons in the initial situation
would choose two rather different principles: the first requires
equality in the assignment of basic rights and duties, while the
second holds that social and economic inequalities, for example

inequalities of wealth and authority, are just only if they result in compensating benefits for everyone, and in particular for the least advantaged members of society. These principles rule out justifying institutions on the grounds that the hardships of some are offset by a greater good in the aggregate. It may be expedient but it is not just that some should have less in order that others may prosper. But there is no injustice in the greater benefits earned by a few provided that the situation of persons not so fortunate is thereby improved. The intuitive idea is that since everyone's well-being depends upon a scheme of cooperation without which no one could have a satisfactory life, the division of advantages should be such as to draw forth the willing cooperation of everyone taking part in it, including those less well situated. Yet this can be expected only if reasonable terms are proposed. The two principles mentioned seem to be a fair agreement on the basis of which those better endowed, or more fortunate in their social position, neither of which we can be said to deserve, could expect the willing cooperation of others when some workable scheme is a necessary condition of the welfare of all.[3] Once we decide to look for a conception of justice that nullifies the accidents of natural endowment and the contingencies of social circumstance as counters in quest for political and economic advantage, we are led to these principles. They express the result of leaving aside those aspects of the social world that seem arbitrary from a moral point of view.

The problem of the choice of principles, however, is extremely difficult. I do not expect the answer I shall suggest to be convincing to everyone. It is, therefore, worth noting from the outset that justice as fairness, like other contract views, consists of two parts: (1) an interpretation of the initial situation and of the problem of choice posed there, and (2) a set of principles which, it is argued, would be agreed to. One may accept the first part of the theory (or some variant thereof), but not the other, and conversely. The concept of the initial contractual situation may seem reasonable although the particular principles proposed are rejected. To be sure, I want to maintain that the most appropriate conception of this situation does lead to principles of justice contrary to utilitarianism and perfectionism, and therefore that the contract doctrine provides an alternative to these views. Still, one may dispute this contention even though one grants that the contractarian method is a useful way of studying ethical theories and of setting forth their underlying assumptions.

Justice as fairness is an example of what I have called a contract theory. Now there may be an objection to the term "contract" and related expressions, but I think it will serve reasonably well. Many words have misleading connotations which at first are likely to confuse. The terms "utility" and "utilitarianism" are surely no exception. They too have unfortunate suggestions which hostile critics have been willing to exploit; yet they are clear enough for those prepared to study utilitarian doctrine. The same should be true of the term "contract" applied to moral theories. As I have mentioned, to understand it one has to keep in mind that it implies a certain level of abstraction. In particular, the content of the relevant agreement is not to enter a given society or to adopt a given form of government, but to accept certain moral principles. Moreover, the undertakings referred to are purely hypothetical: a contract view holds that certain principles would be accepted in a well-defined initial situation.

The merit of the contract terminology is that it conveys the idea that principles of justice may be conceived as principles that would be chosen by rational persons, and that in this way conceptions of justice may be explained and justified. The theory of justice is a part, perhaps the most significant part, of the theory of rational choice. Furthermore, principles of justice deal with conflicting claims upon the advantages won by social cooperation; they apply to the relations among several persons or groups. The word "contract" suggests this plurality as well as the condition that the appropriate division of advantages must be in accordance with principles acceptable to all parties. The condition of publicity for principles of justice is also connoted by the contract phraseology. Thus, if these principles are the outcome of an agreement, citizens have a knowledge of the principles that others follow. It is characteristic of contract theories to stress the public nature of political principles. Finally there is the long tradition of the contract doctrine. Expressing the tie with this line of thought helps to define ideas and accords with natural piety. There are then several advantages in the use of the term "contract." With due precautions taken, it should not be misleading.

A final remark. Justice as fairness is not a complete contract theory. For it is clear that the contractarian idea can be extended to the choice of more or less an entire ethical system, that is, to a system including principles for all the virtues and not only for justice. Now for the most part I shall consider only principles of justice and others closely related to them; I make no attempt to discuss the virtues in a systematic way. Obviously if justice as fairness succeeds reasonably well, a next step would be to study the more general view suggested by the name "rightness as fairness." But even this wider theory fails to embrace all moral relationships, since it would seem to include only our relations with other persons and to leave out of account how we are to conduct ourselves toward animals and the rest of nature. I do not contend that the contract notion offers a way to approach these questions which are certainly of the first importance; and I shall have to put them aside. We must recognize the limited scope of justice as fairness and of the general type of view that it exemplifies. How far its conclusions must be revised once these other matters are understood cannot be decided in advance. . . .

Some Remarks About Moral Theory

It seems desirable at this point, in order to prevent misunderstanding, to discuss briefly the nature of moral theory. I shall do this by explaining in more detail the concept of a considered judgment in reflective equilibrium and the reasons for introducing it.[4]

Let us assume that each person beyond a certain age and possessed of the requisite intellectual capacity develops a sense of justice under normal social circumstances. We acquire a skill in judging things to be just and unjust, and in supporting these judgments by reasons. Moreover, we ordinarily have some desire to act in accord with these pronouncements and expect a similar desire on the part of others. Clearly this moral capacity is extraordinarily complex. To see this it suffices to note the potentially infinite number and variety of judgments that we are prepared to make. The fact that we often do not know what to say, and sometimes find our minds unsettled, does not detract from the complexity of the capacity we have.

Now one may think of moral philosophy at first (and I stress the provisional nature of this view) as the attempt to describe our moral capacity; or, in the present case, one may regard a theory of justice as describing our sense of justice. This enterprise is very difficult. For by such a description is not meant simply a list of the judgments on institutions and actions that we are prepared to render, accompanied with supporting reasons when these are offered. Rather, what is required is a formulation of a set of principles which, when conjoined to our beliefs and knowledge of the circumstances, would lead us to make these judgments with their supporting reasons were we to apply these principles conscientiously and intelligently. A conception of justice characterizes our moral sensibility when the everyday judgments we do make are in accordance with its principles. These principles can serve as part of the premises of an argument which arrives at the matching judgments. We do not understand our sense of justice until we know in some systematic way covering a wide range of cases what these principles are. Only a deceptive familiarity with our everyday judgments and our natural readiness to make them could conceal the fact that characterizing our moral capacities is an intricate task. The principles which describe them must be presumed to have a complex structure, and the concepts involved will require serious study.

A useful comparison here is with the problem of describing the sense of grammaticalness that we have for the sentences of our native language.[5] In this case the aim is to characterize the ability to recognize well-formed sentences by formulating clearly expressed principles which make the same discriminations as the native speaker. This is a difficult undertaking which, although still unfinished, is known to require theoretical constructions that far outrun the ad hoc precepts of our explicit grammatical knowledge. A similar situation presumably holds in moral philosophy. There is no reason to assume that our sense of justice can be adequately characterized by familiar common sense precepts, or derived from the more obvious learning principles. A correct account of moral capacities will certainly involve principles and theoretical constructions which go much beyond the norms and standards cited in everyday life; it may eventually require fairly sophisticated mathematics as well. This is to be expected, since on the contract view the theory of justice is part of the theory of rational choice. Thus the idea of the original position and of an agreement on principles there does not seem too complicated or unnecessary. Indeed, these notions are rather simple and can serve only as a beginning.

So far, though, I have not said anything about considered judgments. Now, as already suggested, they enter as those judgments in which our moral capacities are most likely to be displayed without distortion. Thus in deciding which of our judgments to take into account we may reasonably select some and exclude others. For example, we can discard those judgments made with hesitation, or in which we have little confidence. Similarly, those given when we are upset or frightened, or when we stand to gain one way or the other can be left aside. All these judgments are likely to be erroneous or to be influenced by an excessive attention to our own interests. Considered judgments are simply those rendered under conditions favorable to the exercise of the sense of justice, and therefore in circumstances where the more common excuses and explanations for making a mistake do not obtain. The person making the judgment is presumed, then, to have the ability, the opportunity, and the desire to reach a correct decision (or at least, not the desire not to). Moreover, the criteria that identify these judgments are not arbitrary. They are, in fact, similar to those that single out considered judgments of any kind. And once we regard the sense of justice as a mental capacity, as involving the exercise of thought, the relevant judgments are those given under conditions favorable for deliberation and judgment in general.

I now turn to the notion of reflective equilibrium. The need for this idea arises as follows. According to the provisional aim of moral philosophy, one might say that justice as fairness is the hypothesis that the principles which would be chosen in the original position are identical with those that match our considered judgments and so these principles describe our sense of justice. But this interpretation is clearly oversimplified. In describing our sense of justice an allowance must be made for the likelihood that considered judgments are no doubt subject to certain irregularities and distortions despite the fact that they are rendered under favorable circumstances. When a person is presented with an intuitively appealing account of his sense of justice (one, say, which embodies various reasonable and natural presumptions), he may well revise his judgments to conform to its principles even though the theory does not fit his existing judgments exactly. He is especially likely to do this if he can find an explanation for the deviations which undermines his confidence in his original judgments and if the conception presented yields a judgment which he finds he can now accept. From the standpoint of moral philosophy, the best account of a person's sense of justice is not the one which fits his judgments prior to his examining any conception of justice, but rather the one which matches his judgments in reflective equilibrium. As we have seen, this state is one reached after a person has weighed various proposed conceptions and he has either revised his judgments to accord with one of them or held fast to his initial convictions (and the corresponding conception).

The notion of reflective equilibrium introduces some complications that call for comment. For one thing, it is a notion characteristic of the study of principles which govern actions shaped by self-examination. Moral philosophy is Socratic: we may want to change our present considered judgments once their regulative principles are brought to light. And we may want to do this even though these principles are a perfect fit. A knowledge of these principles may suggest further reflections that lead us to revise our judgments. This feature is not peculiar though to moral philosophy, or to the study of other philosophical principles such as those of induction and scientific method. For example, while we may not expect a substantial revision of our sense of correct grammar in view of a linguistic theory the principles of which seem especially natural to us, such a change is not inconceivable, and no doubt our sense of grammaticalness may be affected to some degree anyway by this knowledge. But there is a contrast, say, with physics. To take an extreme case, if we have an accurate account of the motions of the heavenly bodies that we do not find appealing, we cannot alter these motions to conform to a more attractive theory.

It is simply good fortune that the principles of celestial mechanics have their intellectual beauty.

There are, however, several interpretations of reflective equilibrium. For the notion varies depending upon whether one is to be presented with only those descriptions which more or less match one's existing judgments except for minor discrepancies, or whether one is to be presented with all possible descriptions to which one might plausibly conform one's judgments together with all relevant philosophical arguments for them. In the first case we would be describing a person's sense of justice more or less as it is although allowing for the smoothing out of certain irregularities; in the second case a person's sense of justice may or may not undergo a radical shift. Clearly it is the second kind of reflective equilibrium that one is concerned with in moral philosophy. To be sure, it is doubtful whether one can ever reach this state. For even if the idea of all possible descriptions and of all philosophically relevant arguments is well-defined (which is questionable), we cannot examine each of them. The most we can do is to study the conceptions of justice known to us through the tradition of moral philosophy and any further ones that occur to us, and then to consider these. This is pretty much what I shall do, since in presenting justice as fairness I shall compare its principles and arguments with a few other familiar views. In light of these remarks, justice as fairness can be understood as saying that the two principles previously mentioned would be chosen in the original position in preference to other traditional conceptions of justice, for example, those of utility and perfection; and that these principles give a better match with our considered judgments on reflection than these recognized alternatives. Thus justice as fairness moves us closer to the philosophical ideal; it does not, of course, achieve it.

This explanation of reflective equilibrium suggests straightway a number of further questions. For example, does a reflective equilibrium (in the sense of the philosophical ideal) exist? If so, is it unique? Even if it is unique, can it be reached? Perhaps the judgments from which we begin, or the course of reflection itself (or both), affect the resting point, if any, that we eventually achieve. It would be useless, however, to speculate about these matters here. They are far beyond our reach. I shall not even ask whether the principles that characterize one person's considered judgments are the same as those that characterize another's. I shall take for granted that these principles are either approximately the same for persons whose judgments are in reflective equilibrium, or if not, that their judgments divide along a few main lines represented by the family of traditional doctrines that I shall discuss. (Indeed, one person may find himself torn between opposing conceptions at the same time.) If men's conceptions of justice finally turn out to differ, the ways in which they do so is a matter of first importance. Of course we cannot know how these conceptions vary, or even whether they do, until we have a better account of their structure. And this we now lack, even in the case of one man, or homogeneous group of men. Here too there is likely to be a similarity with linguistics: if we can describe one person's sense of grammar we shall surely know many things about the general structure of language. Similarly, if we should be able to characterize one (educated) person's sense of justice, we would have a good beginning toward a theory of justice. We may suppose that everyone has in himself the whole form of a moral conception. So for the purposes of this book, the views of the reader and the author are the only ones that count. The opinions of others are used only to clear our own heads.

I wish to stress that a theory of justice is precisely that, namely, a theory. It is a theory of the moral sentiments (to recall an eighteenth century title) setting out the principles governing our moral powers, or, more specifically, our sense of justice. There is a definite if limited class of facts against which conjectured principles can be checked, namely, our considered judgments in reflective equilibrium. A theory of justice is subject to the same rules of method as other theories. Definitions and analyses of meaning do not have a special place: definition is but one device used in setting up the general structure of theory. Once the whole framework is worked out, definitions have no distinct status and stand or fall with the theory itself. In any case, it is obviously impossible to develop a substantive theory of justice founded solely on truths of logic and definition. The analysis of moral concepts and the a priori, however traditionally understood, is too slender a basis. Moral philosophy must be free to use contingent assumptions and general facts as it pleases. There is no other way to give an account of our considered judgments in reflective equilibrium. This is the conception of the subject adopted by most classical British writers through Sidgwick. I see no reason to depart from it.[6]

Moreover, if we can find an accurate account of our moral conceptions, then questions of meaning and justification may prove much easier to answer. Indeed some of them may no longer be real questions at all. Note, for example, the extraordinary deepening of our understanding of the meaning and justification of statements in logic and mathematics made possible by developments since Frege and Cantor. A knowledge of the fundamental structures of logic and set theory and their relation to mathematics has transformed the philosophy of these subjects in a way that conceptual analysis and linguistic investigations never could. One has only to observe the effect of the division of theories into those which are decidable and complete, undecidable yet complete, and neither complete nor decidable. The problem of meaning and truth in logic and mathematics is profoundly altered by the discovery of logical systems illustrating these concepts. Once the substantive content of moral conceptions is better understood, a similar transformation may occur. It is possible that convincing answers to questions of the meaning and justification of moral judgments can be found in no other way.

I wish, then, to stress the central place of the study of our substantive moral conceptions. But the corollary to recognizing their complexity is accepting the fact that our present theories are primitive and have grave defects. We need to be tolerant of simplifications if they reveal and approximate the general outlines of our judgments. Objections by way of counterexamples are to be made with care, since these may tell us only what we know already, namely that our theory is wrong somewhere. The important thing is to find out how often and how far it is wrong. All theories are presumably mistaken in places. The real question at any given time is which of the views already proposed is the best approximation overall. To ascertain this some grasp of the structure of rival theories is surely necessary. It is for this reason that I have tried to classify and to discuss conceptions of justice by reference to their basic intuitive ideas, since these disclose the main differences between them.

In presenting justice as fairness I shall contrast it with utilitarianism. I do this for various reasons, partly as an expository device, partly because the several variants of the utilitarian view have long dominated our philosophical tradition and continue to do so. And this dominance has been maintained despite the persistent misgivings that utilitarianism so easily arouses. The explanation for this peculiar state of affairs lies, I believe, in the fact that no constructive alternative theory has been advanced which has the comparable virtues of clarity and system and which at the same time allays these doubts. Intuitionism is not constructive, perfectionism is unacceptable. My conjecture is that the contract doctrine properly worked out can fill this gap. I think justice as fairness an endeavor in this direction.

Of course the contract theory as I shall present it is subject to the strictures that we have just noted. It is no exception to the primitiveness that marks existing moral theories. It is disheartening, for example, how little can now be said about priority rules; and while a lexical ordering may serve fairly well for some important cases, I assume that it will not be completely satisfactory. Nevertheless, we are free to use simplifying devices, and this I have often done. We should view a theory of justice as a guiding framework designed to focus our moral sensibilities and to put before our intuitive capacities more limited and manageable questions for judgment. The principles of justice identify certain considerations as morally relevant and the priority rules indicate the appropriate precedence when these conflict, while the conception of the original position defines the underlying idea which is to inform our deliberations. If the scheme as a whole seems on reflection to clarify and to order our thoughts, and if it tends to reduce disagreements and to bring divergent convictions more in line, then it has done all that one may reasonably ask. Understood as parts of a framework that does indeed seem to help, the numerous simplifications may be regarded as provisionally justified. . . .

Concluding Remarks on Justification

I shall not try to summarize the presentation of the theory of justice. Instead I should like to end with a few comments about the kind of argument I have offered for it. . . .

Philosophers commonly try to justify ethical theories in one of two ways. Sometimes they attempt to find self-evident principles from which a sufficient body of standards and precepts can be derived to account for our considered judgments. A justification of this kind we may think of as Cartesian. It presumes that first principles can be seen to be true, even necessarily so; deductive reasoning then transfers this conviction from premises to conclusion. A second approach (called naturalism by an abuse of language) is to introduce definitions of moral concepts in terms of presumptively non-moral ones, and then to show by accepted procedures of common sense and the sciences that the statements thus paired with the asserted moral judgments are true. Although on this view the first principles of ethics are not self-evident, the justification of moral convictions poses no special difficulties. They can be established, granting the definitions, in the same fashion as other statements about the world.

I have not adopted either of these conceptions of justification. For while some moral principles may seem natural and even obvious, there are great obstacles to maintaining that they are necessarily true, or even to explaining what is meant by this. Indeed, I have held that these principles are contingent in the sense that they are chosen in the original position in the light of general facts. . . . More likely candidates for necessary moral truths are the conditions imposed on the adoption of principles; but actually it seems best to regard these conditions simply as reasonable stipulations to be assessed eventually by the whole theory to which they belong. There is no set of conditions or first principles that can be plausibly claimed to be necessary or definitive of morality and thereby especially suited to carry the burden of justification. On the other hand, the method of naturalism so-called must first distinguish moral from non-moral concepts and then gain acceptance for the definitions laid down. For the justification to succeed, a clear theory of meaning is presupposed and this seems to be lacking. And in any case, definitions become the main part of the ethical doctrine, and thus in turn they need to be justified.

Therefore we do better, I think, to regard a moral theory just as any other theory, making due allowances for its Socratic aspects. . . . There is no reason to suppose that its first principles or assumptions need to be self-evident, or that its concepts and criteria can be replaced by other notions which can be certified as non-moral.[7] Thus while I have maintained, for example, that something's being right, or just, can be understood as its being in accordance with the relevant principles that would be acknowledged in the original position, and that we can in this way replace the former notions by the latter, these definitions are set up within the theory itself. . . . I do not hold that the conception of the original position is itself without moral force, or that the family of concepts it draws upon is ethically neutral. . . . This question I simply leave aside. I have not proceeded then as if first principles, or conditions thereon, or definitions either, have special features that permit them a peculiar place in justifying a moral doctrine. They are central elements and devices of theory, but justification rests upon the entire conception and how it fits in with and organizes our considered judgments in reflective equilibrium. As we have noted before, justification is a matter of the mutual support of many considerations, of everything fitting together into one coherent view. . . . Accepting this idea allows us to leave questions of meaning and definition aside and to get on with the task of developing a substantive theory of justice.

The three parts of the exposition of this theory are intended to make a unified whole by supporting one another in roughly the following way. The first part presents the essentials of the theoretical structure, and the principles of justice are argued for on the basis of reasonable stipulations concerning the choice of such conceptions. I urged the naturalness of these conditions and presented reasons why they are accepted, but it was not claimed that they are self-evident, or required by the analysis of moral concepts or the meaning of ethical terms. In the second part I examined the sorts of institutions that justice enjoins and the kinds of duties and obligations it imposes on individuals. The aim throughout was to show that the theory proposed matches the fixed points of our considered convictions better than other familiar doctrines, and that it leads us to revise and extrapolate our judgments in what seem on reflection to be more satisfactory ways. First principles and particular judgments appear on balance to hang together reasonably well, at least in comparison with alternative theories. Finally we checked to see in the third part if justice as fairness is a feasible conception. This forced us to raise the question of stability and whether the right and the good as defined are congruent. These considerations do not determine the initial acknowledgment of principles in the first part of the argument, but confirm it. . . . They show that our nature is such as to allow the original choice to be carried through. In this sense we might say that humankind has a moral nature.

Now some may hold that this kind of justification faces two sorts of difficulties. First, it is open to the general complaint that it appeals to the mere fact of agreement. Second, there is the more specific objection to the argument I have presented that it depends upon a particular list of conceptions of justice between which the parties in the original position are to choose, and it assumes not only an agreement among persons in their considered judgments, but also in what they regard as reasonable conditions to impose on the choice of first principles. It may be said that the agreement in considered convictions is constantly changing and varies between one society, or part thereof, and another. Some of the so-called fixed points may not really be fixed, nor will everyone accept the same principles for filling in the gaps in their existing judgments. And any list of conceptions of justice, or consensus about what counts as reasonable conditions on principles, is surely more or less arbitrary. The case presented for justice as fairness, so the contention runs, does not escape these limitations.

In regard to the general objection the reply is that justification is argument addressed to those who disagree with us, or to ourselves when we are of two minds. It presumes a clash of views between persons or within one person, and seeks to convince others, or ourselves, of the reasonableness of the principles upon which our claims and judgments are founded. Being designed to reconcile by reason, justification proceeds from what all parties to the discussion hold in common. Ideally, to justify a conception of justice to someone is to give him a proof of its principles from premises that we both accept, these principles having in turn consequences that match our considered judgments. Thus mere proof is not justification. A proof simply displays logical relations between propositions. But proofs become justification once the starting points are mutually recognized, or the conclusions so comprehensive and compelling as to persuade us of the soundness of the conception expressed by their premises.

It is perfectly proper, then, that the argument for the principles of justice should proceed from some consensus. This is the nature of justification. Yet the more specific objections are correct in implying that the force of the argument depends on the features of the consensus appealed to. Here several points deserve notice. To begin with, while it should be granted that any list of alternatives may be to some extent arbitrary, the objection is mistaken if it is read as holding that all lists are equally so. A list that includes the leading traditional theories is less arbitrary than one which leaves out the more obvious candidates. Certainly the argument for the principles of justice would be strengthened by showing that they are still the best choice from a more comprehensive list more systematically evaluated. I do not know how far this can be done. I doubt, however, that the principles of justice (as I have defined them) will be the preferred conception on anything resembling a complete list. (Here I assume that, given an upper bound on complexity and other constraints, the class of reasonable and practicable alternatives is effectively finite.) Even if the argument I have offered is sound, it only shows that a finally adequate theory (if such exists) will look more like the contract view than any of the other doctrines we discussed. And even this conclusion is not proved in any strict sense.

Nevertheless, in comparing justice as fairness with these conceptions, the list used is not simply ad hoc: it includes representative theories from the tradition of moral philosophy which comprises the historical consensus about what so far seem to be the more reasonable and practicable moral conceptions. With time further possibilities will be worked out, thereby providing a more convincing basis for justification as the leading conception is subjected to a more severe test. But these things we can only anticipate. For the present it is appropriate to try to reformulate the contract doctrine and to compare it with a few familiar alternatives. This procedure is not arbitrary; we can advance in no other way.

Turning to the particular difficulty about the consensus on reasonable conditions, one should point out that one of the aims of moral philosophy is to look for possible bases of agreement where none seem to exist. It must attempt to extend the range of some existing consensus and to frame more discriminating moral conceptions for our consideration. Justifying grounds do not lie ready to hand: they need to be discovered and suitably expressed, sometimes by lucky guesses, sometimes by noting the requirements of theory. It is with this aim in mind that the various conditions on the choice of first principles are brought together in the notion of the original position. The idea is that by putting together enough reasonable constraints into a single conception, it will become obvious that one among the alternatives presented is to be preferred. We should like it to happen that the superiority of a particular view (among those currently known) is the result, perhaps the unexpected result, of this newly observed consensus.

Again, the set of conditions incorporated into the notion of the original position is not without an explanation. It is possible to maintain that these requirements are reasonable and to connect them with the purpose of moral principles and their role in establishing the ties of community. The grounds for ordering and finality, say, seem clear enough. And we can now see that publicity can be explained as insuring that the process of justification can be perfectly carried through (in the limit so to speak) without untoward effects. For publicity allows that all can justify their conduct to everyone else (when their conduct is justifiable) without self-defeating or other disturbing consequences. If we take seriously the idea of a social union and of society as a social union of such unions, then surely publicity is a natural condition. It helps to establish that a well-ordered society is one activity in the sense that its members follow and know of one another, that they follow the same regulative conception; and everyone shares in the benefits of the endeavors of all in ways to which each is known to consent. Society is not partitioned with respect to the mutual recognition of its first principles. And, indeed, this must be so if the binding action of the conception of justice and of the Aristotelian principle (and its companion effect) are to take place.

To be sure, the function of moral principles is not uniquely defined; it admits of various interpretations. We might try to choose between them by seeing which one uses the weakest set of conditions to characterize the initial situation. The difficulty with this suggestion is that while weaker conditions are indeed to be preferred, other things equal, there is no weakest set; a minimum does not exist short of no conditions at all and this is of no interest. Therefore we must look for a constrained minimum, a set of weak conditions that still enables us to construct a workable theory of justice. Certain parts of justice as fairness should be viewed in this way. I have several times noted the minimal nature of the conditions on principles when taken singly. For example, the assumption of mutually disinterested motivation is not a demanding stipulation. Not only does it enable us to base the theory upon a reasonably precise notion of rational choice, but it asks little of the parties: in this way the principles chosen can adjust wider and deeper conflicts, an obvious desideratum. . . . It has the further advantage of separating off the more evident moral elements of the original position in the form of general conditions and the veil of ignorance and the like, so that we can see more clearly how justice requires us to go beyond a concern for our own interests.

The discussion of freedom of conscience illustrates most clearly the assumption of mutual disinterest. Here the opposition of the parties is very great, yet one can still show that if any agreement is possible, it is that on the principle of equal liberty. And, as we noted, this idea can be extended to conflicts between moral doctrines as well. . . . If the parties assume that in society they affirm some moral conception (the content of which is unknown to them), they can still assent to the first principle. This principle therefore appears to hold a special place among moral views; it defines an agreement in the limit once we postulate sufficiently wide disparities consistent with certain minimal conditions for a practical conception of justice.

I should now like to take note of several objections that are independent from the method of justification and concern instead certain features of the theory of justice itself. One of these is the criticism that the contract view is a narrowly individualistic doctrine. To this difficulty, the preceding remarks supply the answer. For once the point of the assumption of mutual disinterest is understood, the objection seems misplaced. Within the framework of justice as fairness we can reformulate and establish Kantian themes by using a suitably general conception of rational choice. For example, we have found interpretations of autonomy and of the moral law as an expression of our nature as free and equal rational beings; the categorical imperative also has its analogue, as does the idea of never treating persons as means only, or indeed as means at all. Further, in the last part the theory of justice has been shown to account for the values of community as well; and this strengthens the earlier contention that embedded in the principles of justice there is an ideal of the person that provides an Archimedean point for judging the basic structure of society. . . . These aspects of the theory of justice are developed slowly beginning from what looks like an unduly rationalistic conception that makes no provision for social values. The original position is first used to determine the content of justice, the principles which define it. Not until later is justice seen as part of our good and connected with our natural sociability. The merits of the idea of the original position cannot be assessed by focusing on some single feature of it, but, as I have often observed, only by the whole theory which is built upon it.

If justice as fairness is more convincing than the older presentations of the contract doctrine, I believe that it is because the original position, as indicated above, unites in one conception a reasonably clear problem of choice with conditions that are widely recognized as fitting to impose on the adoption of moral principles. This initial situation combines the requisite clarity with the relevant ethical constraints. It is partly to preserve this clarity that I have avoided attributing to the parties any ethical motivation. They decide solely on the basis of what seems best calculated to further their interests so far as they can ascertain them. In this way we can exploit the intuitive idea of rational prudential choice. We can, however, define ethical variations of the initial situation by supposing the parties to be influenced by moral considerations. It is a mistake to object that the notion of the original agreement would no longer be ethically neutral. For this notion already includes moral features and must do so, for example, the formal conditions on principles and the veil of ignorance. I have simply divided up the description of the original position so that these elements do not occur in the characterization of the parties, although even here there might be a question as to what counts as a moral element and what does not. There is no need to settle this problem. What is important is that the various features of the original position should be expressed in the simplest and most compelling way.

Occasionally I have touched upon some possible ethical variations of the initial situation. . . . For example, one might assume that the parties hold the principle that no one should be advantaged by unmerited assets and contingencies, and therefore they choose a conception of justice that mitigates the effects of natural accident and social fortune. Or else they may be said to accept a principle of reciprocity requiring that distributive arrangements always lie on the upward sloping portion of the contribution curve. Again, some notion of fair and willing cooperation may limit the conceptions of justice which the parties are prepared to entertain. There is no a priori reason for thinking that these variations must be less convincing, or the moral constraints they express less widely shared. Moreover, we have seen that the possibilities just mentioned appear to confirm the difference principle, lending further support to it. Although I have not proposed a view of this kind, they certainly deserve further examination. The crucial thing is not to use principles that are contested. Thus to reject the principle of average utility by imposing a rule against taking chances in the original position would render the method fruitless, since some philosophers have sought to justify this principle by deriving it as the consequence of the appropriate impersonal attitude in certain risk situations. We must find other arguments against the utility criterion: the propriety of taking chances is among the things in dispute. . . . The idea of the initial agreement can only succeed if its conditions are in fact widely recognized, or can become so.

Another fault, some may contend, is that the principles of justice are not derived from the notion of respect for persons, from a recognition of their inherent worth and dignity. Since the original position (as I have defined it) does not include this idea, not explicitly anyway, the argument for justice as fairness may be thought unsound. I believe, however, that while the principles of justice will be effective only if men have a sense of justice and do therefore respect one another, the notion of respect or of the inherent worth of persons is not a suitable basis for arriving at these principles. It is precisely these ideas that call for interpretation. The situation is analogous to that of benevolence: without the principles of right and justice, the aims of benevolence and the requirements of respect are both undefined; they presuppose these principles already independently derived. . . . Once the conception of justice is on hand, however, the ideas of respect and of human dignity can be given a more definite meaning. Among other things, respect for persons is shown by treating them in ways that they can see to be justified. But more than this, it is manifest in the content of the principles to which we appeal. Thus to respect persons is to recognize that they possess an inviolability founded on justice that even the welfare of society as a whole cannot override. It is to affirm that the loss of freedom for some is not made right by a greater welfare enjoyed by others. The lexical priorities of justice represent the value of persons that Kant says is beyond all price.[8] The theory of justice provides a rendering of these ideas but we cannot start out from them. There is no way to avoid the complications of the original position, or of some similar construction, if our notions of respect and the natural basis of equality are to be systematically presented.

These remarks bring us back to the common sense conviction, which we noted at the outset, that justice is the first virtue of social institutions. . . . I have tried to set forth a theory that enables us to understand and to assess these feelings about the primacy of justice. Justice as fairness is the outcome: it articulates these opinions and supports their general tendency. And while, of course, it is not a fully satisfactory theory, it offers, I believe, an alternative to the utilitarian view which has for so long held the preeminent place in our moral philosophy. I have tried to present the theory of justice as a viable systematic doctrine so that the idea of maximizing the good does not hold sway by default. The criticism of teleological theories cannot fruitfully proceed piecemeal. We must attempt to construct another kind of view which has the same virtues of clarity and system but which yields a more discriminating interpretation of our moral sensibilities.

Finally, we may remind ourselves that the hypothetical nature of the original position invites the question: why should we take any interest in it, moral or otherwise? Recall the answer: the conditions embodied in the description of this situation are ones that we do in fact accept. Or if we do not, then we can be persuaded to do so by philosophical considerations of the sort occasionally introduced. Each aspect of the original position can be given a supporting explanation. Thus what we are doing is to combine into one conception the totality of conditions that we are ready upon due reflection to recognize as reasonable in our conduct with regard to one another. . . . Once we grasp this conception, we can at any time look at the social world from the required point of view. It suffices to reason in certain ways and to follow the conclusions reached. This standpoint is also objective and expresses our autonomy. . . . Without conflating all persons into one but recognizing them as distinct and separate, it enables us to be impartial, even between persons who are not contemporaries but who belong to many generations. Thus to see our place in society from the perspective of this position is to see it *sub specie aeternitatis:* it is to regard the human situation not only from all social but also from all temporal points of view. The perspective of eternity is not a perspective from a certain place beyond the world, nor the point of view of a transcendent being; rather it is a certain form of thought and feeling that rational persons can adopt within the world. And having done so, they can, whatever their generation, bring together into one scheme all individual perspectives and arrive together at regulative principles that can be affirmed by everyone as he lives by them, each from his own standpoint. Purity of heart, if one could attain it, would be to see clearly and to act with grace and self-command from this point of view.

NOTES

1. As the text suggests, I shall regard Locke's *Second Treatise of Government,* Rousseau's *The Social Contract,* and Kant's ethical works beginning with *The Foundations of the Metaphysics of Morals* as definitive of the contract tradition. For all of its greatness, Hobbes's *Leviathan* raises special problems. A general historical survey is provided by J. W. Gough, *The Social Contract,* 2nd ed. (Oxford, The Clarendon Press, 1957), and Otto Gierke, *Natural Law and the Theory of Society,* trans. with an introduction by Ernest Barker (Cambridge, The University Press, 1934). A presentation of the contract view as primarily an ethical theory is to be found in G. R. Grice, *The Grounds of Moral Judgment* (Cambridge, The University Press, 1967). See also § 19, note 30.

2. Kant is clear that the original agreement is hypothetical. See *The Metaphysics of Morals*, pt. I (*Rechtslehre*), especially §§ 47, 52; and pt. II of the essay "Concerning the Common Saying: This May Be True in Theory but It Does Not Apply in Practice," in *Kant's Political Writings*, ed. Hans Reiss and trans. by H. B. Nisbet (Cambridge, The University Press, 1970), pp. 73-87. See Georges Vlachos, *La Pensée politique de Kant* (Paris, Presses Universitaires de France, 1962), pp. 326-335; and J. G. Murphy, *Kant: The Philosophy of Right* (London: Macmillan, 1970), pp. 109-112, 133-136, for a further discussion.

3. For the formulation of this intuitive idea I am indebted to Allan Gibbard.

4. In this section I follow the general point of view of "Outline of a Procedure for Ethics," *Philosophical Review*, vol. 60 (1951). The comparison with linguistics is of course new.

5. See Noam Chomsky, *Aspects of the Theory of Syntax* (Cambridge, Mass., The M.I.T. Press, 1965), pp. 3-9.

6. I believe that this view goes back in its essentials to Aristotle's procedure in the *Nicomachean Ethics*. See W. F. R. Hardie, *Aristotle's Ethical Theory*, ch. III, esp. pp. 37-45. And Sidgwick thought of the history of moral philosophy as a series of attempts to state "in full breadth and clearness those primary intuitions of Reason, by the scientific application of which the common moral thought of mankind may be at once systematized and corrected." *The Methods of Ethics*, pp. 373f. He takes for granted that philosophical reflection will lead to revisions in our considered judgments, and although there are elements of epistemological intuitionism in his doctrine, these are not given much weight when unsupported by systematic considerations. For an account of Sidgwick's methodology, see J. B. Schneewind, "First Principles and Common Sense Morality in Sidgwick's Ethics," *Archiv für Geschichte der Philosophie*, Bd. 45 (1963).

7. The view proposed here accords with the account in § 9 which follows "Outline for Ethics" (1951). But it has benefited from the conception of justification found in W. V. Quine, *Word and Object* (Cambridge, M.I.T. Press, 1960), ch. 1 and elsewhere. See also his *Ontological Relativity and Other Essays* (New York, Columbia University Press, 1969), Essay 4. For a development of this conception to include explicitly moral thought and judgment, see Morton White, *Toward Reunion in Philosophy* (Cambridge, Harvard University Press, 1956), pt. III, esp. pp. 254-258, 263, 266f.

8. See *The Foundations of the Metaphysics of Morals*, pp. 434-436, vol. IV of the Academy Edition.

Bibliography

Barry I. Chazan and Jonas F. Soltis, editors, *Moral Education*. New York: Teachers College Press, 1973.

The editors have brought together a group of previously published articles and selections which cover the range of concerns typically discussed by philosophers of education. Topics covered include: morality and philosophy, justification in ethics, moral principles, moral sense and autonomy, teaching and morality. This book is especially recommended to those who want to understand the diverse approaches to moral education presently discussed.

C. M. Beck, B. S. Crittenden and E. V. Sullivan, editors, *Moral Education*. New York: Newman Press, 1971.

Comparable in scope to the Chazan and Soltis collection, in this book the reader will be able to study Lawrence Kohlberg's developmental theory in greater detail. A recent theoretical chapter by Kohlberg begins the volume and Brian Crittenden provides an analysis of the several positions articulated throughout the book in his concluding chapters. Other contributors to the book include such figures as: Ausubel, Baier and Hunt.

Nicholas Rescher, *Introduction to Value Theory*. Englewood Cliffs, New Jersey: Prentice-Hall Inc., 1969.

Despite its title this original book by a leading American philosopher is a comprehensive view of valuation from the perspective of logical analysis: The author's emphasis and illustrations deal with the way value concepts function in "everyday affairs." That is, the study is geared toward social decision-making.

Paul W. Taylor, editor, *The Moral Judgement*. Englewood Cliffs, New Jersey: Prentice-Hall, Inc., 1963.

> Taylor includes the major exponents of philosophical positions on morality and valuation: objectivism, subjectivism, the emotive-imperative theory, and instrumentalism. The book includes selections from such philosophers as: A. J. Ayer, Kurt Baier, John Dewey, Ralph Barton Perry, and C. L. Stevenson.

The reader will also benefit from reading the full works by John Rawls and Raths, Harmin and Simon, excerpts from which have been reprinted in the foregoing section.

Concluding Commentary

It is recognized by some educators that the effects of education are limited and difficult to anticipate. One cannot assert, for example, that religion studies will produce better people, whatever that might mean. Although religion is closely related to value structures and the development of hierarchies of preference and world-view, no single generalization can be made about that relation and no single behavioral outcome is a realistic expectation. Even as schools alone cannot solve such social problems as racism, neither can anyone anticipate that religion studies will resolve the numerous moral problems in this nation or the world.

Such a proviso, however, does not undercut the legitimacy and the intellectual merit of the developments described in this book. As much as anything it indicates a skepticism about guarantees that religious practice or studies about religion lead to the behavioral result of better people.

Religion does exist. It is a powerful force in individual life and social existence. Insofar as we wish to comprehend ourselves, our heritage and our context religion needs to be studied. It is part of the tapestry of life along with the natural and social sciences and literature and art, etc.

In a public school, however, such study must respect the rights of the individual. One of the central elements of the American experience has been the emphasis on the individual's integrity, even if there has not always been a total regard for the principles articulated in the Bill of Rights. As public institutions, the schools of the nation are not to be an arm for a political or religious or economic majority. They are to serve the total population, the individual as well as the group.

Accordingly, in religion studies sectarian bias or traditional prejudice needs to be recognized for what it is—a partial view of experience. But acting impartially is not the solution to the problem of partiality. Human pretense is such as to mask from us the partiality and the hidden agendas embedded in our impartial attempts.

276

Instead therefore of attempting some simple "objectivity" in such studies it seems wiser to amplify our understanding of the objective study mandate laid down in the *Schempp* decision. Admitting one's bias and recognizing the elements of prejudice in our arguments or proceeding toward "disciplined inter-subjectivity" is an honest and human approach to the problem of objectivity.

Further, from the standpoint of the educator (the teacher, the school administrator, the curriculum planner) it is well to recognize that no single approach to studies about religion exists. There are many provocative approaches and some of them have been portrayed here. In turn, that indicates a lack of need for a singular or uniform approach to such study. Instead, if one grants not only religious pluralism on the social level but individual difference among learners, attempts at uniformity may well be held suspect. Religion is a personal matter perhaps only in the sense that individuals in a free society decide about it individually. Even though cultural forces no doubt exert profound influence on that decision, the decision still rests with the individual. There is also considerable evidence to suggest that where society may not grant such freedom of choice, the sensitive person does so anyway.

To make such determinative life decisions the learner needs clarity not indoctrination. He needs to question others, including those in authority. Above all, he needs to question his own authority and argue his position through with himself as well as with others. Especially if American public education should assume a prominent role in value development (I would hope along with the family and the church) clarity and sensitivity become important elements in the learning process.

Recent events on many fronts (youth culture, the peace movement, consumerism, etc.) suggest that individuals are seeking a way to live that at once might be respectful of others and diminish the sense of alienation derived from impersonal social systems unresponsive to individual need. Can the schools contribute to such sensitivity in the population?

One of the ways in which an educational contribution can occur is in the promotion of clarity of thought and incisiveness of analysis particularly with respect to those things we value the most. The magnitude of social happenings and the pervasive sense that we are moving into the future at an ever accelerated pace could easily overwhelm us all. The school years are crucial not merely in and of themselves but as instruments for developing rational skills for sorting out what is occurring in and around us. Can the schools contribute to such clarity of thought in the population?

A positive answer to both questions could be crucial for our immediate destiny. To retreat from what we deem to be important or to hide our thoughts in confusion could be disastrous or demeaning or both. Religion, of course, cannot be the sole source for sensitive and clear thought. But it deserves little attention in schools unless it attempts to stimulate both, sensitivity and clarity.